Listening for God

Listening for God

RELIGION AND MORAL DISCERNMENT

by

HOWARD LESNICK

Fordham University Press
New York
1998

LC 98-18062
ISBN 0-8232-1860-0 (*hardcover*)
ISBN 0-8232-1861-9 (*paperback*)

Library of Congress Cataloging-in-Publication Data

Lesnick, Howard, 1931–
   Listening for God : religion and moral discernment /
by Howard Lesnick.
      p.   cm.
   Includes bibliographical references and index.
   ISBN 0-8232-1860-0.–ISBN 0-8232-1861-9 (pbk.)
   1. Religion and ethics.   2. Religious ethics.   3. Lesnick,
Howard, 1931—   .   I. Title.
   BJ47.L37   1998
   291.5—dc21   98-18062
                                                        CIP

Printed in the United States of America

Who will believe my verse in time to come,
if it were fill'd with your most high deserts?

This book is dedicated to my daughter
ALICE LESNICK
who has "long known the secrets of my heart"
and now
through this book
has helped me to learn them too

First we sing, then we understand.

—ABRAHAM JOSHUA HESCHEL

CONTENTS

ACKNOWLEDGMENTS

When my daughter Alice graduated from college fourteen years ago, I inscribed my gift of a set of Shakespeare with the opening lines of his Seventeenth Sonnet. As they seem no less apt today, I have used them as the epigraph on the Dedication page. Some years before, Alice and I exchanged the realization that for each of us a special power of Robert Bolt's classic account of Sir Thomas More, *A Man for All Seasons*, lay in his portrayal of the relationship between More and his daughter Margaret. "You have long known the secrets of my heart" were his last words to her. For me, they are, hopefully, but the most recent expression of an ongoing awareness of gratitude. Alice teaches (for want of more fully descriptive words) literature and education, currently at Bryn Mawr and Haverford Colleges.

The candle on the cover is the work of Abby Lesnick, my younger daughter, who is now a high-school student at Germantown Friends School in Philadelphia. Crafted some years ago, her candle expresses to me the flickering illumination of discernment, the quality I most needed in order to know what it was I wanted to say in this book.

Along with discernment, however, I have needed a fair degree of courage, for this book is far from the typical work-product of a law teacher. Neither quality would have become available to me without the aid of a great many people throughout the period of the book's gestation. My debt to them is beyond full acknowledgment.

First (with Alice) are two whose love and insight made it quite literally possible for me to recognize, at each decision point, what I wanted this book to be, and to act on those moments of recognition: Carolyn Schodt, my wife, founder and director of A Quaker Ministry to Persons with AIDS, and my companion in spiritual exploration and much else; and Emily Fowler Hartigan, a sometime teaching colleague and constant spiritual and intellectual mentor, who is a member of the law faculty at St. Mary's University in San Antonio.

Two teachers of mine whose gifts were indispensable are Rabbi Marcia Prager, of P'nai Or Religious Fellowship in Philadelphia, and Rebecca Kratz Mays, of the Quaker Study and Retreat Center at Pendle Hill in Wallingford, Pennsylvania, who, respectively, enabled my reengagement with the Jewish tradition and my first receptive engagement with Jesus and the Gospels.

I am especially grateful to three University of Pennsylvania colleagues: Seth Kreimer and Leo Levin, whose wisdom and learning were for me a well of guidance and encouragement often drawn on along the way; and Heidi Hurd, whose acuity and spirit generated an extraordinarily perceptive critical presentation to our colleagues of a set of ideas that, while congruent with hers in certain fundamental ways, are set forth here in a context that must have struck her as truly bizarre.

Thanks are owing too to a number of fellow law teachers who read drafts of the manuscript and were sources of extremely valuable input and affirmation: Milner Ball (Georgia), Robert Burt (Yale), Marie Failinger (Hamline), Thomas Shaffer (Notre Dame), Howard Vogel (Hamline), and James Boyd White (Michigan).

I am also the beneficiary of the thoughtful responses of University of Pennsylvania Professor of Religious Studies Stephen Dunning, and two former CUNY colleagues, friends, and mentors, Jack Himmelstein and Judy Sullivan (the Red Queen); of the wisdom that two former students—students of the Law School, teachers of me—have shared with me from their immersion in the Jewish and Catholic traditions, respectively: Ben Berlin, now a New York lawyer, and John J. Grogan, founder and director of the Camden (New Jersey) Center for Law and Social Justice; of important moments of encouragement from Professor Mary Rose O'Reilley, of Pendle Hill and College of St. Thomas in St. Paul, and Father Ed DePaoli, of St. Gabriel's Roman Catholic Church, in Stowe, Pennsylvania, and of the boundless bibliographical skill and unflagging responsiveness of Ronald Day, Head of Reference Services, Biddle Law Library (and Lecturer in the academic program), University of Pennsylvania, and indeed of the entire reference staff at Biddle.

Finally, I am grateful to two groups of people—my faculty colleagues at the University of Pennsylvania Law School, for the reception they gave my work at a Legal Theory Workshop, and the members and attenders of Chestnut Hill (Pennsylvania) Monthly Meeting, Religious Society of Friends, which has over the past decade increasingly become a spiritual home for me, and a source of much that is reflected in the book—to my Dean, Colin S. Diver, and the following sources of research support during a sabbatical year and several summers: The Cades Memorial Fund, Sparer Memorial Fund, Fred Carr Fund, Raymond G. Pearstine Fund, and Louis J. Goffman Fund.

None of these could save me from errors large and small, for which I accept sole responsibility.

INTRODUCTION

September, 1953. After three years, active warfare in Korea had recently yielded to a truce, but for how long I could not then know. I did know, as I enrolled as a doctoral student in American History at Cornell, that my student deferment from the draft would not be renewed and that within a few months I would receive a notice to report for induction into the armed forces.

In that same month, a fellow New Yorker, about whom I would read a dozen years later, reached his eighteenth birthday, entered college, and registered for the draft. Four years on, his student deferment still in effect, Daniel Seeger, the son of practicing Roman Catholic parents, with two uncles in the clergy, applied for exemption from military service as a conscientious objector. The Selective Service Act then in force exempted from the draft anyone who "by religious training and belief is conscientiously opposed to participation in war in any form." It defined "religious training and belief" as: "an individual's belief in relation to a Supreme Being involving duties superior to those arising from any human relation, but does not include essentially political, sociological, or philosophical views or a purely personal moral code."

In completing a form whose printed yes-or-no questions tracked the language of the statute, Seeger placed quotation marks around the word "religious." He left blank his answer to the question about belief in a Supreme Being, adding this explanation: "The existence of God cannot be proven or disproven, and the essence of His nature cannot be determined. I prefer to admit this, and leave the question open rather than answer 'yes' or 'no.'" He explained the basis of his claim for exemption in these words:

> It is our moral responsibility to search for a way to maintain the recognition of the dignity and worth of the individual. I cannot participate in actions which betray the cause of freedom and humanity. War, with its indiscriminate crushing of human personality, cannot preserve moral values. To resort to immoral means is not to

preserve or vindicate moral values, but only to become collabora-
tors in destroying all moral life among men.

Seeger was interviewed according to established procedures by
the FBI, and given a hearing by the Department of Justice, which
unreservedly acknowledged that he was sincere and honest. Nevertheless, both the Justice Department and the Selective Service
System rejected his claim, because it was not grounded in belief
"in relation to a Supreme Being," as the statute required. Classi-
fied 1-A and ordered to report for induction, Seeger did report,
but refused to submit to induction and was convicted of a felony.[1]

I tell this story, and begin with it, because of the remarkable
disposition of Seeger's appeal by the courts to which he appealed
his conviction. The government made an argument that had a lot
of plain common sense behind it. Congress sought to differenti-
ate, the Justice Department contended, between those beliefs that
are "solely the result of individual reflection" and those that "the
believer assumes to be the product of divine commands." Citizens
whose refusal is based on "obedience to a power higher than that
exercised by a mortal Congress" are entitled to have their refusal
respected, even though most of their fellow citizens hear the
voice of God differently, because God trumps Congress and in
our pluralist society neither an agency of government nor a plebi-
scite can claim to have authoritatively discerned the will of God.
Congress therefore agreed to respect a sincerely held belief that
service in the armed forces would violate a draft registrant's obligation to his God. But those who "merely invoke their own fallible judgment" against that of the legislature stand on weaker
ground. If a citizen is listening only to an internally generated
voice, he must accept the contrary judgment of the representa-
tives of the community.

The Court of Appeals called this argument "persuasive" but
not "dispositive." The Constitution forbids discrimination among
religious beliefs, and religion may not, the court held, constitutionally be limited to belief in a Supreme Being. In part, the court
reached this judgment out of recognition of the increasing religious diversity of the country. We have religions that not only are
not based on the Bible, but are wholly nontheistic. More fundamentally, however, the court said that: "Today, a pervading commitment to a moral ideal is for many the equivalent of what was

historically considered the response to divine commands. For many, the stern and moral voice of conscience occupies that hallowed place in the hearts and minds of men which was traditionally reserved for the commandments of God."

The court thus rejected a distinction between "internally derived" and "externally compelled" beliefs, concluding that, when Seeger insists that he is "obeying the dictates of his conscience or the imperatives of an absolute morality," he is "bowing to external commands in virtually the same sense" as one who "defers to the will of a supernatural power."

In affirming the Court of Appeals' decision, the Supreme Court interpreted the statute to adopt the view held by the lower court to be constitutionally required: "The statute does not distinguish between externally and internally derived beliefs." To both courts, then, it was the *binding force* of the constraint upon the conscience that is critical. The *source* of a belief within or outside the person was explicitly held irrelevant to its "religious" quality. A moral belief generated wholly from within is not necessarily a "merely personal moral code" (declared by the statute to be insufficient to warrant exemption); "personal" it may be, the courts in effect declared, but not "merely" so if held with a force comparable to that thought to reside in a "supernatural power."

The Court quoted (among many others) these words of the leading Protestant theologian, Dr. Paul Tillich, as indicative of the accepted breadth of the concept of religious belief:

> I have written of the God above the God of theism, [in which] the God of both religious and theological language disappears. But something remains, . . . in which meaning within meaninglessness is affirmed. The source of this certitude within doubt is not the God of traditional theism but the 'God above God,' the power of being, which works through those who have no name for it, not even the name God.

This book is designed in large part to describe my own experience of the "certitude within doubt" of which Tillich wrote. I have come to find in religious language and practice an expression of a belief in that for which I "have no name," and which I can locate neither wholly within nor wholly outside myself, but which nonetheless illuminates and inspires my efforts to live a moral life and to understand myself and the world.

That illumination is at times powerful enough to take on the quality of an imperative, but it is not accurately described as the "dictate" of an "external command." The Court of Appeals revealed the constricted quality of its understanding of religious sources of obligation when it used words like "commands," "commandments," "dictates," and "imperatives" to describe the nature of the constraints on Seeger's conscience, and "compelled" and "bowing" to describe the nature of his response. The court's implicit view of the relation between humans and God is that of servant to master, one who gives orders and one who carries them out. But, for that view not to be fatal to Seeger's claim, we must supply (for the judges did not) an answer to the objection that it is incoherent to speak of one's dictating to oneself, or "bowing" to one's own "commands." For that objection asserts as self-evidently true that either the self is bound or it is free, and that the term "self-imposed obligations" is an oxymoron: If their source is recognized as within the self, they are not obligations; if they are imposed on the self, they must perforce have an external source.

This book will seek to express a notion of "obligation" that denies the conclusiveness of this objection, and finds in a version of the religious tradition a way out of the dilemma that it seems so logically to pose. It is a point of view that locates the problem in the vigorously hierarchical words I have quoted.

The journey of my thinking has in large measure been made in dialogue with two polar world-views, each widely held, that unite in denying that what I am drawn to has any coherence. I don't know which is Scylla, which Charybdis, but my effort has been to avoid foundering on either pole, while giving each a full measure of respectful attention.

To many who identify themselves as religious, my approach to religious language and practice would be a misappropriation of the term. Judged by the beliefs of most who call themselves believers, I am not a believer, for (like Daniel Seeger before his draft board) I cannot avow the reality of a being that exists outside human experience. I acknowledge the widespread reality of this understanding of religion. However, I have found it important to attend to those aspects of the religious tradition—and I will write primarily of Judaism, my own religion, and Christianity, but also of Buddhism and fleetingly of Islam—that have been hospitable to a broader understanding of religious belief. I want in this book to describe the ways in which I have come to a religious outlook that many religious people would call nonreligious.

The polar objection comes from a secular stance, which looks wholly within human thought and experience to understand the world. On such a view, Seeger's "obligation" arose outside of himself only in the sense that the principles of rational decision-making are universal. His obligation, not to engage in warfare if there is sufficient reason to abstain from it, was grounded simply in his being a person.[2] To speak in religious terms is simply a mystification, a projection onto the external world of the contents of one's mind. To such people, the failing is not in my world-view, which they (like those who are religious) would character-ize as essentially nonreligious, but in my clinging to the obfusca-tory use of religious language and practices.

I can illustrate these polar critiques, and triangulate my own view on them, with an example drawn from the Christian Scrip-tures. It is the story of the disciples setting out in a boat for Beth-saida. Mark describes Jesus, alone on the land at evening time:

> When he saw that they were straining at the oars against an adverse wind, he came towards them early in the morning, walking on the sea. He intended to pass them by. But when they saw him walking on the sea, they thought it was a ghost, and cried out; for they all saw him and were terrified. But immediately he spoke to them and said, "Take heart, it is I; do not be afraid." Then he got into the boat with them and the wind ceased [Mark 6:47–51).[3]

The question I ask myself about this story is not, Do I believe that it happened as reported on a night in Galilee some two thou-sand years ago? I ask, rather, What does it teach me about my life and the world? I learned an answer only recently, from a woman of my acquaintance, in hearing her answer that latter question for herself. First, she said, "I am often like those disciples in the boat, tossed on the sea and afraid, and I realize that if I let Jesus into the boat," when I live my life experiencing God as present with me, "the winds buffeting me will quiet themselves."

But also, she went on, "I realized a more striking truth. A good friend was hospitalized with cancer, and his family was under great stress," straining at the oars against an adverse wind. "I spent time last week visiting my friend, sitting with his wife, running errands for them, and helping the children at home. Like Jesus, I got into the boat with the family, and for a time at least the winds were easier for them to bear."

I hear both the religious and the secular voices of which I have spoken respond with some exasperation to this account. To the former, I am eliding, first, the fact that I am a Jew and don't "believe in Christ," and therefore don't believe that Jesus could walk on water. (To many religious people, Jewish and Christian, I simply have no business telling Christian stories, in any event.) More fundamentally, if I acknowledge, as I do, that I don't believe that God makes the seas swell and settle as acts of "His" "will," I am misusing a sacred story to support a purely personal (the words of the *Seeger* statute) psychological insight.

The secular voice is glad that I don't "believe" the story, and may even think that my friend's account contains some important truths. But what, this voice complains, is the point of dressing them up with ancient supernaturalisms? In seeking to buttress the authority of my point by cloaking it in the voice of a God that I acknowledge isn't "really there," I am simply evading my responsibility to support the validity of my supposed truth with some respectable mode of proof.

My effort in this book is to articulate the ways in which I have found it illuminating to turn to religious language, religious metaphors, and religious images, not as a source of metaphysical knowledge or belief, but as an aid to understanding and inspiration, an aid to discernment of moral truth and strengthening of the will to act accordingly. Judged by that standard, the story carries truth. (I will also say why I use this form of words, rather than simply say that the story "is true"). That truth is there for a Jew to see as well as a Christian, indeed, I will suggest, for an avowed secularist also. It speaks in Christian terms because it is *told* by a Christian, in the Christian language, if you will. But what it is saying is no more foreign, or unacceptable, to me than it is to hear a French person speak, in his or her own language, words that draw me when they are uttered in mine, or when I understand the French. While there are certainly secular modes of access to the truth that the story points toward, I have come to apprehend, and will try to give voice to, the special ways in which religious language and practices do the work of discerning it.

The Catholic theologian Daniel Maguire writes of religious symbols in these terms: "Symbols, like classics, are invitational, not intrusive or impositional. . . . symbols may speak to any open mind."[4] In quoting these words, I recognize that reasons abound for regarding some, perhaps most, religious symbols as mightily intrusive and impositional. I will speak to the possibility of incorporating that recognition into any attempt to move beyond it. As must be obvious, I do not turn to the scriptures, or other sources of religious language, for "authority" in the traditional sense of a metaphysical trump card.[5] Here, too, there are strands in the religious tradition, Jewish and Christian, that support a less vigorously hierarchical notion of the relation between humanity and divinity.

In what is to follow, I mean to avoid, as best I can, two endemic difficulties. The first is to rely too much on words—more precisely, to rely on too many words. Much of what I want to write about can be more accurately evoked than fully described, evoked through images and, indeed, through silence. Discernment can be aided by silence, and can too easily be overwhelmed by a tidal wave of discourse. Scripture teaches that it is in silence that "the heavens" pour forth constantly their knowledge of "the glory of God": "There is no speech, nor are there words; . . . yet their voice goes out through all the earth, and their words to the end of the world" (Ps. 19:1–4).

There is an obvious tension in trying to write in silence. I recognize that, as a law teacher, and neither a poet nor an artist, I can speak to others (especially the anonymous multitudes who might read this book) only in the very words of which I am wary. I ask the reader to pause over some of the images, stories, and scriptural passages that I will use, to allow himself or herself space to recognize and "be with" his or her own responses, rather than hurrying on to hear only mine.

Almost all talk about religion has the potential to trigger strong reactions, to which I might at times fail to attend sufficiently to enable you to go immediately on with me. For example, the sentence above, about grounds for experiencing religious images as "mightily intrusive and impositional" certainly warrants extended elaboration. If you are a Jew, or a refugee from almost any religion of origin, you will be able to supply that elaboration, but might feel the need to have me provide some, to validate the strength of your feelings. If you have always been comfortable with your religious tradition and its place within the mainstream of American culture, you might not immediately understand the point of what I said so briefly. In either case, I ask you to read at times in a frame of mind that is both receptive and dialogic.

The second hazard is for me, or you, to take what I will say as an argument, a position taken in debate. This book is not a contribution to the chorus of recent writing, much of it by law professors, seeking to determine what public policy ought to be toward the use of religious language, principles, and practices in public life.[6] Much popular writing on this subject tends too much simply to celebrate or to "view with alarm" either the presence or the absence of religiously informed contributions to public policy. Academic writing tends to be what law teacher and classicist James Boyd White calls structurally coercive, "in the sense that the writer seeks to prove something to an unwilling reader who [is] forced by factual or logical demonstration to yield."[7] My goal is to invite you to try on the spectacles with which I see the world, and ask yourself to what extent they fit you, rather than to seek to prove to you that you cannot responsibly refuse them.[8]

An "invitation" is not an argument, although the tendency for it to lead to one is ever present. The difference between the two inheres principally in the fact that the former is addressed to the person of the hearer, what the late professor Warren Lehman termed "speaking to the spirit" of the other.[9] It speaks from the person of the speaker, calling on reasons in a manner that neither masks underlying world-views nor seeks to impose them, either by force of position or by force of rhetoric. I am not simply singing in the shower, for in writing I am motivated in part by a desire to affect your world-view. To that extent, my "invitation" shares with argument an instrumental quality. But I want what I write not to be dominated by that quality. I am not simply hammering a nail into a board. I write also out of a desire to present myself authentically to you, the reader, and to evoke an authentic response. So, in responding to these polar voices, I will not be seeking to invalidate them logically or empirically, to justify a demand that they be still, that they accede to my view or be found deficient in reasoning or integrity. Rather, I will speak from a stance that acknowledges them as coming only in part from others, a stance that acknowledges that they speak in part for me as well.

The great twentieth-century Jewish philosopher Franz Rosenzweig has written of the importance of this stance in felicitous terms:

> I really believe that a philosophy, to be adequate, must rise out of thinking that is done from the personal standpoint of the thinker. To achieve being objective, the thinker must proceed from his own subjective situation. The single condition imposed upon us by objectivity is that we survey the entire horizon; but we are not obliged to make this survey from any position other than the one in which we are, nor are we obliged to make it from no position at all. Our eyes are, indeed, only our own eyes; yet it would be folly to imagine we must pluck them out in order to see straight.[10]

It is necessary, therefore, to begin (but, following Rosenzweig, only to begin) by acknowledging the difference between explanations and justifications or arguments, between causes and reasons. I probably believe as I do because of the life I have lived, rather than only because of the reasons that seem to warrant or compel belief or doubt. That is, in setting out to examine the compatibility of my beliefs with my self-concept as an honest and reflective person, committed to intellectual integrity, I need to start by acknowledging my own subjectivity. It is only in that way that I can honestly be in dialogue with my subjectivity, and with you.

Justice Holmes's most famous aphorism asserts that experience, not logic, has been the life of the law.[11] He certainly did not mean, and I do not mean, to exclude logic or other forms of reasoning from a critical role in testing and shaping our understanding of truth. Indeed, experience, along with intuition and emotion, can inform reason as well as distort it, can aid the search for truth as well as derail it. I begin with an acknowledgment of my own subjectivity because, if I can speak only the truth that I have perceived to be so, I must share with you something of who I am.

If, however, we only acknowledge and do not go beyond our individual subjectivities, dialogue is impossible. More precisely, we could then interact only by making the hearing of another's account of his or her life experiences an aspect of our own life experience; we could read, and write, only autobiography. I look therefore for reasons, not only causes, that might explain—to myself, as well as to you—why I cannot say that I believe as many who call themselves believers do, and why I nonetheless find it legitimate and important to turn to the religious tradition for guidance.

I say "explain," however, rather than "justify" or "persuade." For an honestly self-reflective process of subjecting one's beliefs to the scrutiny engendered by reason and experience, though essential, is not sufficient; it can too easily lose its moorings in the self, can become transformed into a debate, a search for compelling, respectable, or impressive arguments, and lose, unnoticed, its grounding in the actual person. The question is not alone whether a reason is persuasive, but also whether it is in fact salient. So, even when being rational, I must stay in close touch with my subjectivity. I must begin with the way that the course of my life has shaped the evolution of my outlook on the world of religion.

1
Odyssey

> If you want to know who I am, I can provide some
> categories in which to place me: citizen of the United
> States, member of the United Methodist Church, male,
> white, seminary professor, and so forth. But if you really
> want to know who I am, you will have to let me share
> my story with you.
>
> —JOHN B. COBB, JR.[12]

I am a Jew, born in 1931. I grew up in the shadow of the Great
Depression and the Third Reich. My father, the eldest of six children, left school in ninth grade to add to his family's resources the
six dollars he was able to earn weekly. The week that he and my
mother were married, his wages, having risen over the years to
thirty dollars, were cut to twenty-five, and the first five years of
my life (I later learned) were for him a searing struggle to find
and hold on to work.

In 1936, a job offer took us to a small town in Pennsylvania,
and I spent what I recall as five happy years there. Our family was
one of twenty Jewish families in a town of five thousand. My
being a newcomer to a community in which change was not
much a part of everyday life, and my having to wear glasses from
the age of eight, likely contributed as much to my growing into
a settled feeling of being an "outsider" among my school friends
as my being Jewish. That latter quality meant little more than my
having to supply a note of explanation from home when I stayed
out of school on the High Holy Days. My parents were not observant of the home-based practices, Friday evenings and the
Passover service, that are so much a part of Jewish ritual, and the
town had no synagogue or rabbi. Except for reading the Genesis
story in my child's encyclopedia, I had no exposure during those
years to Judaism—or to Christianity either, so far as I can recall,

since the public school imported no religious observances into the day and my Protestant friends and classmates did not bring their religious practices into our daily lives.

I recall no moments of anti-Semitism among my classmates or the community during those years. It certainly existed, but my memory is only of my father's account of two prior incidents, which he told me as warrants of the ready willingness of the "town fathers" to keep it in check. One concerned a druggist who, having competed first in traditional ways with the other druggist in town, placed a sign in his window urging the citizenry to "buy at a Christian store." "They made him take it down," my father told me—not as current news but as a source of pride in the ethos of our neighbors. The other involved the local chapter of a national fraternal organization, which operated on a "blackball" system whereby any brother could prevent the acceptance of a proposed new entrant. My father was not the only Jewish member, because our immediate neighbor (and landlord) had responded a few years earlier to a move to blackball the first one by threatening that he (and after his death, his son) would thereafter blackball every new prospect proposed for membership, until the chapter simply died out. Again, the message of my father's account was not so much the animus of the would-be blackballers as the prompt and potent recognition by the "better element" that anti-Semitism must be kept in check.

Whether during those years I had any awareness of the rise of Hitler and Fascism, I cannot now recall, except that in 1938 two Jewish couples arrived in town as refugees, one Viennese and the other from Berlin. In characteristic Eastern European fashion, the town's Jews welcomed the Austrian couple, and quickly wrote off the "Germans" (as to us they were) as typically haughty and superior.

When I was ten years old, my father was transferred by his company to New York City. My world now became one of many Jewish relatives, friends, and neighbors; of a wider Christian community that for the most part we regarded as mildly to virulently anti-Semitic; and of a growing awareness of, and emotional commitment to, the war against the Axis Powers. As I became more aware of politics and history, I learned of the power of the native fascist movement that was so much a part of the '30s. A local chapter of the German-American Bund was headquartered near the swimming pool that we went to from time to time. Father Coughlin, Gerald L. K. Smith, and *The Brooklyn Tablet* became palpable realities in my consciousness.[13] Yet, with Franklin Roosevelt as my President, and Fiorello LaGuardia as my mayor, I had no doubt that "America" stood for everything that the Nazis and their domestic sympathizers stood against. Neither my Jewish consciousness nor what I later recognized as a nascent Left-oriented approach to politics led me to feel out of synch with the national mood. Patriotism was on *my* side, the side of all who sought inclusion in the promise of the Four Freedoms—Hank Greenberg as well as Jesse Owens and Joe Louis, Sidney Hillman as well as Sacco and Vanzetti and Tom Mooney.[14]

My parents had joined a Conservative temple, and I soon became a conventionally religious practitioner of the mild variety of Conservative Judaism that the temple observed. Comfortable with the fit between my emergent Jewish consciousness and my emergent liberal universalism, I responded strongly to the Jewish liturgy. My parents were emotionally taciturn, and the communal expression of emotion carried by the melodies chanted by the cantor and the congregation drew me strongly, while the textual messages—a clarion call for constantly renewed ethical self-searching, and a profession of hope for the perfectibility of human life under an enduring divine love and protection—contributed to and were validated by the political outlook that I was developing. Virtually alone among my friends, I continued to attend synagogue for several years past my becoming *bar mitzvah*. Through me—the silent act of my going to services, for it would never have occurred to me to urge it on him, or even to realize (as must have been the case) that I was happy to have him do it—my father began to attend as well.

I remember being startled to learn, as my political awareness broadened a bit, that many leftists had fundamental problems with religion. It was not Judaism itself, but the linking of it to a needless hostility to others, that troubled me. I recall my revulsion to hear our Hebrew School teacher take his rejection of Christianity and its Bible so far as to contend that there probably was never any such person as Jesus of Nazareth. We could reject the theology of the Jesus story, and certainly disdain two millennia of Christian anti-Semitism, but it was hardly necessary for us to claim that the whole thing was a fabrication. In those days, however, such excesses of parochial zeal were to me simply individual aberrations, to be rejected and forgotten. They were not an inherent aspect of Jewish consciousness.

I cannot recall what my "metaphysical" views were during those years. Like most boys given religious instruction only in preparation for becoming *bar mitzvah*,[15] I could read Hebrew (in which the service was for the most part conducted) but understood little of what I was reading. Conservative synagogues, however, used a prayer book that presented the liturgy in translation across from the traditional Hebrew. I was therefore necessarily made aware of what was being asserted in the chants that I had grown to love. Along with those aspects of the liturgy with whose sentiments I felt a powerful resonance were of course repeated professions of faith that I later came to understand as propositional assertions about the nature of reality. My best guess now is that during my teen-age years I tacitly ignored those that I thought plainly "not true"—"Blessed is God, . . . who raises the dead"— but fairly easily accepted the truth of most of the liturgy without much thought. That acceptance too, however, was more emotional than propositional, a distinction that would not have occurred to me at the time.

The break came after my first year of college, when I began a long period of alienation from Judaism. To the extent that change was not produced by intrapsychic factors now beyond my capacity to disinter, it had two sources. First, I came to think that I could no longer fail or refuse to see religious faith or belief as the acceptance of the truth of a set of propositions about the nature of reality—what much later I read of as "faith *that*" rather than "faith *in*." While I was comfortable with the Jewish version of those propositions for a while, I had to acknowledge, suddenly, that I just did not believe it. If it was not in fact true that the earth is supported on the back of a giant elephant, which is in turn supported by four enormous turtles,[16] it was no more true that there ever was a Garden or a Flood, and the appearance of neither a ram on Mount Moriah nor a set of Tablets at Sinai was the willed act of a transcendent being to choose to enter the world of time and space.

That disavowal acknowledged, I found it hypocritical to continue to observe Jewish rituals for cultural or social reasons. One either accepted the tenets of a religion or one didn't, I rather scornfully asserted, and if one didn't accept them, it was unworthy to go to a synagogue to wear suits, to make friends or meet girls, or because one was more comfortable in the company of fellow Jews or liked chicken soup and potato pancakes. During the years in which I was able to accept (even though a bit tacitly) the religious side of Jewish observance, I had felt superior to my contemporaries who participated in Jewish activities for "lesser" reasons; when I could no longer avoid acknowledging that I found the religious grounding infirm, I felt superior to those who participated at all. I would not participate in a Judaism that had come to appear only as what, decades later, Professor Paul Mendes-Flohr termed "a mere sediment of memory and sentiment, . . . a matter of ethnic pride and solidarity."[17]

Ethnic pride and solidarity were not merely thin reeds on which to base a religious consciousness. Increasingly I came to see them as affirmatively flawed, and grew unable to ignore the ways in which Judaism was parochial and triumphalist. Reading the Scriptures was a painful exercise. I found them too full of stories of the slaughter, in the name of God, of one tribe after another. I was attracted in college to Tom Paine's observation that the Israelites prayed only for victory in battle. Christianity, of course, was a far more dismal chronicle of crimes committed, against Jews and against millions of others (many of them Christians) as well, but it was only by reason of the good fortune of the Jews to have been deprived of temporal power for two millennia that Judaism could appear less malign.

For too many Jews, an enduring legacy of anti-Semitism was the adoption of an insular disdain for anything "goyish," which I could not accommodate to the postwar universalism that I had embraced. After all, we had won the War, and for all that might have been said (much of which I only later became aware of) about the complicity of the West in the near-destruction of European Jewry,[18] the defeat of Nazism was largely brought about by Christians. In 1948, after 1900 years, a Jewish State was once again established, and immediately recognized by the United States. The Arab attempt to render it stillborn was to me the work of Hitler's agent in Jerusalem, the Grand Mufti Haj Amin El-Husseini, and its result was an enlargement of Israel's borders. The United Nations seemed about to usher in "One World" (the title of an influential book by FDR's 1940 Republican opponent[19]), a world implicitly grounded in a vision of the expansion of an improved version of Western liberal democracy.

In two years of military service, surrounded by Southerners and Midwesterners, mostly farm boys, both Catholic and Protestant, I heard but two expressions of anti-Semitic sentiments. Although neither was directed *at* me, both prompted an immediate disavowal: in one case, a public challenge; in the other, a private apology, from a fellow soldier who heard the statement. Anti-Semitism was certainly alive and well in the postwar world, but there hardly still seemed justification for the garrison mentality I had come to think of as inseparable from religious Judaism.

So matters stood for a generation. My wife (also Jewish) had been brought up in a strongly secular environment, and was not receptive to religious practices as an adult. Neither of us believed in bringing religion into the home "for the sake of" our daughter. Indeed, one of my objections to religious observance was the way in which it seemed inevitably to inculcate in children attitudes of superiority of their parents' religion over others. And a secular interaction with the world seemed wholly able to meet my needs, spiritual no less than intellectual and political.

The change began in ways that I was not even aware of. The foundations were probably laid by the undermining of any easy optimism about liberal democracy and its expansion, an optimism that for me as for many was tested but not destroyed by the rise of the Cold War and the new "Red scare" of the '50s, and more seriously compromised by the wrenching events of the '60s: the Viet Nam war, the assassinations of Martin Luther King and Bobby Kennedy in the spring of 1968, and the rapid evaporation of the egalitarian impulse that was the nation's first reaction to the Civil Rights Movement (or, more precisely, to the white Southern response to it). More of all that in Chapter 5. (Also there of the effect of changes in my personal life. My wife and I separated in 1971, and I was married again in 1976.)

Changes in my interaction with the study, practice, and teaching of law also affected my attitude toward religion. A law teacher since 1960, I began in the late '70s to work with a group of teachers interested in trying to make our work more expressive of our values and aspirations. This experience affected my approach to my work in many ways, which I will speak more about below. But it also had a powerful effect, after a rather long period of latency, on my interaction with religion. Although the content of our work was secular, it featured an explicit focus on our subjective experience, and on the importance and difficulty of acknowledging the need to search for meaning in our work. This bringing out of seldom expressed aspirations, for ourselves and for the world, that animated our choice to study law and become teachers of law, was an opening to the spiritual, notwithstanding that neither I nor my colleagues would have put it that way at the time.[20]

Shortly after my remarriage, my wife, Carolyn Schodt, and I began to attend Quaker Meeting. I cannot now recall how or why that happened; my daughter Alice was a high-school student at Germantown Friends School in Philadelphia, which provided an attractive but fairly remote window on Quaker thought and practice. The emphasis at Meeting on listening, on receptivity, was an arresting contrast with the didactic volubility of Jewish liturgy. Each person spoke for himself or herself alone, for the most part sharing what the speaker thought without telling us that we should do likewise. Some who spoke were traditionally religious, some specifically Christian, while others were plainly at least as wary as I was of being either. The idea that silence was a mode of communal activity, and a source of understanding and insight, drew me powerfully. "We sit in silence," says a classic Quaker aphorism, "and we wait upon the Lord." I came to understand that *waiting* is not a passive process, but an active, extremely challenging receptivity, and to understand as well that receptivity need not entail a willingness to submit to externally imposed direction: "The Lord," rather than being a wholly transcendent personage, is to be found within each of us. The Meetinghouse that we first attended had on one of its walls an exhortation that affected me noticeably: "Turn in, turn in, I beseech thee; there ye need Christ, and there ye must find Him."[21] If "Christ" is within, these folks meant something different about "him" than my presuppositions suggested. The focus was moved away from externally imposed beliefs, which one was compelled to accept, or to reject, as a matter of authority, to the authority of (as the Friends like to put it) one's Inner Guide, a term that, to Quakers, is synonymous with the Christ, or the Light, Within.

A traditional Quaker song speaks of the "Light" that shines "in the Turk and the Jew."[22] While I bridled more than a little, and still do, at the oblivious, happy-go-lucky condescension that is embedded in this message, I recognized that there was something more going on here than a fairly benevolent variety of triumphalism. The reconciliation of my participation in Quaker meeting with my *being* Jewish—not merely being "of Jewish origin"—was and has remained a complex affair, but the experience of complexity and wariness has its origin in the experience of attraction and a sense of opening, which I plainly felt.

A few years later, mostly by accident, we spent a summer vacation at a Zen Buddhist farm near the Pacific Ocean in California. We returned nearly every summer for the next ten years. Quakerism rejects all "outward forms," while Buddhism pays meticulous attention to an endlessly structured set of forms. One is closely linked with Christian modes of understanding reality; the other is not theistic at all. Yet both are much alike, in their pursuit of a spiritual practice emphasizing silence as an aid to receptivity, and meditation as an opening to awareness of self and compassion for others. My attraction to both, despite their plainly observable differences, began to loosen the hold on me of the association of religion with sectarian claims to exclusive possession of the truth, and to enable me to see the common ground of practice and aspiration underlying credal diversity.

The Zen emphasis on "practice" as pervading every moment of mundane life has had an ever-deepening effect on me. I have many times come back to a wonderful, quintessentially Zen, incident when, on returning to Green Gulch Farm for our second stay there, I told a resident who greeted me warmly that this time I was hoping to find ways to learn more about Buddhism. He smiled happily, and said: "Great! Just go into the kitchen, and start doing the dishes!" I have also recalled often, with a sigh at the depth of its call on me, the initial question of one of the senior teachers there, when Carolyn first met with him for *dokusan* (practice counseling): "What has been your practice outside of the *zendo* [meditation hall]?" In a profession that lives on words, I normally would seek to explicate such brief and cryptic messages as fully as possible, provided that my vigilantly exercised powers of evaluation found them worthy of the effort. I began instead to learn just to *be* with them, to let them live in my consciousness, returning to them over and over, sometimes silently, sometimes in speech, watching for moments when their salience would suddenly become manifest. This too was an opening to the spiritual.

I also began to be powerfully affected by the opportunity to observe at close hand the lives of the residents of Green Gulch Farm as members of a monastic community. Most of us are doing well if we manage to align our lives with our deepest values to the extent we can, given our commitments to our work, our mortgages, our children, and the like. A monastic community reverses the dependent and independent commitments: It chooses its work, and its lifestyle, so as to minimize the tension with its values. Green Gulch is relaxed and even playful about the seriousness of its commitments, but it constantly seeks to monitor the tendency to let the "real world" limit its ability to remain faithful to those commitments. So, it is a farm, a model of organic agriculture, but the residents continually strive to remember that their farming, like their meditation, is an aspect of their practice; they are not farmers who also do Buddhist meditation. When, for example, a newcomer objected to feeding the snails, which attack the flowers, to the ducks (a practice that they came to after much reflection), asserting that killing any "sentient being" was inconsistent with Buddhist precepts, they readily honored the individual's refusal to participate, and would have responded hospitably as well to a serious call to reflect again on their decision.

This firsthand encounter with the pervasive orienting effect of a religious grounding on daily life-decisions moved my focus from an obsession with the propositional truth of the central stories of specific religions. When, for example, I asked a resident, who had become a friend, whether he "really believed" in reincarnation, he said, "Do you want to know what the principle of reincarnation means? It means that our acts have consequences that extend far beyond what we can perceive."

Carolyn has always been a deeply spiritual person. She had left the Roman Catholic Church, in sorrow and anger, as a young adult, remaining keenly aware of the loss attendant on that decision, compelled though it was. I say "the Church" rather than Catholicism, or Christianity, because she had come to experience the institutional apparatus of her faith as a barrier between her and her religious consciousness, rather than a vehicle for expressing it. Her link with God (if I may put it that way) remained, in a latent state for want of a means of expression.

At the time we met, although I would not have thought of myself as a "refugee" from Judaism, my alienation from it was deeper, reaching to questioning religious faith itself as well as the institutional trappings of Judaism. In our marriage ceremony, we spoke respectfully of our own and each other's religious traditions, and the positive common legacy that their underlying witness had given us. In this, we spoke sincerely, albeit our desire to speak was heavily influenced by our desire to help our parents in their admirable efforts to respond positively to a marriage, and a marriage ceremony, that could not have been what they most would have wished for.

Our choice to speak words of hope, and let those of judgment stand aside for the moment, had a generative quality; they made themselves come true, more than they reflected present truth. To me, the Catholic Church of my youth—the Church of the Pope of Silence, Pius XII, of the Concordat with Franco, and of the Legion of Decency, Cardinal Spellman, and Bing Crosby—was a malign force in the world.[23] Fiercely parochial, in ways that were more authoritatively promulgated and of far greater temporal consequence than the manifestations of a similar tendency in Judaism, it cared only for its own power. Overseas, it would lie down happily with the Devil—Franco in Spain, the pro-Nazi wartime regime in Croatia, a repressive dictatorship in Viet Nam—as long as its own status was protected.[24] At home, it uncompromisingly sought to influence public policy in ways that would enable it to maintain its hold on its communicants. From them, it demanded unquestioning obedience to a religious ethic that seemed to value little more than deference to authority and repression of sexuality, and was wholly indifferent to the suffering that its policies inflicted. (I recall hearing often the admonition that a couple about to give birth should *never* use a Catholic hospital, lest in an unanticipated crisis the medical staff be disabled from choosing the mother's life over the child's.)

By the time that Carolyn and I were married in 1976, the radical changes in the Church (including the attitude toward its historic anti-Semitism) that followed the Second Vatican Council, the social teachings of Pope Paul VI, and the participation of many priests and nuns in the civil rights and anti-war movements, had opened for me a window on Catholicism, indeed, on Christianity and religion generally.[25] Beyond that, and perhaps more important, there was something, which even now I cannot fully articulate, about marrying into a Catholic family that was part of what drew me back to religion. Observing Christianity through Carolyn's parents, as it appeared from "inside," helped in a non-cognitive way to complement, and probably to crystallize, the impact on my outlook of the public factors I have mentioned. When our son, Caleb, was born in 1977, he was baptized in the Roman Catholic Church, and circumcised in the Covenant of Abraham, not as the compromise action of an intermarried couple, but as a claiming and celebration of the richness of his heritage.[a] We saw that claim as more than simply cultural or ethnic, difficult though it remained to give expression to its religious content. Indeed, much as with our marriage ceremony, the decision was something we discovered ourselves drawn to do. The affirmation of a link with our parents was only in part a desire to accommodate them. It reflected, but also helped to bring further into being, a turning toward the grounding of our own lives.

In recent years, Carolyn has been willing again to enter a church, and we have begun attending Mass at Christmas and Easter, and on Sundays that we are visiting with her folks in Philadelphia or Erie. I have found myself able to experience the Mass without being dominated by the two-millennia overlay of which any Jew must remain conscious. It has a depth and power that is palpable for me. When the priest recites the words "Do this in remembrance of me," I am neither a participant nor a spectator. I can experience something of what Catholic and Episcopalian friends mean when they have said to me that the Mass is about transcendent love, in a way that does not put in issue the difference between the meaning of the Eucharist for them and for me. Dr. Blu Greenberg, an Orthodox Jew, put the point well, speaking of her experience in a Sikh temple: "I wasn't praying and yet I wasn't just standing there coldly and observing. It wasn't a religious experience for me in the Sikh sense, but it was a religious experience."[26]

When we attended Mass as a family for the first time with Carolyn's parents, and I suddenly felt the need to say something explanatory to our children when their grandparents rose to join

---

[a] "[M]y servant Caleb showed a different spirit; he followed me with his whole heart" (Numbers 14:24).

most of the others present, but not us, at the Communion rail, I was able—because I gave the question no prior thought at all—simply to say, "Catholics believe that, at the moment that they take the wafer and the wine, they come into contact with God." I immediately thought to myself, Is *this* the doctrine that has for centuries been so profound a source of alienation and rancor, so tragic a source of oppression and death?

I have spoken of the overlay of which any Jew must be conscious. I came to realize that there was another overlay, which burdened Carolyn and so many who were raised Catholic in the days before Vatican II, that was part of my intellectual awareness but carried no personal emotional sting. I have in mind the strongly authoritarian, hierarchical stance of traditional Catholicism, with the figure of the priest at the altar, almost literally standing in for Christ. What struck me so powerfully when I encountered the Mass was its strong relational, egalitarian quality. One example, which a long-time Catholic might smile at as trivial, but which to me is momentous, will suffice to make the point.

Several times during the service, the priest invokes God's blessing on the congregation, in the words "The Lord be with you." The congregation responds, "and also with you." I find this exchange stunningly transformative. By it, the priest moves from being one with a privileged access to God, who dispenses his blessing to the faithful, to one who initiates a communal acknowledgment that *all* are in need of blessing and *all* are empowered to confer it on another. And in those services I have attended, the remainder of the liturgy, and the homily, have been consistent with this spirit.[27]

My conscience stirred by the realization that I seemed able to become open to every religion but my own, I would go from time to time to synagogue. I would find myself again drawn powerfully by the liturgy, which I would read silently before the service began, hearing in my mind the traditional melodies with which it was chanted, and moved by meditations added to the prayer book that I had never seen before, only to find myself quickly repelled by a ritualized service that seemed arid and lifeless, except as a cultural rite.

In the last several years, however, this last barrier too has crumbled. It was probably not coincidental that the process began with my interaction with Christianity and Buddhism, with reincarnation and the Eucharist, rather than with the parting of the Red Sea or the Revelation at Sinai. Perhaps it is easier to see variousness in the religious tradition of others than in one's own. My mindset had surely been that a religion "belongs" to its orthodox branch (whatever the denomination involved), that I am free to accept or reject, but not to appropriate to a radically revised world-view, the old-time religion. Finding resonance with the practices of religious faiths that I did not feel called upon to accept or reject probably moved me along toward recognizing that I could do the same with my own faith tradition.

Yet any real blossoming of that recognition became possible only once we became aware of a practice community, and its teachers, to guide the search. Encouraged by Carolyn to seek further, we found practitioners of a Jewish spirituality that is free of the qualities that had for so long alienated me from my own religion. Largely through the inspired teaching and learning of Rabbi Marcia Prager, and the practices and writing to which she has opened my mind, I have become willing to let go of the belief that accepting Judaism means going back to a Jewish version of the elephant and the turtles, accepting certain assertions about a God who created the world and rules and intervenes in human history, who chooses whether to make the rain fall and the wind blow, and a lot of metaphysics that I just do not believe. It has been a slow process of recognizing that that does not have to be what the stories mean.

That process has been aided by my exposure to the vast well that is the rabbinic tradition. I am learning from that tradition (among much else) a way of learning which finds in its stories a truth that depends not on their narrative historicity but on their capacity to open a channel of understanding and insight. I have also experienced the variousness of Jewish spirituality, and the profound commonalities that it shares with the Christian mystical tradition, Catholic and Quaker; with creation spirituality and the religion of Native peoples; and with Buddhism.[28] This experience has cleansed Judaism, as I am coming to understand it, of the triumphalist parochialism that for so long kept me at a distance from it.

More than that, in a way that may sound paradoxical but which I do not experience that way, the process has for the first time settled the question of my religious identity: I will live as I was born, a Jew. My experience parallels that of Rodger Kamenetz, who participated in a number of manifestations of Buddhist, Hindu, and Sikh practice during a visit with the Dalai Lama in a group of practicing Jews:

> In Delhi, facing the multiplicity of religious expressions, and the obvious quality of devotion in several of them, I could feel the pressure of competing identities burst and melt. . . . Paradoxically, this did not make me feel less a Jew. Rather, I gained a much broader view of the power of all religions, including my own.[29]

The great Protestant theologian H. Richard Niebuhr says of himself: "In one sense I must call myself a Christian in the same sense that I call myself a twentieth-century man. To be a Christian is simply part of my fate."[30] Except for the connotation of the stoic acceptance of bad luck, I think that this idea captures the thought, and provides a simple escape from the notion that, to remain secure in our particular religious tradition, we must assert its exclusive or superior claim to truth. My experience has confirmed the insight of the leading twentieth-century historian of religion, Mircea Eliade, "that knowledge of the religious ideas and practices of other traditions better enables anyone to understand his or her own. The history of religions is the story of the human encounter with the sacred—a universal phenomenon made evident in myriad ways."[31] As a Jew, I enter into the language, and with it the experience, of Judaism, and also of other faiths and their communicants. I experience that latter entry empathically, and in a way that is more than merely empathic. In both ways, however, it enhances rather than undermines or draws into question my Jewish spirituality.

2

Speaking of God

> When I was through, he spoke hesitatingly, then, carried away by the importance of his subject, ever more passionately. "How can you bring yourself to say 'God' time after time? How can you expect that your readers will take the word in the sense in which you wish it to be taken? What you mean by the name of God is something above all human grasp and comprehension, but in speaking about it you have lowered it to human conceptualization. What word of human speech is so misused, so defiled, so desecrated as this! All the innocent blood that has been shed for it has robbed it of its radiance. All the injustice that it has been used to cover has effaced its features. When I hear the highest called 'God,' it sometimes seems almost blasphemous."
>
> —MARTIN BUBER[32]

When I speak of God, when I use religious modes of expression or participate in a religious practice, what do I mean to be doing? This chapter is my attempt to answer that question. To do that adequately, however, I need to engage more fully with the two polar voices to which I referred in the Introduction. Both question the "religious" character of the beliefs that undergird my answer.

The first of these voices regards my answer as insufficiently religious to justify the term, and challenges the coherence, and perhaps the legitimacy, of my appropriating religion to what it views as an essentially secular world-view. I find in religious language and practices a different sort of truth than do many, perhaps most, who speak in religious terms and follow a religious practice. To some such, the belief that underlies my speech and practice is not religious belief at all, but a misuse of words and actions that lie close to the core of their identity. That at times this objection is expressed in self-righteous and triumphalist terms does not warrant dismissing it. I want therefore to consider very seriously what I will call the challenge of warrant, the legitimacy of my claiming sufficient grounds for speaking religiously in the way that I do.

The polar voice questions not the legitimacy but the value of my resort to religious language and practices. It agrees with the first set of objectors that (notwithstanding my protestations) my consciousness is essentially secular, but believes that I am simply obfuscating my speech and thought by needlessly sacrificing clarity to a usage that is vague and unhelpful at best and, in light of the history of religion, positively harmful. I will call that challenge one of diversion, and will address it in the final section of this chapter.

STANDING TODAY AT SINAI

> Buddha's teaching is only a raft
> to help you cross the river,
> a finger pointing to the moon.
> Don't mistake the finger for the moon.
>
> —THICH NHAT HANH[33]

What do I mean when I say that I find truth in (some) religious language and practices? Why do I resist simply saying that the religious talk that I believe "is" true? Why do I persist in calling myself a non-believer? I will answer with as much analytical clarity as I can muster, consistent with my belief that, beyond a point, clarity in this area is purchased only at the cost of accuracy and salience.

I need to say first that, despite the changes in my attitude toward religion (see pp. 16–23, above), I still cannot accept the truth of religious narratives, if by "truth" is meant the way we mean it when we say, for example, that the statement that the moon rose here at 8:42 last night is true (or false). It is important to say bluntly, albeit as respectfully as I can, that I do not believe that the central narrative of either Judaism or Christianity—the giving of the Torah on Mount Sinai, or the incarnation of divinity in the person of Jesus—ever happened, in the usual sense of that word. It is for this reason that I resist thinking of myself as a believer.[34]

It is not as easy as it might seem to say exactly why I have this lack of belief. At bottom, I can say little more than that a propositional understanding of religious narratives as accounts of specific events at particular moments in human history is premised on an understanding of God that I cannot recognize as God. It is a conception of God as super-potentate, as in the practice, in portions of Jewish liturgy, to refer to God as "the King of the King of Kings," because the "Great King" of the ancient world, the ruler of Persia, was accorded the title "the King of Kings."[35] More fundamentally, the meaning that it gives to the idea of "the will of God" rests on a conception of the relation between time and eternity, space and infinity, Earth and Heaven, humankind and divinity, creature and creator, that I experience as reductionist. I want to say no more about this in the present context, where I am seeking to articulate what I do believe.

I do not regard this skepticism as disabling me of justification for continuing to respond to the power that religious metaphors and religious narratives have to illuminate my path. The truth that they have lies in their capacity to open a channel of understanding and insight, and this much I do avow:

- the story that, at Sinai, Heaven bent down to touch the earth and, as Moses crossed the boundary between time and eternity, all of us who would ever be born stood with the Israelites at Sinai to receive the great gift of God's grace, the Law, making possible our transformation from runaway slaves into free men and women;
- the story that, in Bethlehem, divinity crossed that boundary in the form of a child, born to "a displaced person and a refugee, the daughter of an oppressed people," by which act humans were enabled to find a way to apprehend their worthiness to be loved, and their capacity to love one another.

These stories carry a truth that illuminates my understanding of human life and its meaning, and for me avowing their truth does not entail avowing that they "really happened."[36]

I acknowledge that the preceding sentence implicates some difficult questions about what it means to say that a statement "is true" or "carries truth." Scholars and practitioners, theologians and mystics, with far more learning and wisdom than I, have struggled to express an understanding of the meaning of truth like that which I am employing. I will say what I can about it in a moment. First, however, let me indulge a lawyer's habitual preference, to use a specific context as a vehicle for more fully expressing my belief.

The text that I will use, the opening verses of what is known as the Holiness Code, Leviticus 19, surely has few rivals for centrality in Western religious thought:

> The Lord said to Moses: "Speak to the whole Israelite community and tell them: 'Be holy, for I, the Lord your God, am holy.' "

Do I believe, first, that God did indeed speak to Moses, to us through Moses,[37] while the Israelites were in the wilderness, and, second, that we are admonished by God to be a holy people, that we are charged to be sacred beings?[b]

It is important to realize at the outset that the English term "the Lord" is a translation that significantly changes the meaning of the text, by reducing what is ineffable and untranslatable to what is familiar. Here and elsewhere, the Hebrew text identifies that which speaks to Moses as the Tetragrammaton, the four-consonant "word" (in English, YHWH) that it is both forbidden and impossible to vocalize.[38] To name a being is to "de-fine" it, to mark off its essence from that which it is not, and is necessarily an ascription of finitude. Adam is said to have given "every living creature" its name (Genesis 2:19). Having a name is an attribute of creatureliness, and the ancient belief that to utter the name of God was to invite immediate destruction gave readily understandable force to the profound philosophical insight that "God" can have no name, and that to refer to God by a name is to identify as God that which is (necessarily) less than God. Such an act is of course the paradigmatic act of idolatry.

Prohibition apart, the Tetragrammaton can be said without vowels only by an exhalation of breath. Some Jews today at times render the name of God as "the Breath of Life"; such a term, or terms like "Being itself" or "Ultimate Reality," embody a far different understanding of divinity, and seem to me more faithful

---

[b] The word " holy" is unfortunately associated in current usage with a judgmental or self-righteous piety. The word "sacred" better fits the sense, which I will develop below, of openness to awe.

to what is being said in the Torah, than the appropriation of a relationship suggested by temporal hierarchies, ancient or medieval.

It would be improbable beyond belief to suppose that the human understanding of what is expressed by "The Lord said to Moses" has not changed in two or more millennia.[39] Whatever might have been true as to biblical Israel, I imagine that few believe today that the statement means what it would mean for me to say, "my friend said to me _____," that God had decided to vocalize a sentence of Hebrew to Moses, as a pitcher chooses to throw a fast ball to a catcher. Yeshiva University President Norman Lamm, an Orthodox rabbi, accepts "unapologetically the verbal revelation of Torah," but does not "take seriously the caricature of this idea which reduces Moses to a secretary taking dictation." He goes on: "Exactly how this communication took place no one can say; it is no less mysterious than the nature of the One who spoke. . . . *How* God spoke is a mystery; how *Moses* received this message is an irrelevancy. *That* God spoke is of the utmost significance, and *what* He said must therefore be intelligible to humans in a human context."[40] I find pregnant meaning in the rabbinic teaching that, when Scripture says that Moses spoke to God "and God answered him by a voice" (Exodus 19:19), the implication is "that God answered Moses with the voice of Moses himself."[41]

A Quaker practice of an earlier age, now not entirely gone from use, was to introduce what one was about to say on rising to speak in Meeting: "It has come to me from the Lord to say. . . ." While this preamble bespeaks a level of confidence that I can readily experience as off-putting, it serves to make manifest that the statement "The Lord said to Moses" contains a dual affirmation. First, it is a statement about Moses: that he experienced the admonition to be holy as an accurate understanding of the divine "will," as a true affirmation about ultimate reality; beyond that, it asserts that Moses's understanding was in fact true, that it *is* God's will that we be a holy people, that we be sacred beings.

As to the first, it is not of great importance to me to ask whether, given what little I know of biblical scholarship, I believe that anything at all happened involving the man Moses and this passage during the wandering in the desert. My sense of what Sir Thomas More, for example, or St. Francis of Assisi said and did during their lifetimes comes to me as much from Robert Bolt and Nikos Kazantzakis as it does from history,[42] and for the purposes for which I find it important to attend to their teaching it is not of controlling significance that my apprehension of it is a blend of what reductively can be distinguished as history and legend, as "fiction" and "non-fiction." Indeed, it is inherent in people and events that have a scriptural or quasi-scriptural dimension that their presence in our lives, even if rooted in historicity, is configured to a significant degree by the contours of the presence that they have had in the lives of our ancestors (which is, after all, another form of historicity). Michael Lerner, suggesting from the evidence of its detailed retelling from generation to generation that "something happened" at Sinai, goes on to suggest that "there is another way to look at the story":

> that the something that happened was the telling itself. The very fact that this kind of story has been told, has taken root, and has held the moral and spiritual imagination of a people for twenty-four hundred years is itself the story of a revelation. The ability of a people to grasp, hold, imaginatively transform, and yet remain loyal to a story of liberation may be the very thing that happened.[43]

"Moses" is in this sense a mythic figure, by which I mean, not that he did not in fact walk the earth some twenty-five hundred years ago, but that his life and teaching have been constituted in significant part by the millennia during which those who came after have struggled to understand, and follow, his teaching. The poet and novelist Marge Piercy has made the point in these words: "We say words shaped by ancient use like steps worn into rock."[44]

So, then, I answer the first question, yes, I do believe that Moses believed and avowed that he had correctly divined God's plan for humanity, recognizing that, to traditional religionists and secular rationalists alike, both of whom tend (despite my epithet of reductionism) to insist on a sharper differentiation between fact and fiction, what I have avowed is in fact a disavowal: To such persons, I have really said that I do not believe it, that I do not care whether it is true or false.[45]

The second question may not so readily be put to one side. Do I believe that Moses was (or would have been) right to avow the admonition "Be holy" as God's will? I acknowledge first, that, I do not find in the fact that the Torah *says* "The Lord said to

Moses" a sufficient reason for me to believe it (or a sufficient reason for me to act as if I did). I do not give the Scriptures, even the Pentateuch, that sort of authority. It is for that reason that I am not a believer in the orthodox sense (using the word with a lower-case "o," because the point is salient with respect to Scripture-based religion generally, not only Judaism).

The evident fact of the belief of Moses and the Israelite community through the centuries does play a substantial part in the process of my coming to my beliefs. The beliefs of a great teacher or of a community of faith are a powerful heuristic, and on this ground the fact of Moses's and traditional Judaism's belief leads me no little part of the way toward sharing it. Indeed, on this ground, through its authority as teacher, the entire Torah deserves the most respectful attention.

But I do not find the fact of another's belief sufficient reason for my own, for my own efforts at discernment are (necessarily) involved, in interaction with those of my teachers. I therefore need to take into account the *content* of Moses's and the Israelites' belief. Whether as a matter of its own authority, or that of a teacher or faith community, the mere fact that a belief has a given source—what philosophers call a "content-independent" reason—does not end the inquiry.[46]

I must ask, therefore, what is it that Moses says, and the community of faith believes, is God's will? What Moses says in Leviticus 19:2 is that God's will is that we be holy, for God is holy. I do believe that, and that is why I claim warrant for writing and speaking in religious terms. I want to say—to the extent I can, for here there is great danger that speech will be more reductive than clarifying—what I *mean* when I say that I believe the statement, putting to one side for the moment the questions *why* I believe it, and how I *justify* that belief, indeed, what it means to justify such a belief.

I experience "Be holy" as a statement of moral truth. To reach to live a life grounded in an affirmation of the sacred is a good, surely one of the highest goods. I do not *know* that it is so, that I have correctly discerned the truth; I tend to think (although I am not sure of this either) that the content of moral truth lies beyond what we can call our knowledge.[47] So far as I best can judge, however, the statement "to reach to live a life grounded in an affirmation of the sacred is a good" is true; indeed, that is what I mean to say when I say that I believe it.

I will, as I said, postpone the question, why I have this belief, and attempt more fully to describe its content. The Christian feminist Dorothy Soelle has given content in these words to the idea that I have called an affirmation of the sacred:

> The directive is clear: We, not only God, are destined to be holy. We are beckoned to approximate God. We are invited to acquire and practice the quality of holiness that characterized God by doing the work of love and justice. . . . [T]he rabbinical insistence on the supreme holiness of God still does not negate the emphasis on our human capacity for holiness. Created in the image of God, we therefore are able to imitate God. "What means the text, 'Ye shall walk after the Lord your God'?" In answer to this rhetorical question the Talmud replies that the meaning of the text is "to follow the attributes of the Holy One, blessed be He: As He clothed the naked, so do you clothe the naked, as He visited the sick, so do you visit the sick. . . ."[48]

Soelle's emphasis on "the work of love and justice" surely finds support in portions of the Holiness Code itself. It includes admonitions addressed to the terms of contemporary social life that, taken to heart, powerfully constrain both personal self-seeking and public policy:

> When you reap the harvest of your land, you shall not reap to the very edges of your field, or gather the gleanings of your harvest. You shall not strip your vineyard bare, or gather the fallen grapes of your vineyard; you shall leave them for the poor and the alien: I am the Lord your God.
>
> You shall not steal; you shall not deal falsely; and you shall not lie to one another. And you shall not swear falsely by my name, profaning the name of your God: I am the Lord.
>
> You shall not defraud your neighbor; you shall not steal; and you shall not keep for yourself the wages of a laborer until morning. You shall not treat the deaf with contempt or put a stumbling block before the blind; you shall fear your God: I am the Lord.
>
> You shall not render an unjust judgment; you shall not be partial to the poor or defer to the great: with justice you shall judge your neighbor. You shall not go around as a slanderer among your people, and you shall not stand idly by the blood of your neighbor: I am the Lord.
>
> You shall not hate your brother in your heart. Though you may have to reprove your neighbor, do not incur guilt because of him. You shall not take vengeance or bear a grudge against any of your

people, but you shall love your neighbor as yourself: I am the Lord. . . .

When an alien resides with you in your land, you shall not oppress the alien. The alien who resides with you shall be to you as the citizen among you; you shall love the alien as yourself, for you were aliens in the land of Egypt: I am the Lord your God.

You shall not cheat in measuring length, weight, or quantity. You shall have honest balances, honest weights, an honest ephah, and an honest hin: I am the Lord your God, who brought you out of the land of Egypt . . . [Leviticus 19: 9–18, 33–36].

These passages are a clarion call—an echoing blast of the *Shofar*—that stands in far-reaching judgment on the lives that most of us lead, and on our polity. Yet their eloquence and salience should not obscure the fact that we are concerned with more than goodness, more than politically just acts and institutions. Holiness requires justice, but is more than justice; holiness is goodness, but is more than goodness. To that extent, conservative religionists are right to complain of religion that seems to reduce itself to good works. Rabbi Abraham Joshua Heschel found in both Judaism and Christianity "the conviction that without the holy the good will be defeated": "The good is the base, the holy is the summit. Things created in six days He considered *good*, the seventh day He made *holy*." To live as a sacred being is to seek to live in Sabbath consciousness the week long.[49]

To say that holiness is more than goodness is very different from saying that it is unrelated to it. Rudolf Otto characterizes as the "greatest distinction of the religion of ancient Israel, at least from Amos onwards," the avowal of "precisely the intimate coalescence" of the good and the holy.[50] Daniel Maguire insists that "that which does not enhance human and terrestrial good is in no sense sacred. Religion can take root only in genuine moral awareness. The foundational moral experience is the foundation of religious experience."[51] This, to me, is the teaching of God's response to Abraham's challenge regarding Sodom, "Shall not the judge of all the world act justly?" (Genesis 18:25) (see, more fully, p. 75, below).[52]

To express in words the "more" of holiness, or sacredness, is not easy, and much profound teaching, written and oral, has been devoted to the effort. Rudolf Otto coined the word "numinous," to describe that "more," associating it with the *mysterium tremendum*, the feeling of the presence of an awesome power before which we are wholly submerged.[53] To Mircea Eliade, the sacred manifests itself as reality, a reality "of a wholly different order from 'natural' realities."[54] In the Jewish tradition, there is much that associates holiness with purity. Indeed, the remainder of the Holiness Code, the passages that I have not quoted (Leviticus 19:19–29), is concerned with matters of sexual, dietary, and other forms of purity, and one writer concludes that in Jewish law the concept of holiness "is associated more frequently and strongly with the dietary laws than with any of the other 613 biblical commandments."[55]

Unifying these seemingly disparate conceptions is what, to me, undergirds them: an openness to awe, triggered less perhaps by the apprehension of awesome power than by the "appreciation of the possibility of meaning and moral order," of an "overpowering, nonrational appreciation of purity and completeness in the world and purpose and caring in all life."[56] This is the stance that Rabbi Heschel felicitously called "radical amazement," the experience of time as tinged with eternity, finitude with infinity, the mundane as embodying the transcendent.[57] It is a stance that has been given expression in a wonderful variety of ways. The Hasidic sage, Rabbi Nachman of Breslov, enjoined us: "Seek the sacred within the ordinary. Seek the remarkable within the commonplace"; Rabbi Joseph Soloveitchik describes holiness as "the appearance of a mysterious transcendence in the midst of our concrete world. . . . [It] does not wink at us from 'beyond' like some mysterious star that sparkles in the distant heavens, but appears in our actual, very real lives"; and Rabbi Harold Schulweis writes of "miracles" in this vein:

> A miracle is an intimation of an experience of transcending meaning. The sign-miracle does not refer to something beyond or contrary to logic or nature. It refers to events and experiences that take notice of the extraordinary in the ordinary, the wonder in the everyday, the marvel in the routine. . . . To see the divine in the natural and the rational, in the application of human intelligence and goodness, is a major insight of the Jewish tradition.[58]

The most prosaic object can be the subject of this awareness. Writing about the iconic tradition of Eastern Christianity, law professor Richard Stith quotes an eloquent instantiation of this idea in a Christian context: "What is a nut if not the image of Jesus Christ? The green and fleshy sheath is His flesh, His humanity. The wood of the shell is the wood of the Cross on which His flesh suffered. But the kernel of the nut from which men gain nourishment is His hidden divinity."[59]

A well-known quatrain of William Blake's is as good a rendering of the idea in words as I know:

> To see a World in a Grain of Sand
> And a Heaven in a Wild Flower
> Hold Infinity in the palm of your hand
> And Eternity in an hour.[60]

As Blake's words suggest, there is a sense of the sacred that is not theistic. I will say more below about the relation of the spiritual to the dichotomy between the religious and the secular. What is essential, however, is that this openness, this experience, not be confined to time spent in church, synagogue, or mosque, listening to a Beethoven Quartet, or standing before crashing waves or a brilliant sunset, but be sought in the moment-to-moment hurly-burly of everyday life. In Rabbi Heschel's words, "There is no worship, no music, no love, if we take for granted the blessings or defeats of living. No routine of the social, physical, or physiological order must dull our sense of surprise at the fact that there *is* a social, physical, or physiological order. [Our goal is] to experience commonplace deeds as spiritual adventures, to feel the hidden love and wisdom in all things."[61]

Compare Vanessa Ochs's eloquent personal testimony, "I knew what the sanctified life was not. Not a life filled with more rituals, more scrupulously observed. Not more praying. Not becoming a better person, being more charitable, more concerned with everyone else's pains. Sanctifying had something to do with a sense of constant wonder—feeling gratitude and finding significance everywhere, in every action, relationship, and object."[62]

"Awe enables us," Heschel emphasizes, to "feel in the rush of the passing the stillness of the eternal."[63] It is through such an integration that openness to the sacred becomes a matter of moral, not only metaphysical, truth.

What is added when I say that I believe not only that "Be holy" is a moral truth, but also that it is "God's will"? That is, what is added by expressing what I perceive as moral truth in religious terms? Obviously, I do not mean that it is "commanded" by the Ultimate Commander-in-Chief. You surely noticed Soelle's

choice of words, to express the manner by which she understands
God to speak to humanity: We are "destined," "beckoned," "invited." The denial of an analogy to military, imperial, or corpo-
rate hierarchy in this locution should not hide the fact that what
is postulated is in some manner a bilateral communication. The
imperative to act, rooted in a sense of awe, does not come wholly
from within. William Penn, the Quaker founder of the Com-
monwealth of Pennsylvania, put the thought this way: "Some
seek it in books, some in learned men; but what they look for is
in themselves, but not *of* themselves."[64] A beautiful teaching in
the Talmud takes this form: "When there are [one or more] sitting together and occupying themselves with Torah, the *Shechinah*
[the divine presence] abides among them."[65] The Jewish feminist
Judith Plaskow has described the experience in words that have a
different ring, but perhaps not a radically different meaning:

> [A]s we join with others, in a way that only human beings can, in
> shared engagement to a common vision, . . . we find ourselves in
> the presence of another presence that is the final source of our
> hopes and intentions, and undergirds and sustains them. . . . [I]t is
> through the struggle with others to act responsibly in history that
> we come to know our own actions as encompassed and empow-
> ered by a wider universe of action and thus come to know God in
> a profound and significant way.[66]

My avowal that this "presence" *is* God is definitional: It is what
I mean by "God." My teacher Rabbi Marcia Prager speaks of the
word "God" not as a name, but as a job description. Part of the
job is to "beckon" us toward the discernment of moral truth.
Rabbi Harold Kushner expresses the thought in these words:

> God is the name we attach to the fact that we find certain things
> possible and meaningful in the world and in our lives and the fact
> that we find ourselves stirred to move in the direction of realizing
> these possibilities . . . , the name given to that force existing in the
> cosmos and in every one of us which helps us to identify that which
> is good and true and worthwhile and which moves us to pledge
> ourselves to live up to it.[67]

Pascal has God say: "You would not seek me, if you had not
already found me,"[68] while the title of a book on Zen Buddhist
meditation puts the thought in words that are (characteristically)
at once bewildering and clarifying: "That Which You Are Seeking Is Causing You to Seek."[69] In saying that I believe that "Be

holy" is "God's will," I am saying not only that I have come to believe the admonition as moral truth, but also that I experience that discernment as not coming wholly from within me. I am drawn by the truth, even as I seek it.

I come away from this reflection on Leviticus 19:1–2 concluding that the text has truth, when read in the rather complex way that I have read it. I prefer to say that it "has truth," or "carries truth," rather than that it "is true," for two reasons. First, these latter words suggest, although they do not compel, a more narrowly semantic understanding of what the text says than I (and not only I) have given it. Law teacher and classicist James Boyd White has remarked on the tendency "naturally to accept the view that . . . meaning . . . is propositional in character," a tendency that rests on "an image of language as transparent: our talk is about what is out there in the natural or conceptual world, to which it is the function of language to point." He goes on to suggest that, although this mode of discourse has important uses, "it is essential to recognize":

> that [some] texts work on a very different sense of thought and meaning indeed. They are not propositional, but experiential and performative; . . . not purely intellectual, but affective and constitutive. . . . Texts of this sort are . . . invitational: they offer an experience, not a message, and an experience that will not merely add to one's stock of information but change one's way of seeing and being, of talking and acting.[70]

Philosophers Kent Bendall and Frederick Ferre illustrate the point with telling simplicity:

> We are confronted with [a] function of Christian discourse that is more similar to an act—a pledge of allegiance or an oath of loyalty and trust—than to a claim of knowledge. Reciting the creeds may . . . resemble most closely a public performance like kissing the ring of the pope. As a "performative" utterance it is no more "true" or "false" than is the custom, practiced by some devout Christians, of making sure that the Bible never rests underneath a pile of books but is always on top, a wordless symbol of its authority.[71]

Second, "is true" suggests also a more static version of a so-called "correspondence" theory of truth—a statement is true if it corresponds to reality—than I mean my statement to embody, for human language and thought, embedded in finitude, cannot "correspond to" a reality that (if it is there at all) lies outside of time and space. Indeed, "outside" and "there" are themselves inaccurate depictions, for they are words *of* time and space, and can only demark boundaries within them. In Rabbi Abraham Joshua Heschel's felicitous words, "[W]hen trying to hold an interview with reality face to face, without the aid of either words or concepts, we realize that what is intelligible to our mind is but a thin surface of the profoundly undisclosed, a ripple of inveterate silence that remains immune to curiosity and inquisitiveness like distant foliage in the dusk."[72]

The scriptural text "is true," in the sense that it points to reality, it illuminates reality, it aids in discerning the truth, more than it describes reality. It is, if you will, a heuristic rather than a template—in the lines of the Vietnamese monk Thich Nhat Hanh that open this section, "a raft to help you cross the river, a finger pointing to the moon."

This insight was expressed in these words by the eighteenth-century Quaker writer Robert Barclay: "Because [the Scriptures] are only a declaration of the fountain, and not the fountain itself, therefore they are not to be esteemed the principal ground of all truth and knowledge, nor yet the adequate, primary rule of faith and manners."[73] A Lutheran expression is similar:

> [T]he Bible is not to be treated as a repository of propositional knowledge about God or the world. God's moral demand is set forth in personal address to the People of God through Moses, the prophets, and Christ; and the implications of what was said at certain moments are to be drawn out and grappled with by every generation of God's people amid the vortex of claims that make up their specific historical situations.[74]

Torah is a finger pointing to the truth, and as such it "carries truth." It is a powerfully special "finger," but it is not the truth itself, for only the truth is the truth itself. Recognizing that this is not an orthodox religious view, I draw some special support for it from the fact (as I understand it to be) that the word "*Torah*," most commonly translated as "Law," may be more accurately rendered as "teaching," and is related etymologically to the verb forms "guide," "point out," or "shoot" (as an arrow).[75] The life and teaching of Moses and the Prophets, the Holiness Code, the Pentateuch and the entire Hebrew Scriptures, as well as the teachings, written and oral, of the rabbinic tradition and Jewish communities of faith throughout the centuries (to speak only of

Jewish discernments) are a treasure house of light, of illumination, pointing us deep into the mystery. In the Jewish tradition, they are collectively known as Torah. With millions before me, and (may it be so) millions that are to come, with you if you choose it so, I stand today at Sinai, to receive God's great gift.

THE CHALLENGE OF WARRANT

I can most usefully engage with the challenge of warrant as it has been raised by a colleague in the law teaching profession for whom I have the greatest respect, Thomas L. Shaffer, former dean of Notre Dame University Law School and a teacher whose work in professional responsibility, legal education, and law and religion has been of enormous value to me, as to many others. In a review of *Two Jewish Justices*, a study by law teacher Robert Burt of Justices Brandeis and Frankfurter, Shaffer poses a question to Burt that strikes home to me. The book examines the relation of those Justices' consciousness to their having been Jewish, and (in Shaffer's words) "invokes Judaism as the culture of aliens and prophets." Shaffer finds this troubling, not because of quarrels with Burt's perception of Judaism, but because the author "uses religious metaphor . . . without wanting to surrender—or even to significantly erode—an agnostic jurisprudence." Shaffer finds this "confusing":

> We cannot tell if those who use religious symbols mean to use as well the theology that is behind the symbols. . . . [W]hen a writer uses metaphors from the religious tradition [the question] is whether he is attentive to the religious narrative he uses. A writer . . . may have tapped into the religious tradition in a purely verbal way. . . . A writer could, of course, make use of religious metaphor as one for whom the religious traditions, such as the stories of Israel and of the Cross, carry truth and give meaning to human suffering. . . . [T]his is an issue Burt does not resolve; . . . we who work from the religious tradition in social and professional ethics would like to know what he is up to. If he would like to know why we make such a demand on his scholarship, I would answer that coherence requires it.[76]

I take this set of questions very much to heart. (Indeed, I will write of them as addressed to me, rather than Burt). What *am* I up to, in finding it increasingly helpful, as I do, to ground my work and my consciousness in the religious tradition, and in finding "religious metaphors" uniquely illuminating, while remaining wary of the "theology" behind them for fear that it will turn out to be the elephant and the turtles?[77] I can think of few questions that are at once so reasonable to ask and so difficult to answer.

Do I believe that religious metaphors "carry truth and give meaning to human suffering"? My short answer (as the preceding section suggests) is that the capacity of religious metaphors to give meaning to human life, including its suffering, is the truth that they carry. I suspect that, for Tom Shaffer as for many others, working "from the religious tradition" presumes quite a bit more by way of belief, and his questions crystallize a concern that has been with me for some time: Lacking some avowal of such a greater level of belief in "religious narratives," am I using them simply as a literary or rhetorical adornment?

The question has bite for me on two related grounds: First, although Shaffer, respectful as he is of views that differ from his own, does not challenge the permissibility of a "purely verbal" use of religious metaphors,[78] I am not sure that I would give myself similar permission. Daniel Maguire offers as a definition of religion "the response to the sacred,"[79] and in claiming warrant for legitimately terming my own belief system "religious," I claim, and therefore acknowledge, that I am evoking the sacred. Although my belief in God differs from Shaffer's (and many others'), it is not only my sense of the sacred that is entitled to my respect. I need not believe that the Decalogue is literally a set of "Commandments" to take very seriously its admonition that the name of God not be taken in vain. This is not to say that, to be respectful of the sacred as perceived by others, my use of their religious images must express their sense of the sacred. I do believe, however, that it must at the least express mine, that is, it must be more, qualitatively more, than a rhetorical or literary adornment.

My terming religious images "theirs" suggests my second concern. It arises out of the long-held mindset to which I referred earlier, that a religious tradition "belongs" to its orthodox branch. Much of what I have termed my "Odyssey" has been an account of a liberation from that stricture, but I am plainly not wholly comfortable laying claim to an unimpeded right to "work with" the tradition however I may come to discern it. For the present, however, I have thought it better to allow that discomfort, rather than seek either to suppress it entirely or to let it dominate and constrain my modes of expression.

My belief in the truth of religious narratives and metaphors differs significantly from that of many others, who account themselves believers. However, it diminishes the ways in which the narratives I have described above do carry truth to characterize them, viewed as I understand them, as "simply" metaphors or a "merely human" product, not worthy of being called religious. Either metaphoric, or parabolic, ways of conveying religious truth have validity as a mode of truth-saying or they do not, but they are in no way "lesser" avowals than a more direct, apparently more lucid, propositional assertion. The letters of the Hebrew word *olam*, which means both "world" and "forever," also form the root of the word for "the hidden," or "secrets of wisdom."[80] Religious supernaturalism has in common with secular rationality the belief that, in the one case through reason and scientific inquiry, in the other through revelation and faith, existence can be made manifest. The God for whose will we strive to listen may or may not be "hidden," but to think that it is so, to think that only indirect modes of description are able to do the job, is far from a "lesser" form of belief.[81]

Nor do I understand why it is that positing a wholly transcendent God, one entirely independent of human existence, avoids making of that God a "merely human" product. Most devoutly religious people do not claim to have had a direct personal revelation, but base their faith (including in some cases their belief in the divine authority of their community of faith) on a centuries-old tradition, and their own history. There is nothing disreputable about this source of faith, but it is as "merely human" as it is to believe the opening words of the Quaker maxim (originating, I believe, with St. Teresa of Avila), "God has no hands but our hands, no eyes but our eyes, no voice but our voice."[82] Those who have had a direct personal revelation of divinity are as "merely human" as the rest of us, and I question whether my intuition, insight, wisdom, and discernment partake of the divine any less than does another's experience of revelation. We all are at risk of error.

We should, I believe, resist the tendency to dichotomize entirely human and divine products. In a wonderfully pregnant teaching, Rabbi Harold Schulweis challenges this tendency by noting that the traditional Jewish blessings are over bread and wine, not wheat and grapes. "Baking bread is as miraculous as dividing the sea. . . . Wine, not grapes, represents the fullest expression of the holy, the transaction between the godly human and non-human nature."[83] Most fundamentally, such powers of discernment as we have to know God and the truth—indeed, even our powers of reason, which one often sees contrasted with revelation as being "merely human"—are a product of our creatureliness, all of it a gift of God.

The illumination that I seek can certainly be aided by, and expressed in, secular modes of thought. Yet, for me—and I will speak more to the question in Chapter 4—the religious tradition has a unique depth and power which reflects more than merely its art or rhetoric. And it is a power not only to illuminate but also to inspire, to fuel the will.

On my office wall is a copy of a 1953 woodcut by Fritz Eichenberg, *Christ of the Breadlines*. It shows a file of ragged men and women, shabbily dressed and worn down by poverty and despair, patiently standing in a line that extends in both directions off the picture. In the center, waiting in line with the rest, is Jesus. The "holding" of that picture would take more than a sentence or two of political philosophy to express, and would hardly be improved by that clarification. But what is it doing on my wall? I am not a Christian, or even a believer, as that term is usually used. To be "coherent," would it be more appropriate for me to replace it with the dustjacket of *A Theory of Justice* or *The Grapes of Wrath*? The loss in any such change would not merely be in effectiveness, in rhetorical or literary power. The woodcut says more fully and plainly what I want to say, and it says it in a way that I feel more as coming from the core of me. And that fidelity is not undermined by the fact that I am not a Christian, or a believer.

There is a Talmudic story about Elijah the prophet, who was said to be immortal and to travel regularly between heaven and earth. A rabbi asked him, "When will the Messiah come?" "Go and ask him himself," Elijah responded, and to the rabbi's reply, "Where is he sitting, . . . and by what sign may I recognize him?" the prophet answered that the Messiah was sitting outside the gates of Rome, among a group of other lepers, changing his bandages.[84]

The story goes on, but the portion I have told is not unlike Eichenberg's in its propositional content. The picture it conjures up seems a bit too graphic for a place on my wall, but if I did hang it there I would not want to feel that I was thereby avowing the historicity of the event it depicts, or my belief in Elijah's postmortem corporeal presence in human history. Nor, I hope, would I simply be using the Talmud or the rabbinic tradition to make a political or ethical statement.

THE CHALLENGE OF DIVERSION

The second challenge, although it also characterizes my stance toward religion as essentially secular, has a very different complaint with it. It is made by one who in traditional terms is less rather than more religious than I. Such a person (like the first group of challengers) is troubled that my religious beliefs do not even purport to rest on any "real" authority, and sees my use of religious language as merely ornamental. The objection, however, is, not that its credal base is rather pallid, but that it needlessly gets in the way of understanding. In part, this occurs because, for readers attracted to religious language, its emotional or aesthetic appeal can be a substitute for clear thinking, while for those who are (sensibly) repelled by the dismal role that religion has played in history, resort to it inevitably brings with it a lot of baggage that cannot so easily be put aside.

I heartily agree that the "baggage" should not lightly be put aside. It is important, I believe, to begin by acknowledging fully that one who sees in religion a means of access to moral truth has a lot of explaining to do. One need not adopt the view attributed to Voltaire, that religion arose when the first fool met the first knave, to recognize that religion has more to answer for than it ever could. (Understand that I am speaking here of all religions that have had temporal power, but especially of the Abrahamic religions that are central to the history of the West.) Along with much good, religion has done much evil, and we should not too quickly pass quietly over one for the sake of recognizing the other. Its sins are of three sorts, and in each category are grievous, pervasive, and enduring.

First are the ways in which it has blighted the lives of millions of its communicants. It has terrorized children (and adults as well) with images of an awaiting hell. It has inculcated in its adherents feelings of worthlessness, of self-blame for their misery. It has told countless grieving children (and adults) that the God who loves them, and whom they must love, needed their dead parent (or child) more than they did. It has upheld obedience to other mortals as obedience to God. It has condemned much in human life that is a source of joy, and emphasized a grim, punitive, life-denying morality over even the religion's own joyous aspects. It has too rigidly dichotomized male and female, and upheld one over the other, robbing women of their birthright, impoverishing both men and women, and legitimating a sexual fragmentation of humanity that is at the base of much of the war and oppression that has afflicted human life.[85]

Second is the sorry record of the world's religions through the centuries in serving so pervasively to support unjust social orders, to serve the priestly function of legitimation far more often than the prophetic function of reconciliation. Religion has spoken often in the voice of St. Paul—"The powers that be are ordained by God. . . . Therefore whoever resists authority resists what God has appointed" (Romans 13:2)—and far too seldom in that of Amos:

> I hate, I despise your festivals,
>   and I take no delight in your solemn assemblies.
> Even though you offer me your burnt offerings
>   and grain offerings,
> I will not accept them;
>   and the offerings of well-being of your fatted animals
>   I will not look upon.
> Take away from me the noise of your songs;
>   I will not listen to the melody of your harps.
> But let justice roll down like waters,
>   and righteousness like an ever-flowing stream [5:21–24].

This religious legitimation of injustice is in an important respect more than simply an historical fact.[86] It is built into the perfectionist vision that religious consciousness typically has. As legal philosopher Roberto Unger has expressed it, "the extraordinary representation of the ideal" in religion "can offer the self temporary refuge": "In this sense, the extraordinary is a mystification, the aroma that sweetens the air of the established order. Its very availability makes the absence of the ideal from everyday life seem tolerable and even necessary. . . . [E]verything in the ordinary world can become all the more relentlessly profane, prosaic, and self-regarding."[87]

This insight suggests the great difficulty, even in a religious consciousness that seeks always to remain open to the prophetic tradition, of keeping that openness itself from operating to foster complicity in profound temporal injustice. The truth, however, as philosopher and Reformed Church Elder Merold Westphal has put it, is that openness to the prophetic tradition has seldom competed successfully with credal orthodoxy for the attention of organized religion:

> [O]rthodoxy has been defined historically in terms of metaphysical issues, such as those growing out of trinitarian, christological, and sacramental debates, and terms of epistemological issues, such as those growing out of debates over the authority of the Bible, of tradition, and of the magisterium. It has not been defined with reference to the social praxis required by orthodoxy.[88]

Finally, the world's religions have seldom managed to resist the temptation to uphold their particular vision by damning those of others, and to tell their communicants that it is the will of God that they despise, oppress, and in countless instances kill their fellow humans. (As I have noted earlier, the seemingly milder record of Judaism is probably only a reflection of its relative lack of temporal power since the destruction of the Second Temple. Certainly, the Hebrew Scriptures contain many blood-curdling manifestations of this spirit.) Who was it who first observed that people are religious enough to hate one another, but not religious enough to love one another? Religious leaders have often presented their faith in terms that (often literally) demonize that of others, colluding eagerly with the murderous intentions of their nations' secular authorities.

I therefore cannot quarrel with one who, in light of this history and its continuing reenactment in our contemporary world, is simply unable to take seriously the claim that religion can be a source of moral understanding and healing. A logical answer might be to invoke what philosophers term the idea of the "genetic fallacy," that one cannot disprove the truth of a proposition by relying on the failings of its proponents. But centuries of pervasive oppression in the name of God, if not sufficient to establish that it is a false God that is being invoked, certainly warrants a pervasive wariness.[89] All I can say is that, over the last decade or so of my life, my own wariness has eroded significantly, and I have found myself increasingly able to seek a religious consciousness that fully accepts the validity of the bill of indictment that has been laid at the feet of the world's religions, while still believing that history reflects grievous distortions of those religions, and not their essential nature. Men and women seeking power, and inclined to use it at the expense of their fellows, use means of expressing themselves that are prevalent in their society, and religion has served no less than secular philosophy to justify injustice. Neither the presence nor the absence of religious explanations of human life determines the capacity of such people to succeed in their objectives. The acceptance of neither a religious nor a secular stance will ensure that one lives a morally defensible life.

The other aspect of the challenge of diversion objects to reliance on the attractiveness (where it exists) of religious language, as importing an emotional appeal into what should be a rational process. It might, for example, begin its response to my discussion of Leviticus 19:1–2 by attempting (with some exasperation that it should be necessary) to "translate" what I have said into more straightforward, relatively clear language, perhaps something like this: "To live one's life open to a feeling of awe is a moral good. I find myself drawn to this belief from outside (as well as within) myself." If that is what I mean, a challenger of this persuasion would insist, why don't I just say so, and let us get on to the question whether others have any reason to agree? Cloaking my claim in religious language, while it commendably does not invoke the authority that tradition has accorded it (for I myself do not give it such authority), either seems to be seeking to take unacknowledged advantage of a vestigial aura of that authority or is simply an aesthetic practice. Whether one finds the "cloaking" appealing (on account of its poetic language or underlying emotions) or repellent (by reason of the long bloody story of religiously justified oppression), the practice only diverts us from attending to the central question, which is the truth or falsity of what I have asserted.

The challenge of diversion assumes that reducing the scriptural text to "clear" propositional form is all to the good. To me, the reduction is reductive in the pejorative sense: Much of the essence is lost thereby. To say that I should be open to awe is not of the same genre of moral imperative as to say that I should drive within the posted speed limit, but it is difficult to explain this response without falling into a similar reductionism. To any individual reader, my response will probably seem either obvious or obscurantist. The philosopher-classicist Martha Nussbaum, writing about "Form and Content, Philosophy and Literature," makes a point that seems to me salient with respect to the expression of philosophical truth through religious language as well as literature:

> There may be some views of the world and how one should live in it—views, especially, that emphasize the world's surprising variety, its complexity and mysteriousness, its flawed and imperfect beauty—that cannot be fully and adequately stated in the language of conventional philosophical prose, . . . but only in a language and in forms themselves more complex, more allusive, more attentive to particulars.[90]

What I have termed the challenge of diversion is animated by two mutually reinforcing positions: First is a version of secular rationality that tends to accord a very cabined place to the emotions, serving at most as a motivating force, but not a heuristic, indeed, as a phenomenon that must not be allowed to "get in the way" of clear thinking. From this stance, religious language is suspect in much the same way as poetry and literature, and religiously grounded emotions stand no better than others. Moreover, the religious and the rational are viewed as in what James Boyd White calls a "blanket opposition," "as though," he goes on in critical terms, "religion consisted of nothing more than an act of faith about which nothing could be said."[91] I think both these views excessively dichotomize their subjects, a belief that I will say more about (in both aspects) in Chapter 3. For present purposes, however, the problem with this version of rationalism is not so much that it has an answer that I believe is wrong as that it tends to lead its adherents not to notice that there is a question that it has already answered. The rightness of a rationalist answer cannot be found *within* rationalist premises.

As I have noted earlier, religious metaphors and religious narratives can express avowals of moral truths more fully and more directly than secular language does. More salient here, religious consciousness can point toward moral truth, that is, can orient and fuel the moral sense. Religious language and practices aid in linking their specific content to the experience of awe, and to the moral life. There is more to be said here, but for the moment I will only note my belief that much of this process has to do with ways in which metaphors and parables approach their point indirectly, by juxtaposing the prosaic and the cosmic. Protestant theologian Sallie McFague expresses the thought in these words: "In a religious metaphor, . . . the two subjects, ordinary life and the transcendent, are so intertwined that there is no way of separating them out and what, in fact, we learn is not primarily something about God but a new way to live ordinary life."[92]

When Jesus taught that God takes account of the fall of a sparrow (Matthew 10:29), he was not, if I understand it right, primarily making a metaphysical claim. The message of the passage in which the line appears is an ethical one, instructing his disciples how they should go about to "proclaim the good news." He spoke of the sparrow, sold "two for a penny," to say to them, "Do not be afraid" (10:7, 29, 31). The courage that the consciousness of their own worth in the eyes of God was meant to give them would enable them to remain true to their mission.

For each of us, too, there can be no more powerful aid to our ever-faltering efforts to live a moral life, when we are tempted to conclude that what we do or fail to do does not really matter, than to hold in our consciousness the realization of our inherent self-worth; no more arresting awareness, when we are tempted to regard our fellow creatures only as means to our ends, than to be brought up against the realization of the inherent worth of every other person; and no more precious intervention, when the difficulty of living a moral life bids to overwhelm our resolve, than to feel on our shoulders, as a woolen cloak in a chill wind, the arm of the itinerant rabbi of Nazareth, as once again his words come to us through the ages, "Do not be afraid."

Reading the teaching as it speaks to our public life, I think mostly of its pertinence to the moral standing of utilitarian cost-benefit analysis. It is the sense of awe that the natural world inspires, the sense of the sacredness of all of life, even that "worth" only a half-penny, that most powerfully admonishes us to resist defining its value as its market price, fungible with other "things" of like exchange value. Again, I may be wrong to take the admonition to heart in that way, but to establish that surely takes more than the declaration that it is irrelevant. Between my view and a rationalist dismissal of the teaching as a diversion lies a profound difference of view as to the way we find moral truth.

It is heartening, therefore, to find recognition of this view in the world of analytic philosophy. Kent Bendall and Frederick Ferre explain in these words what they call the "conative" significance of the parable of the Lost Sheep:

> What do we mean by the common phrase "the infinite value of every individual"? We certainly are not speaking in terms of economic value or military value or intellectual value. What kind of value is it then? It is the value (we are commonly told) that each man possesses "in the sight of God." Strip this of its metaphysical form to expose its existential functioning and one finds not so much a descriptive as a conative use: the expression of a decision to attempt to value all existing individuals beyond measure and beyond comparison. Within this dimension of meaning, the Parable of the Lost Sheep, for example, may be recited with the existential function of affirming the worth of every man, not self alone. Such a parable then becomes more than a bit of pleasant poetry, more even than an emotive prop for ethical determination; it becomes an instrument of one's existential decision, a reflection of one's voluntarily adopted stance toward oneself and one's fellow mortals. It is a reflection of passionate decision, of personally involved conviction.[93]

In positing this "link" between religious language and practices and the moral life, I am not asserting any logically necessary relation. First of all, it distorts the genius of the heuristic to attribute to it either logical or hierarchical necessity. What the contemporary Protestant theologian Marcus Borg describes with respect to Jesus's teaching has broad salience: "As invitational forms of speech, the parables do not invoke external authority. . . . Rather, their authority rests in themselves—that is, in their ability to involve and affect the imagination. Their voice is invitational rather than imperative."[94] In any event, there are surely secularists who, for example, reject market-measured aggregations of "utility" as a guide to public policy, and religious people who do not. More fundamentally, there are surely secularists whose moral sense is powerfully keen, and religionists whose lives are a disgrace.

My assertion is grounded in my experience. The religious tradition has exercised a powerful force in orienting my perceptions of what the moral life requires of me, and in continually recalling me to struggle a bit harder to act on that perception. That experience is surely not to be set aside as a personal idiosyncracy. An acquaintance in the law teaching profession, a conservative Protestant, has recounted how, when he settled down on a Friday afternoon to what he expected to be an uninterrupted afternoon of writing, only to have a student knock urgently at his door with a knotty problem, it was "as a Christian" that he felt obliged to set his other work aside to respond to another's need. To a reader hearing this, and knowing no more about the person who spoke, the identification may well be off-putting as triumphalist or self-congratulatory. I can only say that, despite the vast gulf between his understanding of religious faith and mine, I unquestionably credit and resonate with what he said. His ever-present awareness that his moment-to-moment actions have deep significance, that it is there that he either bears witness to what he professes or turns his back on it, exercises a constant tug, a spiritual discipline, checking his tendency to act reflexively. One whose practice keeps alive in one's consciousness, for example, the belief that "before every human being comes a retinue of angels, announcing, 'Make way for an image of the Holy One, Blessed be He' " (see p. 110, below), will find that awareness a powerful influence on his or her actions.

I have come to think that a significant part of the way in which the sense of awe that I find at the core of the religious outlook operates to fuel the ethical search is grounded in the heuristic value of the sense of gratitude that it engenders. The centrality of this sense of gratitude is for me no more profoundly embodied than in the Jewish tradition of reciting the Hebrew prayer *Sheheheyanu* on the first occasion of every significant event during the year: Blessed is God, "who has given us life, and sustained us, and brought us to this season." The prayer is more than simply an expression of gratitude, however; it can be a source of it as well, and a powerful transformative force in one's life. What the U.S. Catholic Bishops have termed "grateful hearts" leads us "from self-seeking to a spirituality that sees the signs of true discipleship in our sharing of goods and working for justice."[95]

These words of the Christian theologian James Gustafson speak eloquently to the matter:

> There is in [the experience of gratitude] a matter of trust and of hope which is only in part confirmed in human experience. . . . Honesty requires the admission that it is difficult to be grateful to God for life when it gives no concrete opportunities for human fulfillment, when those who have been sustaining and meaningful to us are brutally taken away, and when whole communities are suppressed and destroyed by the demonic and destructive activities of men, and indeed, of nature. Conscientious religious men have a quarrel with God not only after Auschwitz but after earthquakes, not only in the midst of an unjust war but after assassinations of leaders who have symbolized hope and justice and peace. Like Job and Jeremiah, we too have occasion to curse God for the day that we were born. To gloss over such human experiences would be to engage in cheap religious rhetoric.
>
> Nonetheless, the occasions for gratitude, though they come in small sizes and with less frequency than we might desire, remain as some testimony to the goodness of life and even evoke our celebration. For all our anxieties and struggles, we are grateful to be, to exist. Most of us have been loved beyond our deserving, forgiven when we dared not believe it possible, sustained by the patience of others when they have had grounds to reject us. We have received from the sustaining powers of the sun and the earth, the social order and the culture, more than we can ever claim to deserve. These experiences point to the goodness of God, and they confirm the goodness which we dimly apprehend. And we are grateful.
>
> Gratitude, like dependence, can be oppressive and destructive if it carries also an obligation to cower before those who have given life to us. But it can be liberating if the gifts we receive are given freely, graciously, and in love, rather than as bribes or for the self-glorification of the giver. This is the importance of the experience of God as beneficent and gracious: what is given is freely given in love. It is not merely what we earn by our accomplishments, but it is already there for us to respond to, to appropriate, to participate in.
>
> The experience of gratitude is a pivot on which our awareness of God's goodness turns toward our [moral] life. . . . What is given is not ours to dispose of as if we created it, nor ours to use to serve only our own interests, to mutilate, wantonly destroy, and to deprive others of. Rather, if life is given in grace and freedom and love, we are to care for it and share it graciously, freely, and in love.[96]

As I experience it, the relation of the "awareness of God's goodness" and the moral life is neither one of an authority imposed from without nor simply a projection of what is within. My law teacher colleague and spiritual mentor, Emily Fowler Hartigan, has written of a feminist spirituality that stresses "the wonder and inherent goodness of creation, such that its binding forces are experienced as blessings to be pursued ever more deeply . . . , a gentle draw, more than a compelling force, an invitation more than a command . . . , an 'ought' that beckons more deeply than it threatens."[97]

The religious tradition, in whatever version it speaks to us, is therefore not to be dismissed as a mere ornament to an ethical claim that can more clearly be asserted in secular language. Much of Chapter 4 addresses the process of discerning the truth of ethical claims, of discerning the will of God. Suffice it here to note that, in Quaker parlance, the successful result of that effort is known as "clearness." Again, one person's clarity is another's obfuscation, but it is another thing entirely to assert, as universal objective truth, that "it doesn't matter."

3

Truth Without Triumphalism, Mystery Without Mystification

The God of which I have spoken is both the repository of truth about the moral life, and the force that draws me to struggle to discern and follow it. Embedded in mystery that transcends the limitations of finitude, it resides within me as well. The belief that I have the capacity to seek the truth, and that at the same time it calls to me from beyond myself, grounds and fuels the search. The recognition that, with St. Paul, I "know only in part," that I "see through a glass, darkly" (1 Corinthians 13:12)—the awareness that I do not, and probably cannot, know for certain whether I have accurately penetrated the mystery—is for me (as perhaps it was not for Paul) an integral part of my consciousness, but the faith that there is a truth to be known, and the realization that it lies beyond my ken, are insights that I find mutually reinforcing rather than incompatible. Each without the other would be existentially hazardous: Without the faith to which I refer, I would be driven to what my law school colleague Michael Moore calls the "devastating" conclusion that "the only thing to be said about either watermelons or concentration camps is that some people like them and some people don't";[98] without the realization of my limited capacity to know the truth, I would fall into the triumphalist abyss that religion all too frequently manifests.

To speak about moral truth as something (some thing?) that exists outside of myself, and draws me to it, is to invite immediate dismissal on two primary grounds, which I will call the charges of mystification and triumphalism. First, if I may again quote Michael Moore, such talk "conjures up images of a kind of Aurora Borealis, but without the lights."[99] When the talk is in religious terms (Moore's is not), the image comes with lights, and the charge of mystification is that they dazzle rather than illuminate. I will speak to that charge in the last section of this chapter.

The charge of triumphalism, as I have suggested, reflects the distressingly familiar fact that many who profess a belief, especially a religious belief, in the existence of truth about morality tend to believe as well that they know the truth. A relatively benign form of this phenomenon is the classic account of the two chaplains of differing Protestant denominations expressing the deep regard for one another that their term of military service together engendered. One summed up his learning by saying that he now realized, as he had not before, that "we both worship the same God, you in your way and I in His." Centuries of examples that are in no manner benign are unhappily daily augmented by contemporary press accounts.

I take the objections of triumphalism and mystification very seriously. My intention is not so much to rebut them as (in Emily Hartigan's felicitous phrase) to "enfold their insights"[100] into my understanding of what it means to search for truth, to listen for the voice of God. Let me begin, then, with an example that perhaps most prompts both objections, one that speaks explicitly of a truth that is embedded in mystery, yet known with complete assurance. It comes from a most esteemed source, the great German Christian theologian Rudolf Otto.

SHEDDING THE TRIUMPHALIST LEGACY

> DUKE OF NORFOLK: Does this make sense? You'll forfeit all you've got—which includes the respect of your country—for a theory?
> SIR THOMAS MORE (*hotly*): The Apostolic Succession of the Pope is—(*Stops; interested*) Why, it's a theory, yes; you can't see it; can't touch it; it's a theory. But what matters to me is not whether it's true . . . but that I believe it to be true, or rather, not that I *believe* it, but that *I* believe it.
>
> —ROBERT BOLT, *A Man For All Seasons*[101]

> The Baptists go by water,
> The Methodists go by land;
> If you want to climb
> The hill of the Lord,
> You gotta go hand in hand.
>
> —Traditional Spiritual

Otto, in his classic work *The Idea of the Holy*, begins his discussion of "The Resurrection as a Spiritual Experience" by noting that the Christian confession of faith is both "I *believe* in Jesus Christ, risen from the dead," and (following Job) "I *know* that my Redeemer liveth."[102] The former statement uses the terminology belief-*in*, which one associates with faith-in-the-sense-of-trust, but it can be read also as an avowal of an idea—in Martin Buber's terminology, an acknowledgment of "a thing to be true." The latter sentence, however, despite its use of the term belief- (or knowledge-) *that*, suggesting faith-in-the-sense-of-creed, is (again, Buber) plainly a profession of "contact," contact "with the one in whom I trust."[103]

Knowing, which Otto describes as "faith-knowledge," also connotes a heightened degree of certainty. Martha Nussbaum describes this degree of certainty as a "cataleptic condition," that is, "an absolutely indubitable and unshakable grasp of some part of reality, a grasp which could not have been produced by nonreality."[104] This condition of certainty is intimately connected to its basis or source. To Otto, the "assurance of the Risen Christ" does not arise from empirical data, the evidence of the senses, but is, "in the scriptural phrase, 'the evidence of things not seen'." It relies on no other evidence than "the witness of the Holy Spirit." "To speak of the Resurrection is to utter a mystery," and how faith in that mystery comes to be "is no less a mystery, indeed the greatest of all mysteries."

To Otto, faith-knowledge of a mystery excludes two common sources of justification, one found among believers and the other among skeptics. The first are "naïvely supernaturalistic" explanations, which rely, for example, on "the evidence of the Empty Tomb." These are destructive of that mystery, reducing it to a sort of supernatural empiricism.[105] So, too, are "rationalistic" explanations, which reduce the resurrection account by explaining it as an evolution in the minds of the disciples, from a continuing post-Crucifixion "impression of the person of Jesus," to the conviction that "such a one cannot have remained dead," deepening to take "imaginative and figurative form in visions." To Otto, both interpretations share the failing that they disregard altogether the "mysterious character" of the Resurrection event.

If "faith-knowledge" is the greatest of all mysteries, perhaps there is nothing to be said about it: Whether with respect to

Christianity or any faith tradition, each of us either has faith-knowledge or does not. Otto may be suggesting as much. In describing the source of experiences like knowledge of the Risen Christ, the "summons and ordination" of Isaiah, and Saul of Tarsus's encounter on the road to Damascus, he writes:

> [W]hoever knows anything of the Spirit and its miraculous nature, whoever feels in himself the Spirit active in those mysterious experiences that build up the Christian's life, . . . [h]e alone has the key to the truth of the matter. Just as the Scriptures as a whole . . . require the Spirit if they are to be taught or understood, so too it is with these occurrences. Only a first-hand spiritual experience teaches a man to see and enables him to estimate a spiritual experience of a former day. Possession of the Spirit at first hand becomes here a faculty of "retrospective prophecy", which is recognition in the sense of re-cognition or knowing again for oneself.[106]

I have not had the "first-hand spiritual experience" of which Otto writes, whether with respect to Christian, Jewish, or less specifically sectarian matters. A statement like his, made from within the experience of faith, tends to draw a fairly sharp boundary between those who have shared that experience and those who have not. It tends to trigger in me a reaction like this: If you too have had the experience that enables you to know for yourself the truth of the witness, well, bully for you. The rest of us can do no other than to choose between a wistful longing to join you, if only the highway we are traveling will one day soon turn out to be the road to Damascus, and a more self-assured dismissal of so encapsulated a proffered source of insight into the truth. Neither response prompts much engagement with what is being said.

I have found it helpful, however, in seeking to think further about what Otto wrote, to compare it with a statement that is very similar to his, but made from outside a commitment of faith, one that is framed as a description rather than a manifestation of this source of faith-knowledge. Here is an excerpt from the entry on "Truth" in *The Encyclopedia of Religion*:

> One way of knowing the ultimate truth is the awareness of what-is through the extraordinary experience of spiritual presence(s). . . . The awareness is perceived as an overwhelming disclosure that transcends other norms of validity, such as empirical verification or rational analysis. Such divine disclosure provides a direction for living and a principle for knowledge not available in other norms of validity. . . . The response of faith is one of service in . . . the divine

will. The truth known in such response is validated by the devotee in the experience of being known by the Holy One.[107]

This passage helps me to stay with Otto, to seek more fully to understand rather than react evaluatively to what he is saying. The witness of the devotee that his or her experience validates faith-knowledge may "carry truth" to me, and therefore be true in the heuristic sense of which I wrote in the preceding chapter. The passage is reminiscent of the proposition, "One proves the existence of God by praying." This obvious non sequitur, this ultimate begging of the question, in fact "carries truth" in the profound sense that the acts and statements of "the devotee," like a scriptural text, point a way along which I might look, although what I see may differ from that of the believer. Giving continuing receptive attention to the witness of believers like Otto, neither joining nor dismissing them, teaches me better to discover my own belief.

The God of which I can speak is one mostly hidden from my sight, discernible through the experience of a silent beckoning, the experience (to borrow again Emily Hartigan's words) of "an infinitely deep, infinitely inviting Mystery."[108] For Otto, mystery is the source of clarity, but I have had no "overwhelming disclosure," no "extraordinary experience." Martin Buber describes "life with spiritual beings" in words that come to mind at this point: "[T]he relation is wrapped in a cloud but reveals itself; it lacks but creates language. We hear no You and yet feel addressed; we answer . . . , unable to say You with our mouth."[109] "The Spirit blows where it listeth" (John 3:8), and sometimes, in the silence, I "hear the sound of it," but, yes, I "do not know where it comes from or where it goes."

"Listeth" is today rendered as "wishes," but I would not read this Scripture to suggest a coming-and-going at will (or whim), for I am concerned lest talk of an "extraordinary experience" or "overwhelming disclosure" suggest a passive waiting. I prefer metaphors that suggest patient constancy beyond, and patient searching and receptivity within. To rely yet again on Emily Hartigan: "God is with us, many of our traditions tell us, as *shekhinah* and spirit, but that abiding presence will not fill the space uninvited. God will not trespass upon us."[110]

"We sit in silence, and wait upon the Lord." This classic self-

description of Quaker Meeting for Worship is not, I think, meant
to say that *we* are here, and the Lord may (or may not) show up
today. Carmelite priest Carlos Mesters notes, "When a person
finally takes note of God's presence, God has probably been there
a long time already."[111] Talmud and Gospel agree (see the passages
quoted at p. 36 and note 65) that the Presence *does* abide, that
God is already present, waiting for us. To wait upon the Lord is
an engaged, not a passive, stance. Even "inviting" sounds inadequate, too much a single act, like sitting down and folding (or
opening) one's hands. To "wait" is that, to be sure, but more; it
is to struggle, quietly and endlessly, to open mind, heart, and spirit
to the abiding presence.

So, when I say that I believe that Leviticus 19:2 is true—that
to seek to live as a sacred being is a moral good, and that I experience myself as drawn to that belief, and not merely generating it
from within—I am saying that, in making that avowal, I experience myself as looking into the unknowable Truth and connect-
ing accurately with a portion of it, quietly but with some
substantial confidence. Part of my experience is of a "silent beckoning" from without. The force that beckons is what I mean by
God, and it is the experience of "being beckoned" that leads me
to believe that there *is* a Truth or Reality that resides outside of
me.

I say I "believe" rather than "I know" to keep in mind that
there is simply nothing I can say about Truth, Reality, or God
that escapes the limitation of being an expression of my understanding of Truth, Reality, or God. I cannot even be sure that my
entire experience of a Presence external to myself is more than a
projection of what is within me. What I mean by my statement
of belief is that it has a stabilizing and resonating coherence with
my overall understanding of the world and my place in it. It is
that experience of coherence that leads me to believe that I am
justified in my belief. I keep to the foreground the "non-foundationalist" character of my belief. It rests on no first principles, on
no axioms not needing explanation; it is embedded in other beliefs, which are in turn embedded in it. In Michael Moore's
words: "Justification of any belief . . . is not the locating of indubitable particular judgments from which all else can be known by
induction; no more is it the locating of indubitable first principles
from which all particular judgments can be known by deduction.

Justification of any belief is a matter of its coherence with all the other propositions that we believe to be true."[112]

Otto's faith-knowledge of the Mystery of the Resurrection certainly seems wholly different. His commitment to the truth of his belief discloses no residue of contingency; this single belief grounds so much else of his thoughts and actions; and (as he insists) it has neither a rational nor an empirical basis: These elements seem to make his statement a paradigm case of foundationalist belief. Yet, except for the first factor—he finds it important to emphasize that he *knows*, while I insist on keeping in the foreground that I am speaking of what I discern to be, not of what-is—I am not sure how great the difference is. Living a life continually open to the sacred ("Be holy") may not ring to most ears as equally orienting an avowal as belief in the Risen Christ is, but (as I sought to describe in Chapter 2) it is assuredly no minor matter in my life. And I believe that, whatever rational or empirical reasons I may give for responding to the world with a sense of awe, the response seems less the outcome of some calculus than a constitutive (albeit not necessarily permanent) aspect of my consciousness.

The critical difference between foundationalist and non-foundationalist belief has to do less with the believer's response to his or her own belief than with the response to the refusal of others to share in it. If I am right in reading Otto to be saying that he knows for a certainty, but his "first-hand spiritual experiences" cannot be the ground of my beliefs, I put us on the same side of the line.[113] The words that introduce this section, which Robert Bolt put into the mouth of Sir Thomas More, make this point with eloquent simplicity: "[W]hat matters to me is not whether it's true . . . but that I believe it to be true, or rather, not that I *believe* it, but that *I* believe it."

When More spontaneously began to assert that the Apostolic Succession is not "a theory," he was, I think, saying what Otto says about "faith-knowledge." Yet, his disavowal did not retract anything about the depth of his commitment to his belief/knowledge. He acknowledged that what he meant to profess about his "knowledge" of the world was a statement about his understanding of the world, not a statement about the world.

Triumphalism, to me, is a refusal to make this acknowledgment. My effort in this book is to present a religious consciousness that succeeds in divesting itself of the triumphalist legacy. As I have suggested, I believe that triumphalism is not necessarily triggered by certainty that one has correctly discerned moral truth (the will of God). Even if that certainty is asserted to be grounded more in revelation (God's act) than in discernment (the believer's act), the assertion is not triumphalist so long as it acknowledges that it is the speaker, not God, who is making it. It is true that certainty tends to tempt one to omit the acknowledgment, but it is the response to that temptation, not its existence, that is critical.

It is another matter entirely to dismiss as triumphalist, absolutist, or what-have-you the belief that truth, whether grounded in an idea of God or not, has a reality independent of our opinions of it, as distinguished from the belief that the speaker knows what it is. Excessive confidence that one has correctly discerned the truth can afflict those who are skeptics as well as those who are believers about the existence of moral truth. Again, it is a failing of many believers to conflate the question of the existence of truth with that of its content, but the remedy is not for non-believers to make the same mistake. To dismiss all religious people, for example, as inherently intolerant of non-believers (including believers in another faith tradition), however much most believers throughout history may supply empirical justification, is an inappropriate stereotype and itself a form of secular triumphalism.

A like failing can be laid at the feet of religious folk who dismiss secularists as lacking in moral sense or moral standards. First of all, one need not ground reality in God to believe that its moral strictures are real and demanding. Much of Eastern religion is not theistic, perhaps not "religion" at all, and it is an especially arrogant form of triumphalism to look down on it for that reason. In addition, there is a Western secular natural law tradition that is no less committed than religion to the pursuit of goodness. More broadly, there are countless thoroughly skeptical people, wholly relativist in their moral philosophy, whose lives are an eloquent reproach to those of many who profess their faith loudly and often. Anti-secular or anti-relativist triumphalism stands no better, in my judgment, than the anti-religious variety.

A non-triumphalist consciousness like that which I have sought to express would move the metaphysics of religious language and practices into the background, to emphasize (following James Boyd White, see p. 37, above) their performative rather than their propositional aspect. It fits what I have called a view of truth as a heuristic rather than a template, "a finger pointing to the moon." So, we can leave off disputing, for example, the propositional truth of the tenet that the Torah was written by God and given to Moses, or the doctrines of Transubstantiation or the triune aspect of God, and try instead to look along the line of sight that these (and other) doctrines provide, to see what illumination they can yield us.

What I have written to this point contains many examples of this process, which deemphasizes credal differences, treating different religions as something like different languages: If I speak English and you speak French, neither of us feels called upon to resolve who is right. To say this is not to say that it is of no consequence whether one speaks English or French, or that they are in reality the same language. (To say, in the words of the Spiritual that is at the head of this section, that we need to go "hand in hand" is not to say that we are following the same path.) The question is not so much whether I believe in your creed as what I can learn from the ways in which it aids you to understand the world and live your life.

Rabbi Abraham Joshua Heschel taught in these words about the danger of intellectualizing the professions of religious faith:

> The term, "God of Abraham, Isaac, and Jacob" is semantically different from a term such as "the God of truth, goodness, and beauty." Abraham, Isaac, and Jacob do not signify ideas, principles or abstract values. Nor do they stand for teachers or thinkers, and the term is not to be understood like that of "the God of Kant, Hegel, and Schelling." Abraham, Isaac, and Jacob are not principles to be comprehended but lives to be continued. The life of one who joins the covenant of Abraham continues the life of Abraham, for the present is not apart from the past. "Abraham is still standing before God" (Genesis 18:22). Abraham endures forever. We are Abraham, Isaac, and Jacob.[114]

Rudolf Otto's essay "Silent Worship" gives eloquent testimony to the "kinship" to be noticed between faith traditions that, "viewed externally," that is, defined by their credal avowals, "seem to stand at the opposite poles of religious development, viz., the Quaker Meeting and the Roman Catholic Mass": "*Both* are solemn religious observances of a numinous and sacramental character, *both* are communion, *both* exhibit alike an inner straining not only 'to realize the presence' of God, but to attain a degree of oneness with Him."[115]

Kinship is the appropriate word. Kin are not alike in all important respects, and need not minimize their differences; yet, their recognition of kinship, hopefully, leads them to acknowledge too their unity, and to carry on, different-and-united, with care and respect for one another.

In seeking thus to deemphasize the metaphysics of religions, I am not arguing for an emphasis instead on "dialogue," or to enter the debate about the value of "interreligious dialogue."[116] Professor Paul Griffiths, as part of an attack on dialogue, calls for keeping the metaphysics in the foreground, on the ground that it is "axiomatic" that "all human activity," religion included, "both implies and evinces a commitment to some particular metaphysic."[117] My reaction is that to infer from the truth of such an axiom that we must or should define ourselves by our metaphysical commitments is a singularly academic bias. I have found it far more illuminating, with respect to the teachings of my own religion as well as of others, to view the theological propositions that characterize most creeds as heuristics, as guides to moral truths, rather than as metaphysical claims to be debated.

Professor Griffiths has in mind disputation over principles of a highly rarified sort, not, for example, specifics like the Nicene Creed or the Sinaitic revelation but (with Buddhism in mind) such beliefs as those about "impermanence, the transience of all things, and the absence of any enduring principle that constitutes the identity of human persons."[118] It is difficult to imagine those of us who are not trained philosophers or theologians either taking part or caring much. Indeed, it is a theologian, Sallie Mc-Fague, who counsels against a form of "theological reflection" that is so "anxious" about propositional clarity and definiteness. Language, she contends, "does not only describe," it also "evokes and intimates." She draws an analogy to the description that one writer uses of scientific models: "They are neither literal pictures of reality nor 'useful fictions,' but partial and provisional ways of imagining what is not observable; they are symbolic representations of aspects of the world which are not directly accessible to us."[119]

There is certainly a danger (to use Griffiths's lurid words) of "plunder and expropriation" in using another faith's religious practice as part of one's own. I would say, not that such practices demonstrate a vice inherent in dialogue, but that they illustrate the difficulty of carrying it on in ways that are genuinely aware of its hazards. To seek to cure that vice, as for example in the strictures laid down by the Conference of Bishops against Catholic appropriation of the Passover Seder (p. 64, below), is to take a step toward interreligious *understanding*, something different from, and more fundamental than, dialogue, and which neither validates nor casts doubt on it.[120] This approach enables one to view credal difference in the manner that educational theorist Peter Elbow would apply to dichotomies generally, "holding them unresolved" at the propositional level.[121]

To abjure triumphalism requires more than steering clear of intolerance. One may be genuinely respectful of the right of others to hold different world-views, but be unable to hear or describe them without feeling compelled to say in what ways they are inferior to one's own. It is here that excessive confidence in one's faith, spilling over into a self-satisfied evangelism, becomes a moral hazard. One who is moved to "bear witness" to others—whether in song, prayer, sermon, writing, or conversation, whether by proclaiming either one's good fortune in being "saved" or "chosen" or the special qualities of one's particular faith tradition—is certainly free to act on that call. The need is to remain always conscious of the danger of pulling rank on others, those to whom the testimony is addressed or those spoken about more or less disparagingly.[122]

Rank can inhere in ecclesial authority, in the force of superior numbers, or in a tradition of dominance. So, George Eliot's Adam Bede used his moral authority over Arthur fairly, for it came only from the content of his words, and from his own probity, but her Savanorola oppressed Romola, for, although his moral judgments struck a resonant chord in her own, they came to her cloaked in the authority of their Church. (Cloaking is an especially salient metaphor here, since his clerical robes were as much a part of his message as his words.[123]) It is for this reason that I find disturbingly obtuse the claim of some Christians that their religion is being discriminated against when Native American religious symbols are accepted as public displays and Christian ones are viewed warily.[124]

The same ground supports the judicial decision holding unconstitutional the practice of a judge to open court each day with the statement "Let us pause for a moment of prayer," bowing his head, and reciting a simple "non-sectarian" prayer; certainly, anyone has a right to invoke divine guidance on his or her work, but the fact that he is a judge, exercising great power over those appearing before him, gives to his act, in its time, place, and manner, more than a purely personal significance. The result should have been otherwise had the judge found a manner of expression that made clear that he was speaking only for himself, and not inviting the participation of others present.[125]

Abjuring triumphalism means for communicants of religious traditions with significant strains of it in their history to acknowledge them fully and candidly, and to repudiate them.[126] Where triumphalism is built into Scripture or liturgy, the task is to face up to the question whether a refusal to address those strains is not a renewal of the evils wrought by those who have gone before. The incessant manifestation of disdain for "the Jews" in traditional translations of John's Gospel, and the heedless recitation of the horrific closing passages of the Book of Esther on the Jewish holiday of Purim, are especially egregious examples. The precise contours of one's belief in the sacred quality of Scripture may forbid bowdlerization of "difficult texts," but other responses surely remain available.[127]

The National Conference of Catholic Bishops has given striking recognition of the need to go beyond intolerance in encouraging its communicants who desire to participate in a Seder during Holy Week to do so, while cautioning them that "it is wrong to 'baptize' the seder by ending it with New Testament readings . . . or, worse, turn it into a prologue to the Eucharist. Such mergings distort both traditions."[128]

For my part, I need to be able and willing to listen to Jews who are more traditional, or less traditional, than I, to Christians and Muslims of varying hues, and to secular rationalists as well, without feeling that, if I am to avoid being understood to accept their tenets, I must emphasize only the ways in which we differ, or what I regard as their essential failings. It means also to be able and willing to understand and describe their fundamental beliefs without caricaturing or belittling them. It means that I can recognize that there is something, perhaps much, that I can learn from the belief-systems of others, that dialogue between us can be more than an exchange of defenses of our positions or efforts at proselytization, that what I believe is not put in question by genuinely listening to another's belief system, that I am not necessarily called upon to give or withhold assent to what I hear. As Quaker writer Isaac Penington admonished us in 1659, "Mark, it is not the different practice from one another that breaks the peace or unity, but the judging of one another because of different practices."[129]

So, although I value attempts by contemporary Jews to speak spiritual renewal to those of their co-religionists who have lost or never known the deep spiritual nourishment to be found in the rabbinic tradition, I react differently when that effort leads them to encourage by example the tendency of their readers to belittle the insights of Jesus or Christianity.[130] And when I am in conversation with an Orthodox Jewish friend, and hear him never refer to what he plans to do tomorrow or next week without adding the parenthetical "God willing," my effort is to let go of my reflexive judgment about his apparent metaphysical belief that God is moment-to-moment deciding how to intervene in his life, and allow myself to appreciate the way in which his religious consciousness has trained him constantly to remain aware that his life and good fortune are never to be taken for granted.[131]

When I attend Mass, and hear the priest and the congregation confess their faith in the words of the Nicene Creed, my effort is not to congratulate myself on escaping so bizarre and benighted a set of beliefs, nor to ask myself whether I am on the verge of becoming a Christian after all (and should either follow that leading or get out of there fast). Rather, it is to regard what is being said as seeking to express fundamental truths in a language not my own, and to attempt to "be with" the service at a level that is partially but not entirely cognitive. My hope is that I will thereby be aided in my own efforts to understand and express truth.

There is a wonderful story about a religious meeting between the eighteenth-century Quaker John Woolman and a group of Native Americans, in which Woolman rose to pray. The Chief stopped the translator, and later said to Woolman, of the prayer whose words he did not find it necessary to know, "I love to feel where words come from."[132]

APPROACHING MYSTERY

> Tell all the Truth but tell it slant
> Success in Circuit lies
> Too bright for our infirm Delight
> The Truth's superb surprise
> As Lightning to the Children eased
> With explanation kind
> The Truth must dazzle gradually
> Or every man be blind
>
> —EMILY DICKINSON[133]

> They stood at a distance and said to Moses: "Speak to us yourself and we will listen; but do not let God speak to us or we shall die."
>
> —Exodus 20:19

The charge of mystification is that the grounding of religion in mystery is neither necessary nor helpful to the project of understanding the world, that religion's use of vague and metaphorical language obscures critical questions and evades critical problems. The religious tradition regards mystery as a fundamental truth about reality, as an aspect of reality that is to be celebrated and embraced, not in place of clarity and transparency but along with them. The secular tradition tends to regard mystery as a problem to be overcome if possible, and the assertion that it is not possible as a confession of weakness or defeat.

It seems clear that there is no way to decide which view is right, except from a stance that transcends human knowledge. What appears to one as a preference for obfuscation and fuzzy thinking is to another the only sensible way to avoid reductive clarity and false transparency. At bottom, my aversion to a wholly secular explanation of the world rests on a belief in the importance of grounding our stance toward the world in a palpable sense of wonder. Father Edward M. DePaoli, trained in both the classical and the Catholic tradition, writes that, "If before Descartes all philosophy began in wonder, after him it all begins in doubt."[134] Doubt and wonder, mystery and knowledge, clarity and obscurity, need to co-exist, each to discipline the other. The modern secular tradition too frequently acts as if the expulsion of any sense of wonder is the necessary predicate of any valid or justifiable efforts at understanding the world.[135] Walt Whitman's poem "When I Heard the Learn'd Astronomer" is a classic statement (perhaps itself an excessively polarized statement) of an aversive reaction to this sort of reductionism:

> When I heard the learn'd astronomer,
> When the proofs, the figures, were ranged in columns before me,
> When I was shown the charts and diagrams, to add, divide, and measure them,
> When I sitting heard the astronomer where he lectured with much applause in the lecture-room,
> How soon unaccountable I became tired and sick,
> Till rising and gliding out I wander'd off by myself,
> In the mystical moist night-air, and from time to time,
> Look'd up in perfect silence at the stars.[136]

It is important to recognize, if we are to avoid religious triumphalism, that there is nothing inherent in secularism, in particular in the rejection of theistic approaches, that requires the reduction of wonder to clarity. To me, a secular consciousness that hospitably incorporates a sense of awe and wonder has much in common with a similarly oriented religious consciousness. The use of the word "atheist" as an epithet is a common manifestation of this anti-secular triumphalism. For some, the word "spiritual" rather than "religious" captures one side of a dichotomy that is more significant than that between the religious and the secular. Indeed, it was a parish priest giving an ordinary Sunday homily who I heard explicitly ground his preference for the spiritual over the religious in the tendency of religion, by too often stressing rigid obedience to doctrine, to diminish the openness and flexibility that is at the heart of the spiritual. There is secular spirituality and religious spirituality, just as there are believers as well as nonbelievers in whose consciousness I can discern little or no awareness of the spiritual, of the holy.[137]

The legacy of Stalinism, and the power in the West of the tradition of demonizing communism, have obscured it for many, but the Socialist tradition is undeniably spiritual (notwithstanding its atheism) at its core. The great Christian pacifist A. J. Muste spoke in 1961 of those "who are regarded as unbelievers": "[M]y thoughts constantly shuttle back and forth between the conviction that many of these are the true believers and the wish that I might be able to give them an account of the faith that is in me . . . in language that would be comprehensible to them." Martin Buber wrote of what many, today and in his day, probably would deem self-evidently an oxymoron, religious socialism: "[S]ocialism without religion does not hear the divine address, yet still it responds; religion without socialism hears the call but does not respond." And Robert Bellah has called for a "socialist vision" "linked once again, as it was for Henry James, Sr., and Eugene Debs, with a vision that is moral and religious as well as political."[138]

Nonetheless, there is an evident basis for Cornel West's conclusion that the "preoccupation" of the Marxist tradition with "improving the social circumstances under which people pursue love, revel in friendship, and confront death" has led that tradition to be "silent about the existential meaning of death, suffering, love, and friendship." To West, his Christian perspective, in particular the "rich traditions of the Black Church that produced and sustains [him,] embraces depths of despair, layers of dread, encounters with the sheer absurdity of the human condition, and ungrounded leaps of faith alien to the Marxist tradition." "Social theory is not the same as existential wisdom," and it is the existential issue that to West is critical.[139]

What is central, to me, is less the despair, dread, and absurdity of which Cornel West wrote—although there is plainly more here than I have acknowledged—than the ability and willingness to bring to one's daily life a palpable awareness of awe and wonder, of Rabbi Heschel's "radical amazement."[140] The aim is not to repudiate wholesale the insights and methods of scientific rationality, but to recognize that both are legitimate and important modes of inquiry, which need to be kept in a dynamic relationship to each other. As Emily Hartigan expresses this idea: "Some [understandings] can be brought to the cognitive surface; some can only be lived. We must, in theologian Tad Dunne's words, 'be careful not to think we can explain Mystery; . . . we must be equally careful not to call Mystery those things which Mystery impels us to understand.' "[141]

A rabbinic admonition to similar effect uses the terms "intellect" and "faith" (rather than "rationality" and "mystery") as contrasting sources of understanding: "There are truths that transcend intellect and that can be perceived only through faith. At the same time, utilizing faith for something that can be comprehended is making use of the wrong faculty; intellect must grasp that which is within the reach of intellect. . . ."[142] Made as a broadside dismissal of religious language and practices, the charge of mystification is a form of secularist triumphalism.

I experience the sense of awe and wonder as a beacon illuminating moral truth, not only truth about the physical world. It does this, I believe, largely by generating a deep and abiding sense of gratitude, which I believe is a heuristic of enormous power.[143] A consciousness of gratitude, of blessedness, helps to make recognition of the claims of others on our life choices appear welcome and appropriate, not merely a burden imposed on us by some outside command. In the Jewish tradition, one who does an act of kindness or charity for another, and is thanked for it, is expected to respond, "No, it is I who thank you, for giving me this opportunity." The opportunity is not merely to carry out the obligation to give *tzedakah*; in a less command-oriented consciousness, it is to recognize that one whose life is such that he or she can be of help to one in need of kindness or charity is better off than the one who must seek it from others.[144]

This sense of gratitude surely does not require a religious outlook on the world, but in my experience it is the religious tradition that most fully encourages it and most adequately manifests it. From gratitude flows the awareness of dependence, of transience and mortality, in a context of enduring compassion and trust, not merely acknowledged intellectually, but made part of a regular religious practice, whether the morning-and-evening recital of the *Sh'ma Y'Israel*,^c the daily (or weekly) experience of the Eucharist, the speech-in-silence of Quaker worship, or the overflowing emptiness of Buddhist meditation.

To me, one of the tragedies of the modern era is that the magnificent teachings of the narratives and rituals of the religious tradition have been so pervasively transformed into propositional descriptions of reality, to be accepted as such by fundamentalist versions of each faith tradition and rejected as such by non-believers.

---

^c The Jewish confession of faith, traditionally rendered in English as "Hear, O Israel, the Lord our God, the Lord is One," is to be recited on first arising and immediately before going to sleep.

The philosopher Mortimer Adler, insisting on a pristine "corre-spondence" theory of truth for what he terms "logical" state-ments—for which I have used the term "propositional truth"—acknowledges that "meaning or significance is not de-pendent on the logical truth of what is being said or thought."[145] He recognizes (attributing the view to Augustine) that the reli-gious tradition maintains that, although the message that the Bible conveys "must be true," "since it conveys that message in human words [they] are totally misleading" if read only literally. Yet, de-spite his explicit disavowal, Adler's contrast of the logical truth of philosophy with the "poetical truth" of religion trivializes the latter, partly by the belittling terms "instruction and delight" by which he describes its benefits, but also by his ready acceptance of the idea that, about "poetic" truth, there is nothing that can be said, that it works (or not) in wholly private ways. Emily Dick-inson's insight (in the heading of this section) that to tell "all the Truth" we must "tell it slant" has an epistemological sophistica-tion that analytic philosophy too often lacks.

Catholic theologian Elizabeth Johnson describes religious sym-bols as "a word or image that participates in the reality being signified, opens it up to some understanding, yet never exhausts it completely."[146] Symbols, Paul Dinter asserts, "always involve a tension between their plain meaning and a hidden meaning. They express something about reality, not by naming it or describing it, but by taking a detour and naming or picturing something else. . . . Metaphoric expressions are the best way for us to bridge the gap between ordinary experience and intuitions of the extraordi-nary."[147] In speaking in symbols, metaphors, and parables, reli-gious practice seeks both greater cognitive clarity and more enduring experiential effect than is available through proposi-tional discourse.[148] Indeed, it rejects too great a separation of cognitive from experiential knowledge. It rests on the acknowl-edgment that both are necessary routes to knowledge, that one without the other is incomplete.

This excessive separation, and resultant inadequate acknowl-edgment, is characteristic of rationalist thought. Martha Nuss-baum, writing of literary and philosophical "forms of discourse," calls on philosophy to be "more literary, more closely allied to stories, and more respectful of mystery and open-endedness." She is seeking to integrate a polarity, rather than shift from one pole to the other: Emotions must be trusted as a source of knowledge, for they are "discriminating responses closely connected with beliefs about how things are and what is important," but not trusted blindly, for "the knowledge conveyed in emotional impressions must be systematized and pinned down by the activity of reflection."[149] Tibetan Buddhist Thuksey Rinpoche put the thought this way: "Wisdom is rooted in Compassion; Compassion is made sonorous and active through Wisdom. . . . We call a man a diamond when his heart is a mind and his mind is a heart, when there is no separation between the two, when both are illumined."[150]

That religiously grounded insights often seem to resist a self-reflective quality is not to say that they must. The religious consciousness that I seek to express in this book takes very much to heart this need to integrate trust and reflection. For religion is more than emotion; it responds to what Yeshiva University President Norman Lamm calls the "persistence of [our] metaphysical yearning," involving our intellectual curiosity, spiritual thirst, and quest for transcendent meaning. We need, Rabbi Lamm insists, to abjure the "unspoken certitudes" of a secularist triumphalism that brands all religion as "unworthy of serious consideration," and to recognize instead that the secular and the sacred exist in perpetual tension, each embodying truths "that may be ignored only at the peril of injuring one's intellectual integrity."[151]

I can, again, best get at what I want to say through a specific example, one drawn from the teaching of Rabbi Joseph B. Soloveitchik, a preeminent figure in twentieth-century Jewish thought. He begins with his thesis: "Holiness means the holiness of earthly, here-and-now life." To explicate it, he turns immediately to a wonderful Talmudic account:

> Rabbi Joshua b. [ben; the son of] Levi said: "When Moses ascended on high, the ministering angels spoke before the Holy One, blessed be He, 'Sovereign of the universe! What business has one born of woman among us?' He answered them, 'He has come to receive the Torah.' They said to Him, 'That secret treasure . . . Thou desirest to give to flesh and blood!' . . . The Holy One, blessed be He, said to Moses, 'Return them an answer.' . . . He [then] spoke before Him, 'Sovereign of the universe! The Torah which Thou givest me, what is written therein! I am the Lord Thy God, who brought thee out of the land of Egypt (Exod. 20:2).' Said he to [the angels], 'Did you go down to Egypt? Were you enslaved to Pha-

raoh?, etc. Again what is written therein? Remember the Sabbath day, to keep it holy (Exod. 20:8). Do you then perform work that you need to rest?, etc. Again, what is written therein? Honor thy father and thy mother (Exod. 20:12). Do you have any fathers and mothers? Again what is written therein? Thou shalt not murder. Thou shalt not commit adultery. Thou shalt not steal (Exod. 20:13). Is there jealousy among you; is the Evil Tempter among you?' Straight away they conceded to him."

Here is the lesson he draws from the story:

God does not wish to hand over His Torah to the ministering angels, the denizens of a transcendent world. Rather, he handed over His Torah to Moses, who brought it down to the earth and caused it to dwell among human beings, "who reside in darkness and deep gloom" (Ps. 107:10). The earth and bodily life are the very ground of the halakhic [obligatory] reality. Only against the concrete, empirical backdrop of this world can the Torah be implemented; angels, who neither eat nor drink, who neither quarrel with one another nor are envious of one another, are not worthy and fit for the receiving of the Torah.[152]

I imagine that through the centuries religious Jews have differed over the question whether Rabbi Joshua ben Levi meant to describe an actual conversation that took place in Heaven. I do not know what Rabbi Soloveitchik would say about that. As my discussion of the opening lines of the Holiness Code (Chapter 2, p. 29, above) makes clear, what the story says to me by taking place in the presence of God is that the lesson which Rabbi Soloveitchik takes from it is true, that it and he have accurately "pointed" to the truth.

Attention to Soloveitchik's language helps me to understand in what way the truth that the account expresses is moral truth. He does not say that the angels do not need the Torah, but that they are not "worthy and fit" to receive it. The moral law is given to humankind because of its creatureliness, its "fallenness," if you will, not as a yoke to keep in check its depravity, but as a gift, to enable humanity to find the way through the "darkness and deep gloom" to live a holy life. We are to take it in gratitude, and follow it in joy, as a celebration, rather than a constriction, of our being.[153]

I do not claim that the story *proves* the truth of its lesson. In Emily Hartigan's term, it "illuminates rather than 'proves'"; Christian theologian James Gustafson, in describing the process, uses the same term, referring to "a story [that] does not really prescribe precise conduct but illumines one's choices."[154] The illumination is, however, something of substance. It operates to connect the reader with a non-cognitive recognition of the truth of Soloveitchik's teaching, which his own text alone does not have. It does this to some degree by its antiquity and the teaching authority of its source, and (paradoxically enough, in a manner that I cannot adequately explain) in part by the blatant irrationality of its impossible anthropomorphism. But, since the "illumination" is not deductive, not a matter of entailment, its force is not illegitimate or question-begging. It leaves it to the reader to be drawn by it, to find it a beacon of light, or not.

What I have said of metaphors and parables is true as well of rituals. On a cognitive level, rituals are expressions, not derivations, of belief: One who did not believe it was the will of God would not bother to bind phylacteries on his arm and forehead each morning; one who did not believe in either a Catholic or a Protestant version of the presence of Christ in the Eucharist would not be interested in regularly taking Communion.[155] Yet, I believe that there is more to be said. Doing the act in question is not only, perhaps even not necessarily, a profession of belief. It may be a practice that, like a Talmudic or Gospel story, can teach us mindfulness or awareness, as any spiritual discipline might, or teach us a more specific lesson about the world and the moral life.[156] I will turn in the next chapter to the ways in which ritual can lead us to, and keep us from, a fuller discernment of truth.

4

Listening for the Voice of God

Some time after these events, God put Abraham to the test. "Abraham," he called to him, and Abraham replied, "Here I am." "Take your son, your only son, Isaac, whom you love, and go to the land of Moriah, and offer him there as a burnt offering on one of the mountains that I shall show you." So Abraham rose early in the morning, saddled his donkey, and took two of his young men with him, and his son Isaac; he cut the wood for the burnt offering, and set out and went to the place in the distance that God had shown him.

—Genesis 22:1–3

A man of my acquaintance, a graduate student in religion and a convert to Islam, is often asked (because of the way he dresses) whether he is a Muslim. He likes to answer, "I don't know." To the perplexed reaction that this response inevitably prompts, he replies: "*Muslim* is an Arabic word that means 'one who has submitted to the Will of God.' Only God knows whether I am a Muslim; all I can say is that I try."[157]

There is, I have come to see, more here than first meets the eye. The emphasis on surrender, on obedience, is plain. But it is too easy to polarize the insight and miss its second, more muted but equally fundamental avowal, that of his uncertainty whether he has correctly discerned the will of God. For we are seldom wholly ignorant that we have fallen short when we are confident that we *know* what God asks of us, when (to put those words in the secular terms by which I can express it propositionally) we know the right and wrong of what we are about to do but nonetheless do what we know is wrongful. We are more likely to founder unawares on those occasions when we thought that we had correctly perceived the will of God, but our actions were based on mistaken belief, were wanting in what the Quakers felicitously call discernment. It seems true, then, that although my student acquaintance spoke only of submission, his insight equally embraces discernment.

In a stunning reinterpretation of the story of the *Akedah*, the binding of Isaac, which the passage at the head of this chapter introduces, Michael Lerner has questioned the traditional reading of the story as the quintessential example of obedience to God, even to the point of the murder of one's own son. Abraham's father was not only a worshipper of idols, but an idol-maker, and the son suffered severe punishment for departing from his family's religion. God told him, "Leave your own country, your kin, and your father's house" (Genesis 12:1), but, Lerner maintains, it was easier for him to leave physically than psychically. What Abraham heard, according to Lerner, was, *not* the voice of God, but the "voices of the gods of his past, now in the voice of God, telling him to do to his own son what was done to him." It is only at the last instant, "as he looks into the eyes of the son he has bound for slaughter, [that] he can now overcome the emotional deadness that allowed him to cast Ishmael off into the desert. At the very last moment, Abraham heard the true voice of God, the voice that says, 'Don't send your hand onto the youth and don't make any blemish.'" "Abraham's problem," Lerner concludes, "is our problem: to distinguish between the word of God and the unconscious legacy of pain presenting itself as if it were the voice of God."[158]

This reinterpretation reconciles the story of the *Akedah* with Abraham's earlier encounter with God, where, in what is surely one of the most momentous passages of Scripture, he successfully challenges God's intention to destroy Sodom even though fifty good people might live there among the wicked: "Shall not the Judge of all the world act justly?" (Genesis 22:25). It was, I believe, the pivotal gift of biblical Judaism to the world that the God whom it acknowledged as Supreme Ruler of all is a God of Justice. However one grapples with the problem of the existence of evil in the world, it is unthinkable that God calls on us to do that which is wrong.[159]

Lerner claims that in the centuries after the biblical period the

message of the *Akedah* was transformed in response to the ineradicable injustice and oppression that the Jewish people endured.[160]
I do not know whether biblical scholarship gives sufficient basis
for such a departure from the apparent meaning of the text, and
my resistance to Lerner's reinterpretation does not rest primarily
on textual strictures. Rather, it is based on the centuries of teaching, Jewish and Christian alike, and the role that the story has
played in the death of thousands of Jewish martyrs through the
ages, which have given the traditional reading a sanctity that I
find it difficult to put to one side.[161] Lerner's account does, however, give powerful testimony that obedience alone can never account for a decision taken in obedience to the will of God, for it
always rests on the anterior belief that one in fact knows God's
will.

Quaker sage Douglas Steere recounts a conversation with
Thomas Mann, in which the latter said, "Were I to determine
what I personally mean by religiousness, I would say that it is
attentiveness and obedience." Steere goes on:

> Without attentiveness in both our private and [our] public worship
> there can be only a confirmation of the African proverb that says,
> "When God speaks, He does not wake up the sleeper." But unless
> this precious attentiveness is linked to obedience, the deeper bond
> is missing. To come near to God is to change, and unless there is
> obedience, a change of will . . . , I have failed the love that bid me
> to join God.[162]

The challenge for one who (like me) believes that traditional
religion too often emphasizes obedience, without taking sufficient account of the problem of discernment, is to avoid the polar
error. My tendency is to focus only on discernment, on the difficult process of learning what God calls on me to do, while paying
insufficient attention to the difficulty of acting on my discernments, of mustering the will to heed a call that is plainly experienced, to do what is right and avoid doing what is wrong. It is
for that reason that I will begin with the idea of obligation. I want
to give expression to a sense of obligation that resists dichotomiz-
ing sharply its internal and external sources, and treating as "real"
only the latter, and that rejects too the traditional command-and-
obey concept of obligation.

OBLIGATION

> Jesus then came with his disciples to a place called Gethsemane, and he said to them, "Sit here while I go over there to pray." He took with him Peter and the two sons of Zebedee. Distress and anguish over-whelmed him, and he said to them, "My heart is ready to break with grief. Stop here, and stay awake with me." Then he went on a little farther, threw himself down, and prayed, "My Father, if it is possible, let this cup pass me by. Yet not my will but yours.

> —MATTHEW 26:36–39

If in Christian theology Jesus is fully human and fully divine, it is his human aspect that is here most eloquently portrayed. His words engender in me as I read them the very feelings that Jesus expresses; the passage tears at the heart and, as often as I read it, nearly overwhelms me. Ironically, most of the great martyrs of history are presented to us, in contemporary documents or subsequent reenactments, as embracing their fate enveloped in serenity. I think of Socrates; of Rabbi Akiba, and the countless martyrs in the centuries that followed who died *al kadosh hashem* (for the sanctification of the Name), refusing to surrender or violate their Jewish faith; of T. S. Eliot's Thomas Becket, archbishop of Canterbury, and Robert Bolt's Sir Thomas More, lord chancellor of England; of Mary Dyer, hanged on Boston Common for returning to preach her Quaker faith; and of Martin Luther King, speaking on the last day of his life of a death that perhaps only he (and his assassin) anticipated. Each of these, themselves or through those who have written of them, have left us stirring expressions of a calm willingness to face death rather than turn aside from his or her calling.[163] Has it been Jesus alone who at Gethsemane gave us this example of so passionate and unrestrained an acknowledgment of human frailty, of the desire simply to live out life in peace?

Few of us have had the experience of being called upon to allow ourselves to be subjected to a painful and ignominious death, refraining from taking even a simple action that would protect ourselves. Yet, I—and, I imagine, you as well, but I will speak only of myself—so often shrink from incurring, from even risking, far less malign consequences of far less dramatic choices I face in my daily life. I live a secure, privileged life, and run few even of the truly minor risks that would attend my doing more than I do to work against, even simply to speak against, the manifold injustices that exist in the communities of which I am a part. I say this not to berate myself, for I think that I have made many choices in my life that are responsive to my perception of the good, and in the process have abjured some of the benefits that would have come from making different choices. In both dimensions, where I have measured up and where I have fallen short, I think that the religious tradition plays a powerful role, not only in helping to teach me "the will of God," but in enabling me to follow it.

The traditional means by which religion has reinforced our will to do God's will is through the imperial metaphor of God as Supreme Overlord, the "King of the King of Kings."[164] I find a very different picture of God in Jesus's words at Gethsemane. The "Father" with whom Jesus speaks is far, for example, from the "Father, chiefly known to me by Thy rod," of Herman Melville's Calvinist divine, Father Mapple.[165] Jesus's "submission" is an act of love, reciprocal to the love that he experiences. Robert Bolt understood this (better, I fear, than I do) when he had his Thomas More, hearing his daughter's heartfelt appeal, "haven't you done as much as God can reasonably *want?*", respond that "it isn't a matter of reason; finally it's a matter of love."[166] The weakness that is an ineradicable aspect of Jesus's humanity loosens its grip on his actions in the moment that his prayer brings the human Jesus into intimate relation with God.[167]

It has often been observed that the words "religion" and "obligation" have a common Latin root, *ligare*, "to bind." For many, believers and skeptics alike, religion is the principal ground of obligation. Indeed, many would assert, with Dostoievski's Ivan Karamazov, "If there is no God, then everything is permitted." This idea is most commonly rooted in a conception of God as (in the words of the Selective Service Act, with which this book began) a "Supreme Being,"[168] the Unmoved Mover, who constituted morality by "His Word" and dispenses rewards to the faithful and punishment to the disobedient. This "divine command" view of the relation between divinity and humanity, although tenaciously embraced by segments of orthodoxy in Judaism,

Christianity, and Islam, is today widely rejected by many who deem themselves believers, theologians and others. I reject it, too. But it is important, before dwelling on that rejection, to pay tribute to that aspect of the traditional "kingship" model of divinity which seems to me to carry an essential truth, one uniquely able to ground a moral life.

"If the Lord is my Master, to no man am I a slave." This cry of seventeenth-century English radicals dramatically expresses the way in which traditional religious consciousness can play an emancipatory, radically egalitarian role. Fidelity to the commands of the One True Ruler has served to embolden those who would resist the tyranny of fellow mortals. Through the ages, the immortalized and the unremembered alike have found the strength to question the idolatrous insistence of the powerful on absolute obedience to them in the idea given voice by Sophocles with a simplicity and eloquence unmatched in twenty-five hundred years:

CREON: But tell me thou—and let thy speech be brief—
            The edict hadst thou heard, which this forbade?
ANTIGONE: I could not choose but hear what all men heard.
CREON: And didst thou dare to disobey the law?
ANTIGONE: Nowise from Zeus, methought, this edict came,
            Nor Justice, that abides among the gods
            In Hades, who ordained this law for men.[169]

Modern theology, prompted in many cases by feminist insights, has done us important service in questioning the traditional conception of divine law as an edict from Olympus. It takes nothing away from that fact to bear in mind this two-edged quality of even the most traditional, patriarchal/hierarchical image of divinity. Rabbi Nancy Fuchs-Kreimer recounts a powerful experience, in reflecting on the continuing, contested use in Jewish liturgy of the word *melekh*, usually translated "king" (now, at times, the neutral "ruler"), in the traditional Jewish blessing said on many occasions throughout the day. In German, the Hebrew word is sometimes translated *Führer*, which was the title by which Adolph Hitler chose to be known, and she tells of a group of German Christians who, at great personal cost, responded to the command to acknowledge the decrees of *der Führer* in these words: "We will not obey Hitler. We already know who *our* Fuehrer is." She goes on: "I am perplexed by fellow feminists who reject hierarchy in theology. When I am on my knees during the Rosh Hashana *aleinu*,[d] the hierarchical claim concerning God is my *refutation* of all earthly hierarchies. I would not find 'God as King' a sustaining image if it were my daily liturgical diet. But for grand 'state occasions' like the start of a new year, recognizing God as Fuehrer feels entirely appropriate to me."[170] A textual introduction to the *aleinu* attributes to it like significance: "We worship no earthly power. Only to the only King do we bow and kneel, as a sign of ultimate loyalty to Him alone, and awareness of our mortality."[171]

There is at work here something deeper than simply an instrumental means of strengthening the will to act morally by positing a supernatural sovereign that trumps worldly incentives to do otherwise. The kingship imagery is, I believe, a metaphorical portrayal, in readily recognizable strokes, of a profound response to the experience of awe and wonder, that sense of the sacred embedded in the mundane, that I believe is at the heart of the religious consciousness. That experience generates an imperative, in religious terms a "call" or a "leading," to act, and the language of divine sovereignty serves to crystallize that feeling of being impelled, to keep its force in place in our consciousness, notwithstanding the inevitable ebbing of the immediate experience itself. In the anthropologist Clifford Geertz's felicitous terms, a "repetitive religious experience . . . comes in time to haunt daily life and cast a kind of indirect light upon it."[172] It is as we live what Geertz calls our "commonsense" lives, subject to all that common sense would tell us to do and avoid doing, that the haunting recollection of moments (liturgical or others) when we have experienced ourselves as in the presence of God does its work.[173]

Who now remembers Martin Niemoller? A German Lutheran pastor imprisoned during the War for anti-Nazi activities, he was, to at least one American Jewish teen-ager, a very bright star in a very dark sky. In 1961, now a bishop, he spoke in Philadelphia, and I went to pay my respects as much as to hear him. He had been a U-boat (submarine) commander in the German Navy dur-

---

[d] This magnificent prayer, which has been described as "the proclamation of God as Supreme King of the Universe, and as God of a United Humanity," has since the fourteenth century closed all Jewish services. (See the reference in the endnote that follows the quotation in the text). Its recitation on the High Holy Days is the only occasion on which Jews are permitted to kneel.

ing the First World War, and spoke of how he had subsequently become a pacifist. "I would watch through the periscope for the enemy vessel, and when the crosshairs were amidships of it, I would say, 'fire.' The sailor standing by would press a button, and I would watch the torpedo's wake and the hoped-for explosion. One day, years later, I asked myself, if Jesus of Nazareth had been that sailor, when I ordered, 'fire,' would he have pushed the button?"

Niemoller felt impelled to act as he came to believe Jesus would have acted. But what does that soft word "impelled" really mean? In identifying himself as a Christian, Niemoller had told us what the term meant to him: "A Christian," he said, "is one who accepts Jesus as teacher and brother." Nothing here of the traditional Protestant words of Christ as Lord and Savior, or of anything analogous to Nancy Fuchs-Kreimer's liturgical enactment of obeisance to the Sovereign, let alone of a tone like Isaiah's vision of his call, the Lord sitting on a temple throne, surrounded by angels, the house filling with smoke, and a live coal brought by an angel to sear the prophet's lips and move him to respond to God's "Whom shall I send?" with "Here I am; send me" (Isaiah 6:1–8).

Yet, impelled Niemoller nonetheless was, with momentous consequences for his life.[174] It would be shallow in the extreme to say that, because he experienced Jesus "only" as teacher and brother, rather than as Lord, he was not obliged, but merely chose, to give up warfare. I respond strongly to his story because my own experience of awe, of (again, in Heschel's wonderful term) radical amazement, has little in it of fear and trembling, of God as Judge, in the traditional sense of the source of rewards and punishments. I believe that the deeply embedded equation of obligation with sanction needs to be questioned. So traditional a believer as C. S. Lewis saw a "preoccupation" with reward and punishment as a "corruption" of religion. He spoke, rather, of commands that were "inexorable, but . . . backed by no 'sanctions' ": "God is to be obeyed simply because He was God. Long since, . . . He had taught me how a thing can be revered not for what it can do to us but for what it is. . . . If you ask why we should obey God, in the last resort the answer is, 'I am.' "[175]

My experience is that the good—to use a quasi-secular term—draws me to it. Its compulsion is more like that of gravity than of lightning. I can resist ("disobey"), and there is much in the world that encourages resistance, that encourages me to follow Jonah rather than Isaiah.[176] Religious practice, liturgy, and Scripture strengthen my ability to overcome that resistance, to live as I am beckoned to live.[177]

Nor does Niemoller's story suggest that his own discernment played no role. Jewish tradition has it that within each person there exists an "evil impulse" and an impulse toward the good.[178] To see Christ in the sailor, and listen to his message—the message that the actual sailor was not free to express, perhaps not even to discern—is not simply a vision from the beyond. It assuredly arises from within. Indeed, Niemoller's talk of teacher and brother will doubtless confirm the objection that what I am talking about— the sources of awe, the experience of the good, the beckoning— exists wholly within human experience, and should not be projected "out there" to that which transcends human experience. At bottom, I have no logical answer to the claim of projection, and can say only that my experience is of that which is not wholly within, that the external world *does* provoke my responses. In William James's words (as quoted by Rudolf Otto): "[I]t is as if there were in the human consciousness a sense of reality, a feeling of objective presence, a perception of what we may call 'something there.' . . ."[179] That may indeed be only a projection, but one who thinks so cannot, any more than one who thinks not, say where the truth of the matter lies.

The charge of projection is grounded in the sensible realization that there is a strong element of wish-fulfillment in one's perception of a God that is not wholly a human creation. Kent Bendall and Frederick Ferre wisely point out that this observation does not have the "slam dunk" quality with which it is often invoked:

> Freud himself, no friend of religious faith, distinguishes carefully between "illusion" and "delusion." Illusions, for him, are the product of wish-fulfillment, but they need not be false. Wish-fulfillment may lead away from reality, producing delusion, but the force of "illusion" may equally well serve to motivate fresh scientific discovery, spur risky undertakings, and forward social advance. Wish fulfillment may be behind the contributions of a Columbus, a Pasteur, or a Freud (by his own acknowledgment), as well as a Jesus or a Paul. The assumption of a simple step from wish-fulfillment to falsehood, therefore, is not logically permissible.[180]

In any event, "only a projection" has an unwarrantedly dismissive ring. Consider, in this connection, Bertrand Russell's magnificent essay "A Free Man's Worship." It richly repays reading in full, but I will quote here only a brief portion. Our "true freedom," to Russell, lies in our "determination to worship only the God created by our own love of the good, to respect only the heaven which inspires the insight of our best moments." "[F]or Man, condemned to-day to lose his dearest, to-morrow himself to pass through the gate of darkness, it remains only to cherish, ere yet the blow falls, the lofty thoughts that ennoble his little day; to worship at the shrine that his own hands have built. . . ."[181]

In speaking thus of God as "created by our own love of the good," Russell assumes that, to be "real," in the sense of existing outside human thought, God must be a "thing" of some sort.[182] Rabbi Harold Kushner expresses a different conception of "God," which opens the meaning of God's "existence." To Kushner, "God is not an entity out in space somewhere. . . . 'God' is a name we give to a certain set of realities that we have discovered to be built into the world." The question of God's existence is not one "about the population of Heaven":

> To believe that God is real means believing that the qualities we associate with God are real, that they truly exist in the world. If we have experienced love, trust, generosity, either as donors or as recipients, if we have known the feeling of being honest or helpful, then we know from our own experience, not based on anyone else's philosophy or persuasiveness, that these qualities are real beyond all question. If we have felt the strivings of goodness in ourselves, this is evidence of the reality of God in our own hearts. And if we understand "God" to mean the Power that makes these experiences possible, the reality of these experiences should bear eloquent witness to the reality of God. We cannot prove or disprove whether there is an old man with a long beard dwelling in Heaven, but we can definitely prove that God, the Source of growth, love and truth, does exist.[183]

Not only can the evil impulse obscure the truth from our sight, but it can bid fair to undermine our ability to follow the truth that we do see. The Jesus that Niemoller experienced as in the submarine with him both taught him the truth and gave him courage to act on it. I find, therefore, important learning in the language of obedience, of submission, even of kingship. The very elusiveness of the process of discernment should alert us to the

danger that our inquiry may be distorted by want of will, by what
I have called resistance to the good, to the word of God. Just as
traditional religion can understate the "hiddenness" of the word
of God, and insist on an obedience that too often is blind, so can
one commit the polar error, and give too little recognition to that
within us which would turn us away from an imperative whose
existence we cannot honestly deny.[184]

Discernment

> Can you by searching find out God?
>
> —Job 11:7

> You will say, Christ saith this, and the Apostles say that;
> But what canst thou say?
>
> —George Fox[185]

The question put to Job was plainly intended as a rhetorical one,
carrying its own negative answer. Traditional religion embraces
this answer, seeing in the divine act of revelation a means of access
(perhaps the only means) to moral truth, and seeing in the human
act of faith the source of serenity about both the limited quality
of human understanding and the reality of a world of injustice
and pain. Philosophers differ over the question whether there is a
truth to "find out," or whether goodness and evil exist only as
conventions of culture. Within each camp, or set of camps, they
differ too over the implications of their answer for human searching. I will not in this section focus on secular modes of expression,
since I can most usefully develop my thoughts in dialogue with
the religious tradition.

To traditional religionists, the foundational normative source of
moral truth is Scripture, which is binding authority, obligatory
upon us, because it is "the word of God," revealed to its human
authors. Indeed, the Jewish tradition is not only that Moses entered Heaven to receive the text of the Torah, but that Torah preexists the act of Creation, that "God consulted the Torah and
created the world."[186]

Those who would give to Scripture this degree of authority
necessarily build into their theology the human task of interpreta-

tion, for even one who believes in some literal or quasi-literal way that God "speaks" cannot dispute that those who say what they have heard are human.[187] The actual redactors of Scripture, as well as those who have given content to the divine law over the ages, are understood as acting under inspiration: In Judaism, the "oral Torah," the body of rabbinic opinion that has come down to us and continues to the present, illuminates God's will; in Catholicism, the Church established by Christ as his earthly manifestation carries on its mission under the authority of the divinely ordained successors to Peter the Fisherman. (One should not overstate this institutional quality of Jewish and Catholic seeking, which is significantly leavened by the weight given to "dissenting opinions" in rabbinic Judaism and to freedom of conscience in contemporary Catholic thought.) At the same time, while at least some Protestants may begin from the opposite pole, giving less of a role to a community of faith or clergy and focusing more on a direct interaction between the prayerful individual and the text, the weight traditionally given the text, and the vigor with which many Protestant groups proclaim the incontestable truth of particular readings of Scripture, limit its "individualist" strain.

My problem with authority-oriented religion is, at bottom, its underlying premise that "revelation" is the willed act of a Being who chooses when, to whom, and how to disclose ultimate truth, analogous to the manner in which one person chooses whether, when, and how to disclose or assert something to another. I simply cannot recognize such a conception of God. Martin Buber taught that "whoever goes forth in truth to the world, goes forth to God."[188] I believe that all who search for the truth (whether they are believers or skeptics) are seeking God; that God is there for those who seek "him," at once hidden and manifest; and that in that sense divine inspiration guides our search whenever we devote ourselves honestly to it.

At the same time, I see no escape from acknowledging that the truth that is thought to be or have been found is a fallible discovery, for the search partakes of the human as well as the divine, and therefore remains a human search, subject to error as is everything else about our creaturely life activities. We are partners in the ongoing acts of creation, and they partake of the beyond; our acts are therefore tinged with divinity, but they are not divine acts. Moses and St. Peter may have been far more deeply "tinged" than you or I, but human even they remained.[189]

Those who believe that the speech of any person or institution is wholly that of God have ordinarily come to that belief because of their decision to align themselves with the prior belief of a community of faith. That community is itself tinged with divine inspiration, but not more than that, save by what quickly becomes an infinite regress. A communicant may, by the "faith-knowl-edge" of which Rudolf Otto spoke (pp. 55, above), have come to believe that he or she, or his or her community of faith, has "seen the glory" in a fuller sense. Others who choose to accept the testimony of such persons may have sound reason to do so, but it is a human being on whose testimony they are basing their belief. In legal philosopher David Luban's term, revelation is "es-oteric": "to rely on it is to have faith in the prophets who com-municate the revelation."[190] "There is no truth that truths itself," Robert Bellah felicitously reminds us, "although modern ratio-nalism since the time of Descartes assumes there is."[191]

Recall my reference above (p. 70) to Mortimer Adler's attribu-tion to St. Augustine of the recognition that although the message conveyed by the Bible, being divinely inspired, "must be true," "it conveys that message in human words," which must therefore be interpreted before the theologian can decide what it is that must be believed.[192] It is necessary, therefore, to adhere to two precepts: "Hold to the truth of Scripture without wavering," but "adhere to a particular version only in such measure as to be ready to abandon it if it should prove to be false. . . ."[193] Wolfhart Pannenberg attributes to St. Paul the "critical distinction" that, "while the truth of God's revelation is indeed ultimate, our un-derstanding of that truth is always provisional and will remain so until the end of history."[194] Norman Beck grounds a similar view in the admonition against idolatry:

> [I]t is idolatrous of us to attribute inerrant, infallible, ultimate au-thority either to scriptural traditions or to ecclesiastical institutions. Scriptural traditions and ecclesiastical institutions point to the ulti-mate, they participate in that to which they point, and they open up levels of reality otherwise closed to us, and as such they have been assigned *significant* authority over us by us during various peri-ods of our history. It is apparent, therefore, that the people of any religious traditions may through usage and decree determine that

their scriptural traditions and their institutions have significant authority among them. . . .

Subscription to the significant authority of scriptural traditions and of institutions is appropriate and essential in order that there may be proper accountability within a religious community. Subscription to them as infallible and ultimate authority, however, is idolatrous.[195]

The foregoing has for me two consequences. One is to undermine the action of the most orthodox segments of traditional religion to cabin revelation to defined moments in history. This view, put with maximum rigor by one writer, asserts that: "the moral answers to the questions perplexing mankind since earliest times are known, [and] no new or revised moralistic teachings will be forthcoming from the Author of morality because all revelation from him is full, complete, and binding."[196]

If revelation is potentially open to all, it is continuing rather than complete. It is not only Moses, the Prophets, and the rabbis of old and of the present day, not only the Evangelists (with their accounts of the life and teachings of Jesus), St. Paul, and the Church Fathers of old and of the present day, to whom God has spoken. The Truth may be one and eternal, but one's understanding of it is necessarily situated and partial, and the neighbor or public figure whom I least respect, one to whom I least would naturally turn as a source of divine guidance, even (I remind myself) the authoritarian, conservative religionist from whom I am now distancing myself, may in fact in his or her last utterance have discerned (a portion of) that Truth.

When George Fox, in the famous passage that is at the head of this section, asked each of his hearers, content like most of us to turn to authority for the Truth, "What canst thou say?" he was not responding to some illegitimacy or other infirmity in the authority. For Fox, Christ and the Apostles were history's highest witnesses to the Truth; yet, he admonishes us, the words or thoughts that would come to you, or me, were we to turn to our own Inward Guide, might likewise express the voice of God, might likewise speak the Truth. I should not allow the teachings of authorities to foreclose my own searching; nor should I allow my own confidence in my discernment to close my mind to the teachings of others. For within each of us resides the incarnate God.[197]

I hope it is clear how different what I have written is from "cultural relativism," the dismissive term with which Jesuit theologian Avery Dulles has characterized the belief that "religious truth" is ineffable, able to be expressed only "in symbols and metaphors, but [which] cannot be communicated by propositional language." Far from viewing the teachings of the past "with suspicion," for example, I (like many others whose religion is not orthodox) regard them as having genuine sanctity (see p. 31, above). I do not object to the decision of conservative religionists to believe (as I do not) that "divine revelation can be formulated . . . in irrevocably and universally true credal and dogmatic propositions." I do fault their refusal to allow those who do not join them in their beliefs to have what we do believe taken seriously and described with accuracy and respect; we do not all warrant consignment to a common grave, our headstones labeled "widely prevalent," "sophisticated intellectuals," or "cultural relativists." This kind of sneering polarization is a manifestation of the triumphalist spirit that is conservative religion's tragic flaw.[198]

A second consequence is to prompt the realization that the belief that one has correctly understood God's will can be justified, it can be held with a high degree of confidence, what the Quakers call clearness, but it can never be knowledge, in the sense that it can never be known to be true, for the ultimate metaphysical truth of the matter lies beyond our finitude. In that respect, the question put to Job was rightly put rhetorically. But the more salient response is that, although as humans we never know whether by "searching" we in fact "find out God," as humans we are all able to carry on the search. To me, that means that we are called to listen for the voice of God, to seek to learn God's will, and our efforts in response to that call partake of divine inspiration. The desire to seek moral truth, and the capacity to learn it, are constitutive of our humanity, just as much an aspect of our creatureliness—in religious terms, just as much a gift of God—as the frailty of our desire to know and act on the will of God, and the fallibility of our attempt to discover it.[e]

What does it mean for one's belief to be justified, for one to be "clear" about a moral question, bearing always in mind that

---

[e] I prefer the term "discernment" because "discovery" has too mechanistic a connotation for me.

justification, or clearness, is different from knowledge? In the absence of incontestable first principles in which the work of justification may be grounded, we cannot bridge the gap between justification and knowledge.[199] The process is one that the contemporary political philosopher John Rawls calls "considered judgment in reflective equilibrium."[200] All we can seek to resolve, with respect to any moral question, is whether our considered judgment about it coheres with our moral judgments as a whole. Where it does not, the task is to bring the two into equilibrium by adjusting the specific judgment, the general set of them, or both. Where it does, we are (provisionally) reinforced in our belief.[201]

I prefer to describe the outcome of the process as clearness rather than justification, because the latter term (like the broader one, moral reasoning, of which it is an aspect), has at the outset two unfortunate tendencies: It facilitates, although it does not require, overweighting the role of reasoning, and especially of deductive logic, in the process, and it encourages one to objectify the process, to search for universal (even if provisional) answers, to which "we" will all agree provided we act, in Rawls's words, "conscientiously and intelligently."[202] The process is thus made more of argument and rationalization than of self-awareness and reflection. Rawls's work itself, for all its brilliance and widely recognized value, is a classic manifestation of these problematic qualities.

In expressing concern at the overweighting of rationality in the process of discernment, I certainly do not mean to exclude it, or to uphold irrationality. I have referred earlier (p. 70) to the widely shared (and widely ignored) insight that reason and emotion are not warring forces, but mutually supportive ones, and will add just a word here. Psychologist and ethicist Sidney Callahan points out that, "just as reason tutors and monitors emotion, so too can our emotions tutor reason."[203] As my colleague Michael Moore observes: "[A]nger at unjust treatment need not make reasoned choice more difficult. It may instead make choice easier by highlighting what we otherwise might have missed. Anger at injustice is at least as effective as reciting Kant when keeping the priority of justice before one's mind as one decides how to respond."[204] Indeed, I find wisdom in Callahan's judgment that "in our technological culture the greatest moral danger arises not from sentimentality, but from devaluing feeling and attending to or nurturing moral emotions."[205] To act on this judgment, however, requires recognition that what Moore wrote about anger, the most "respectable" of the emotions, needs to be acknowledged regarding the "softer" emotions as well. It is a well-known psychological datum that expressions of anger often "front" for feelings of pain, for oneself and others, which it is more difficult (especially for men) to acknowledge. We need to think, with educational critic Mary Rose O'Reilley, of "compassion as a mode of critical inquiry," as a route to knowledge.[206] Susannah Heschel, Abraham's daughter, has written of how her father "shattered our assumptions by rejecting the Aristotelian description of God as the 'Unmoved Mover'. Instead, he described God as the 'Most Moved Mover'."[207] Daniel Maguire writes of the "moral centricity" of biblical Judaism, which "does not just involve skills in the subtleties of ethics, but baptism by immersion in the feelings that ground ethics."[208]

The contemporary philosopher Gerald Postema has written wisely, in my view, of the process that he terms practical moral reasoning:

> Practical moral reasoning is wrongly viewed as strictly analogous to theoretical reasoning, the central objective of which is to arrive at correct answers to specific problems. This view of moral reasoning and experience is too narrow, for moral reasoning is not so singularly outcome-determinative. Our evaluations of ourselves and our actions depend not only on getting our moral sums right, but also on having the appropriate attitudes and reactions to the moral situation in which we act. . . .
>
> [I]n cases in which obligations to other persons are correctly judged to be overridden by weightier moral duties, with the result that some injury is done, it is not enough for one to work out the correct course of action and pursue it. It is also important that one appreciate the moral costs of that course of action. This appreciation will be expressed in a genuine reluctance to bring about the injury, and a sense of the accompanying loss or sacrifice. . . .
>
> Moral sentiments are an essential part of the moral life. The guilt or remorse one feels after mistreating a person is not merely a personal sanction one imposes on oneself after judging the action to have been wrong; it is the natural and most appropriate expression of this judgment. Similarly, the outrage we feel at injustice done to another and the resentment we feel at wrong done to ourselves are not just the emotional coloring of detached moral judgments, but the way in which we experience and express these judgments.

Thus, morality is not merely a matter of getting things right—as in solving a puzzle or learning to speak grammatically—but a matter of relating to people in a special and specifically human way.[209]

Many will find jarring this justaposition of so thoroughly secular an analysis to illustrate what I have been expressing in religious terms. I have done this deliberately, to stir the question posed by that reaction, for to me it is simply a case of speaking a different language. There is no reason, save our cultural norms of segmenting (from both directions) religious and secular thinking so thoroughly off from each other, that accounts for the strangeness. Indeed Postema's "voice," even as he counsels against too narrowly analytical an approach—we are not just "getting our moral sums rights"—is just as much an unadorned proclamation of what the reader "must" believe as would be the "testifying" of a fervent evangelist, who would proclaim the answer revealed in Scripture. In neither case should whatever irritation may be prompted by that coercive mode of discourse lead an unsympathetic reader to over-identify the style with the substance, and reject out of hand the position being espoused.

In content, what Postema emphasizes here is very close to a classic Quaker way of expressing a critical aspect of the process of discernment, the importance of "feeling the weight" of a concern. Our emphasis on rationality fits easily with an emphasis on the correctness of one's answer to a difficult question of moral choice. In that frame of mind, the "losing" considerations can too readily be discounted by logical demonstrations of their weakness, and thereupon be dismissed from one's mind. "Feeling the weight" is a discipline that warns us to be with the process a bit more patiently than reason might prompt, and encourages us (in Postema's term) to "appreciate the moral costs" of a right decision, not to undermine it but to influence its meaning and quality, to attend, as well, in Martha Nussbaum's felicitous terms, "to the intrinsic ethical character of the claim that on balance is not preferred." She goes on: "[I]t is good, in a more general way, to focus on these dilemmas and not to go beyond them, or 'solve' them, because to do so reaffirms and strengthens the values in question, in such a way that one will be less likely to violate them in other circumstances."[210]

I want now to look briefly at several non-cognitive avenues of discernment, associated with religious practices, with which I have had direct experience in recent years. The first is silence. In Quaker practice, for example, communal silent meditation is understood as a primary route to discernment. As individuals speak out of the silence into which the Meeting returns, the experience is palpably that of "dialogue" between speech and silence, in a way that is more than merely reflecting on what has been said. Moreover, there appears to be less a sharp dichotomy than a semi-permeable membrane between one individual and another, between an individual and the Meeting. In Zen Buddhist meditation, the silence is unbroken (except very rarely, and only by the abbot, briefly and cryptically), and the community sits side-by-side, looking only at the wall; yet, the experience of community, of interdependence and compassion, as Reality, is again palpable, not only with respect to the others in the room but (in Buddhist parlance) to all sentient beings.[211]

I am not asserting here that the consequence is logically entailed, that it must happen. Indeed, discernment cannot be willed: "God was in the silence. Yet, the moment you began working to create silence, you drove it away."[212] What I am reporting is an experience, what often has happened, to me and to others. In another well-known line attributed to George Fox: "This I know experimentally."[213]

Quaker Meeting is called Meeting for Worship, and most Quakers, no less than communicants of other traditions, think of themselves as at prayer; meditation has too secular, too pale, a ring. It may seem ironic (at best), but in seeking to write as I have of the positive role that religion has come to play in my life and thought, I resist describing what I am doing, whether at Meeting or at Jewish services, as either prayer or worship. The words still seem to me too powerfully embedded in a view of God as potentate, who dispenses the largesse we seek, provided that we are sufficiently flattering in our approach. Intellectually, I know that that is a gross caricature of the prayer and worship of many today (although not of all), but I still resist. God is always there, a "gentle draw,"[214] but always hidden as well, and the work to be done is to be done by us, in opening ourselves to awe and mystery ("worship") and seeking the insight to know God's will and the strength to act on what we know ("prayer"). When we fail, as to some extent we surely will, it is not that God did not "answer" our prayer; perhaps our prayer-work was defective in some way, but perhaps the answer—whether insight or strength—lay too far beyond our grasp.

At Meeting on a November Sunday, I heard an acquaintance speak about All Saints' Day, the Catholic holy day. As I listened, struggling with my resistance to the very idea of saints (God's courtiers), the thought came to me to think of saints as intercessors, not with God on our behalf, but with us on God's behalf, as those who help us to know and follow the will of God. The Dominican priest Thomas F. O'Meara writes: "The saints of Catholicism exist not to witness to miracles but to illlustrate divine life in men and women."[215] In this sense, it is true that we are a congregation of saints, which as I understand it is consistent with Catholic no less than Quaker thought. I still would not be comfortable saying that I "prayed" to St. Francis, to John Woolman, or to a living person who is a source of spiritual insight and inspiration, but there is a sense in which I am simply refusing to use traditional words in untraditional ways, which in other contexts I have found possible and illuminating.

I realize too that, although I have described silence as a communal experience, for the most part I have portrayed myself as searching to know and carry out God's will essentially on my own. The central religious experience of a *community* of faith has not readily spoken to me. Over the course of my lifetime, I have more often found "community" stultifying and coercive than inspiring and illuminating. Yet, I want to acknowledge all that I have gained over the past ten years from the members and attenders at Chestnut Hill Friends Meeting in Philadelphia. In Meetings for Worship, in workshops and presentations, even in committee work, I have learned experientially the truth of the Quaker precept that we are all ministers to one another. Some of this learning has come to me through words, some from being privileged to be able to hear others tell of their own struggles with the task of discerning and choosing a life open to the teachings of the Spirit, some simply from the wholly non-cognitive, non-verbal process of coming together week by week to sit in silence. So many are palpable presences to me, although in many cases I am wholly ignorant of even basic facts about them. I find in the Meeting a constant lodestar, which fuels and guides my halting efforts to know and follow Truth.

For many, religious symbols and rituals are a major route to discernment. The Trappist monk Thomas Merton, writing of the "Desert Fathers," fourth-century Christian monks who lived alone or in small communities in the Middle East, describes eloquently the monk's knowledge that "his Rule was only an exterior framework, a kind of scaffolding with which he was to help himself build the spiritual structure of his own life with God."[216] In the Jewish tradition, with its 613 commandments, their intended effect is described in these words by one scholar:

> [It] is not to drain away energies better spent on moral concerns, but rather to fabricate a system of life in which restraint, self-discipline, and the tendency to relate every facet of human existence, however apparently inconsequential, to the will of God became a matter of instinct. If the moral life has, as one of its vital preconditions, an integrated, disciplined and attentive self, then one important effect of Jewish law, both in its moral and [in its] religious dimensions, was to create this kind of ordered and sensitive personality.[217]

To that end, the Talmud articulates a "rule" that is not satisfied by recitation of prescribed prayers: "Prayer should not be said as if a man were reading a document. . . . If a man makes his prayer a fixed task, his prayer is no supplication." One should pray only when he can "direct his heart."[218]

I recognize the normative force of this perception of the relation between ritual and discernment. Nonetheless, my experience has undermined as much as it has reinforced its salience. Although realizing that ritual is intended as a spiritual discipline facilitating a deeper communion, I have so often found it displacing what it was meant to express.[219] Cognizant too of how for so many others ritual has operated as a barrier to, or a substitute for, opening oneself to God, I have responded positively to the Quaker tradition of viewing rituals and symbols warily. Even the Scriptures, revered as they were by the early Friends, are taken with the caution that it is only "the word," and not necessarily "the words," of God that is Truth. The Spirit is seen in and through Scripture, but it is the Spirit, and not the Scripture, for whose "voice" we listen.

Rabbi Heschel, recognizing the "tension between regularity and spontaneity," and the importance of remaining "loyal to both aspects of Jewish living," drily termed the problem "as easy to solve as other central problems of existence."[220] A contemporary study of Hasidism notes the fundamental basis of the difficulty:

The power of liturgy lies largely in its familiarity. The worshipper is enriched by the words' antiquity: We pray today as did our most ancient ancestors, as our descendants will down to the end of time. So it seems from within the traditional community of prayer. But in this very sameness and constant repetition lies the potential downfall of such prayer, which can degenerate into mere mechanistic recitation.[221]

Law teacher Frank Alexander writes of the tendency for "religious forms [to] decay into inanimate structures and symbols powerless to reach out and embrace." Yet, he goes on, "Nonetheless, within such structures lie a vibrant and powerful spirit of creation, grace, and redemption."[222] During the many years of my estrangement from Jewish practices, the aridity of what struck me as rote use of the liturgy was a major factor in turning aside periodic impulses toward reconsidering my estrangement. Having said this, however, and taking nothing away from it, but recalling Robert Bellah's admonition that "the great antinomies of human life are never resolved by grasping one polarity and forgetting the other,"[223] I want to acknowledge the ways that sacred texts and religious symbols and rituals can illuminate and inspire, not only deflect, the process of discernment, the act of listening for God.[224]

Daniel Maguire characterizes sacred writings as "moral classics, . . . marked by a seemingly inexhaustible fund of meaning and an enduring contemporaneity."[225] I believe that it is their non-cognitive quality that is central to their power. In differing ways, Scripture, liturgy, and the visual accoutrements of ritual, while they speak to our minds, reach deeper within us, first to touch our hearts, our emotions, and yet more deeply still, to a place that, though it lacks a good name and even a metaphoric location within us—"soul" and "gut" have polar failings—is a wellspring of understanding. An obvious example is music, which, I believe, is not a mere adornment to the text but a powerful heuristic, precisely because it "speaks" in non-propositional ways to a less accessible aspect of our being. If the religious experience is most of all opening oneself to awe, music does that work most powerfully. Abraham Joshua Heschel has expressed the idea with characteristic eloquence: "First we sing, then we understand."[226] In some traditions, it is the thundering notes of a massive organ, or the soaring tones of a large choir; in the *davennen* of the Jewish tradition, it is the low-key (often off-key) chanting, in repeated cadences and melodies, of the liturgy itself. When I read some Jewish prayers, wherever I am and whatever the setting, I "hear" what my eyes take in as I first heard them chanted more than fifty years ago.

The antiquity and the sanctity of Scripture and liturgy also contribute non-cognitively to their heuristic value. When we are so palpably in touch with our own parents and theirs, in a procession that reaches back far into the past, we are aided, I believe, in powerful ways in reaching "reflective equilibrium," in placing in a more appropriate perspective the distortions in perception and will to which mundane life gives rise. When, perhaps out of respect for the beliefs of our ancestors, or our friends or colleagues whose wisdom and moral stature we acknowledge, we feel ourselves obliged to struggle with the deeper meaning of "difficult texts," and not to permit ourselves simply to dismiss or revise them, we are more likely to find in them meaning that our minds can accept and that give us both light and strength. "For many people," my law school colleague Heidi Hurd suggests (albeit in her relentlessly rational voice), "moral insight is more easily achieved if they reason [sic] under the guise [!] of interpreting an authoritative text than if they reason with Sartrean self-awareness that everything is up for grabs at once."[227] I hope that more than one example of this heuristic process has come through in what I have written.

In a curious way, sacred texts that, taken literally, express that to which we cannot give our mind's assent serve a special value in this regard.[228] This is the lesson of the Zen koan, which seeks to force upon the serious student a non-cognitive source of understanding by the very fact of its cognitive self-contradiction. I would like to use an example from the Jewish liturgy to illustrate what I mean, and to tread a way through two polar responses to "difficult texts."

The ten days between *Rosh Hashanah* (the New Year) and *Yom Kippur* (the Day of Atonement) are called the Days of Awe. The imagery is that the Gates of Heaven open during that period, and our lives for the coming year are ordained. A central prayer of the extensive *Rosh Hashanah* liturgy is the *U'nsaneh Tokef*, said to have been composed as his dying words during a twelfth-century service by a rabbi who had chosen martyrdom over conversion.[229] It begins (in the standard Conservative translation of the generation in which I grew up): "We will observe the mighty holiness of this day, for it is one of awe and anxiety." (Even as I type these words, I feel once again, across the decades of my life, the change in the mood of the Congregation, and hear the cantor's chant; I feel and hear as well, more dimly but real, the moment repeated in countless congregations throughout the world and across the centuries.) The prayer goes on:

> On this day we conceive Thee established on Thy throne of mercy, sitting thereon in truth. We behold Thee, as Judge and Witness, recording our secret thoughts and acts and setting the seal thereon. Thou recordest everything, yea, thou rememberest the things forgotten. Thou unfoldest the records, and the deeds therein inscribed tell their own story for lo, the seal of every man's hand is set thereto.
>
> The great shofar is sounded, and a still small voice is heard. The angels in heaven are dismayed and are seized with fear and trembling, as they proclaim, "Behold the Day of Judgment!" For the hosts of heaven are to be arraigned in judgment for in Thine eyes even they are not free from guilt. All who enter the world dost Thou cause to pass before Thee, one by one, as a flock of sheep. As a shepherd mustereth his sheep and causeth them to pass beneath his staff, so dost Thou pass and record, count and visit, every living soul, appointing the measure of every creature's life and decreeing its destiny.

Then begins this unforgettable litany:

> On New Year's Day the decree is inscribed and on the Day of Atonement it is sealed,
>
> how many shall pass away and how many shall be born;
> who shall live and who shall die;
> who shall attain the measure of man's days and who shall not attain it;
> who shall perish by fire and who by water;
> who by sword, and who by beast;
> who by hunger and who by thirst;
> who by earthquake and who by plague;
> who by strangling and who by stoning;
> who shall have rest and who shall go wandering;
> who shall be tranquil and who shall be disturbed;
> who shall be at ease and who shall be afflicted;
> who shall become poor and who shall wax rich;
> who shall be brought low and who shall be exalted.

"BUT"—the next line of the prayer is traditionally capitalized—"REPENTANCE, PRAYER AND RIGHTEOUSNESS AVERT THE SEVERE DECREE."

> For according to Thy Name so is Thy praise. Thou art slow to anger and ready to forgive. Thou desirest not the death of the sinner but that he return from his evil way and live. Even until his dying day Thou waitest for him, perchance he will repent and Thou wilt straightway receive him.

May "our name," the prayer concludes, "be forever linked with Thine own."[230]

How shall a contemporary Jew approach this powerful prayer? In the synagogue of my childhood, we chanted it in Hebrew, and read it in English, and were left to ourselves to struggle with the fact that most of us just didn't believe what it appeared to say. Simple piety, respect for our grandparents (who presumably did believe it), enjoined us not to ask questions; we were not really being asked to "believe it," only to repeat it reverently. In some Orthodox congregations, it is presumably taken to express propositional, ontological truth. The renaissance of orthodox religion (not only in Judaism) during the last generation seems to have heightened the identification of religious faith with credal purity.

The Jewish Renewal movement, to its great credit, tends to emphasize the continuously evolving quality of Judaism, and places some priority on the rejection of supernaturalisms. It has given us a reconstruction of the central passage, "Who shall live, and who shall die," that adapts it to current sensibilities:

> When we really begin a new year it is decided,
> And when we actually repent it is determined:
>> Who shall be truly alive,
>>> And who shall merely exist;
>> Who shall be tormented by the fire of ambition,
>>> And whose hopes shall be quenched by the waters of failure;
>> Who shall be pierced by the sharp sword of envy,
>>> And who shall be torn by the wild beast of resentment;
>> Who shall hunger for companionship,
>>> And who shall thirst for approval;
>> Who shall be shattered by storms of change,
>>> And who shall be plagued by the pressures of conformity;
>> Who shall be strangled by insecurity,
>>> And who shall be beat into submission;

Who shall be content with their lot,
   And who shall go wandering in search of satisfaction;
Who shall be serene,
   And who shall be distraught.[231]

Certainly, there is wisdom in the "reconstructed" passage; it is a call plain to see, to (a modern version of) the self-searching and rededication that is central to the Days of Awe. For those who came to Jewish Renewal after exposure to the traditional liturgy, the changed text is heard against the echoing background of the remembered, and weaves its meaning in unspoken dialogue with it.

As a substitute for the traditional version, however, it comes with an enormous cost, for it is precisely the impossible anthropomorphism, the ontological improbability, of the prayer, that is part of its power. One need not believe in the photographic veracity of its portrayal of the Heavenly Tribunal to find its imagery truly stirring. Not only does it speak of "awe and anxiety," it engenders it.[232] Even the logical incompatibility of its segments—is it all decided ("sealed") by Yom Kippur, or is forgiveness always available?—adds to that power.[233] Substituting the far more sensible psychological and ethical insights of the revised version cuts us off, in a few years if not immediately, from the link with the ages that does such a critical part of the work of opening us to renewal.

To do that work, classic texts need not be taken as representational portrayals of ontologic "facts." While I am not at all knowledgeable regarding the tradition, I am aware of at least some traditional Jewish lore consistent with such a non-representational understanding. A wonderful example is a teaching of Rabbi Joseph Hertz, late Chief Rabbi of the British Empire. The prayer known as the Mourners' Kaddish is to be recited at the close of each service for eleven months following the death of a parent or child, and thereafter on the anniversary of the death. Performing this service is thought of as perhaps the highest obligation of piety, and Rabbi Hertz recounts what he terms a "folk legend" about Rabbi Akiba, a towering figure in Judaism, from the time of the Roman occupation. Akiba is said to have encountered a man groaning under a load of wood carried on his shoulders. In response to the rabbi's inquiry, the man replied that he was "one of those forlorn souls condemned for his sins to the agony of hell-fire. I must procure the wood, and myself prepare my place of torment." "And is there no hope for thee?" Rabbi Akiba asked. "Yes, if my little son, whom I left behind an infant, is taught to utter the Kaddish."

Rabbi Hertz concludes the story thus:

> Akiba resolved to search for the family and infant son of the deceased. He found that the mother had married again, this time to a heathen; and that the child had not even been initiated into the Covenant of Abraham. Rabbi Akiba took the child under his care, and taught him to lisp the Kaddish. Soon—the legend continues—a heavenly message assured him that, through the son's Prayer, the father had obtained salvation.

Rabbi Hertz's avowal of the "truth" of this account explicitly embraces a heuristic rather than a representational concept of truth. He begins by noting that "the soundest and saintliest thinkers in Israel have always maintained that all detailed descriptions of Hell or Heaven are but poetic symbols, intended to make abstract conceptions intelligible to mortal minds." "And yet," he goes on in words of incomparable beauty and wisdom:

> [T]his legend of Rabbi Akiba and the child saving his father from hell-torments, contains a wonderful truth. It teaches that parent and child are one. No man has altogether died, even to this world, if he knows that those he leaves behind him will read this Prayer after him, wherever they be scattered in this wide world; that they will reverence his memory as their dearest inheritance, and throughout their days, consider the recital of the Kaddish in his memory as a sacred act. "No one can be called dead whose children continue his work", say the Rabbis. And the Kaddish is the vow which the children pronounce that it is their holiest resolve to live in unity of soul with the parent who departed this life; that the God of the parents shall be their God; and, therefore, in the face of death they exclaim [in the opening words of the *Kaddish*] "Magnified and sanctified is the name of God."
>
> Thus is the Kaddish a bond strong enough to chain earth to heaven. It keeps the living together, and forms the bridge across the chasm of the grave to the mysterious Realm of those whose bodies sleep in the dust, but whose souls repose in the shadows of the Almighty. It teaches our soul to cling in trust and hope to One Whose decree obtains in the daily happenings of our individual lives as well as in the larger destinies of mankind, nay, of the universe. This prayer, in short, is the thread in Israel that binds the generations "each to each in natural piety", and makes the hearts of parents and children beat in eternal unison.[234]

It is the idea, in our time too common to orthodox and skeptics alike, that a literal, propositional understanding of the text is a "higher" form of faith that, to me, is at the core of the problem. As Rudolf Otto maintained with respect to the Christian mystery of the Resurrection, the spiritual dimension of the account is in a very real sense actually reduced by making it a simple supernatural event.[235] In reflecting on the Christian teaching, "Death is swallowed up in victory" (1 Corinthians 15:54), philosophers Kent Bendall and Frederick Ferre "leave to one side . . . the metaphysical issues of survival after death": "The existential function of decision about the permanent significance of human existence is not concerned with weighing the probabilities of post mortem experiences. It is rather a gesture of unterrified confidence in the irreducible meaningfulness of the existing human individual. Christian language of victory and life ably serves at least this use."[236]

Similarly, it is in no way a lesser concept of God to find in the traditional account of the Days of Awe given by the *U'nsaneh Tokef* a heuristic of truth, rather than an ontological proposition. When the ritual recitation works through us, aiding our "turning"—the magnificent word *t'shuvah* traditionally translated as "repentance," more deeply means turning back (toward God)—it is God that is at work, through the reenactment of the 800-years' recitation of it by the Jewish people, through the consciousness of the congregation with which we sit, and through that within us which hears, understands and responds.

LISTENING TO JESUS

> From my youth onwards I have found in Jesus my great brother. That Christianity has regarded and does regard him as God and Saviour has always appeared to me a fact of the highest importance which, for his sake and my own, I must endeavor to understand.
>
> —MARTIN BUBER[237]

It is surely obvious from what I have written that I do not regard my attachment to Judaism as a barrier to my listening for the voice of God in the teachings, beliefs, and practices of other religious traditions. Nor does it weaken that attachment to find, as I often have, discernment and spiritual sustenance there. Indeed, as I have recounted in Chapter 1 (p. 24, above), it was only my growing openness to other religious traditions that moved me toward a rapproachment with my own.

Nonetheless, as should also be obvious, Jesus, and Christianity, present unique difficulties in this regard. Recognizing the extreme sensitivity of the effort for both Jewish and Christian readers, I want to describe as honestly as I can the path by which I have come (if I may appropriate a classic evangelical phrase) to "let Jesus into my heart," and to attend to some of Christian faith and practice.

I must start with the bases of the difficulties. The primary one, of course, is history: the 1500-year record of savagery practiced against the Jewish people by European Christendom, by popes and bishops as well as kings, by pastors and theologians as well as nobility and peasantry, not merely grounded in the fabric of social and political life but also built into the theology, liturgy, and daily teaching of Christian thought and practice. Documenting this assessment here is not my task; illustrating it risks trivializing the matter.[238] The most positive statement one can make is that it took until this century for the long-standing murderous hostility of Christianity to provide a ground out of which arose an attempt to extinguish completely the remnant of Israel. For what was undertaken and almost accomplished by the Third Reich cannot be wholly sealed off from Christianity by a facile reference to the "pagan" or anti-Christian aspect of Nazi ideology. Nearly all Jews, and far too few Christians, remember that Hitler's anti-Semitism was a significant part of his attraction to large numbers of Europeans: to Germans first, but also to millions of Hungarians, Lithuanians, Poles, Russians and, yes, to Frenchmen as well.[239] This was the monstrous obscenity of Ronald Reagan at Bitburg, seeking to cabin responsibility by speaking of "one man's totalitarian dictatorship."[240]

Today, the Roman Catholic Church, and many Protestant denominations, have taken truly major steps to repudiate the crimes and slanders of the past. Much has occurred at the highest levels of the Church, triggered by the incumbency at a critical time of Angelo Roncalli as Pope John XXIII. During the Second World War, Archbishop Roncalli, papal nuncio to Turkey, earned the dismissive scorn of Archbishop Francis Spellman of New York for devoting great effort to the rescue of Jews from the Nazis,[241] and the Second Vatican Council, convened by Pope John soon after his election, saw a fundamental shift in Catholic thought and practice.[242]

What Vatican II set in motion has radiated throughout the Church.[243] For all the manifestations in other areas of his return to the Church's pre-conciliar consciousness, Pope John Paul II has maintained and reinforced his predecessor's decision to set a new course in Christian attitudes toward Jews and Judaism. Selective reference cannot do justice to his acts and statements throughout his papacy.[244] Having grown up in the days when Roman Catholics were forbidden even to be present at a public or private event at which a member of another *Christian* denomination engaged in any religious act, I find most powerfully symbolic of the change Pope John Paul's visit to the ancient Synagogue of Rome, where he concluded his remarks by reciting in Hebrew a scriptural passage that is a central aspect of Jewish liturgy.[245]

It does not denigrate the fundamental importance of these and other manifestations of change[246] to observe that they have differing degrees of penetration, in many places having limited impact "on the ground." One anecdotal example will suffice, to prove nothing, but to make the point sufficiently: I learned recently of a sweet, well-meaning sixteen-year-old, in an enlightened, benign suburb of Philadelphia, who objected to criticism of Hitler, because, as she was taught in her Catholic school, German Jews paid no taxes, and were free to leave Germany in any event! (The anecdote, I need not make clear, is not about the child but about her teacher, and perhaps the school for which he worked.)[247]

In light of this record, I have no quarrel with any Jew who is flatly unwilling or unable to look at the Christian religion, or the man in whose name it was founded, with anything other than fear and loathing. The great Protestant theologian of mid-century Reinhold Niebuhr got it right: "Practically nothing can purify the symbol of Christ as the image of God in the imagination of the Jew from the taint with which ages of Christian oppression in the name of Christ have tainted it."[248] I have lost most of that feeling, and will try to say how the change occurred, and what it has meant to me, but I am not making an argument for the way in which anyone else should respond to the problem. Rather, my argument is with any Christian who is unable to understand a totally aversive response, or who thinks himself or herself entitled to judge or seek too earnestly to change it.

The second barrier is that we have access to the words and actions of Jesus only through the Gospels, where a man who lived and died a deeply observant Jew is presented in a manner that foreshadows and makes sense of the evolution of a group of Jewish followers of a Jewish teacher, first into a group that can best be called Jewish Christians (or perhaps more accurately Christian Jews), and then into a Christian Church of Gentiles and formerly Jewish converts that became a rival with Judaism in the larger Roman world. Christian scholars and theologians are only now beginning to recognize, and acknowledge, the extent to which biblical Judaism, and specifically "the Pharisees," are caricatured in the Gospels, and more fundamentally the extent to which the Hebrew Scriptures, and Judaism itself, have been appropriated to the supersessionist triumphalism of traditional Christianity. This too has, to a significant degree, been repudiated in contemporary Christianity,[249] but it is difficult for a Jew reading the unaltered Gospels to ignore those distortions as he or she seeks to attend to what Jesus taught.

Finally, Christianity is unique, and uniquely challenging among modern religions, in regarding its central teacher as God incarnate, the Word made flesh, "God made visible." Neither Moses nor Elijah, of course, but also neither Gautama Buddha nor Muhammed, is in their faith traditions what Jesus is in Christianity,[250] and simple respect for another religion counsels me against casually appropriating what I find in Jesus's life and teaching, treating him as just another "great teacher," to be appreciated like those I have mentioned, or among a list—as I have heard some liberal Christians say—of such preeminent moral teachers as Socrates, Gandhi, and Martin Luther King. It is especially bizarre to hear King included, for he was a Christian, near as I know in both practice and belief, a minister of the Gospel of Jesus Christ, and I imagine he would have regarded such a list as either sacrilegious or idolatrous. Christianity has had more than one "Christ-like" figure—St. Francis is perhaps the most notable—and has always, as far as I am aware, quickly repudiated any impulse to divinize them, remaining faithful to its commitment to the uniqueness of Jesus. I recognize that one who professes to be a Christian while denying that Jesus is "the uniquely and exclusively true revelation of God"[251] can hold his or her own in contention with those Christians who regard such a stance as definitionally self-contradictory, but it is not for one who is not a member of a faith tradition to explicate it or define its boundaries. I am far more comfortable "working with"—finding the place in my life and thought of—the Holiness Code than the Incarnation.[252]

The fact that my receptivity to Jesus, and to Christian teaching, has to a significant degree broken through these powerful constraints is probably grounded not in my thinking but in my experience. I grew up always aware of anti-Semitism, yet never suffered any but relatively mild forms of it. The fiercely phobic reactions of some of my grandparents' contemporaries, first-generation Americans whose world-views were forged in the ghettos of the nineteenth-century Ukraine, repelled me. Beyond that, when my grandparents and some of their relatives left Russia near the turn of the century, they left the remainder of their families totally behind; my parents, born shortly thereafter, never knew the identity of any cousins on "the other side," and so we knew nothing of relatives in the generations lost to genocide. The closest I have come has been to read, in the Holocaust Museum, the name of my maternal grandparents' village, Belaya Tzerkov, engraved on a glass wall commemorating Jewish communities that were annihilated by the Germans (with the eager help of their Ukrainian sympathizers).

I have recounted in Chapter 1 how my rapprochement with religion began after Carolyn and I were married, and after the dramatic changes in the Catholic Church propelled by the Second Vatican Council. The process has been halting and tentative, and I was able to turn again to Judaism only after, and in an important sense as part of, my gradually expanding openness to Christianity. Carolyn's subsisting spirituality throughout her estrangement from Catholicism, and her eagerness to learn of Jewish spirituality, encouraged in me a reciprocal openness to Catholicism. My life with her family has made Christianity less an abstraction, and given me a window on it as a guiding presence in the concrete lives of specific people. It is a pleasure to be able to invite Carolyn's father to say grace at our table when they are present on a holiday. When he omits the traditional invocation of Father, Son, and Holy Spirit, I appreciate his sensitivity to the fact that in a sense his task is to speak on behalf of all present. But in truth I am as happy when he includes it, for it is he who is speaking, and I am able to be with him in his using the language of his faith to call upon God, without my having either to join in his words or to dissociate myself from them.

It has been my good fortune that, in each tentative (and vigilant) encounter with the Mass, and the parish priests who have celebrated it in the churches we have attended, I have found much to feed my mind and spirit, and nothing to offend my fully attuned Jewish antennae. As I have turned to current and recent writing of the Vatican, of Christian theologians, and of religiously oriented Christian colleagues among law teachers, I have come more and more to see the depth of the repudiation of Christian anti-Semitism and supersessionism, and the willingness to acknowledge responsibility for the crimes of the past. When I read former Notre Dame Law School Dean Tom Shaffer assert, "the God in whom we have faith is the God of the Hebrews," "the God of Abraham, Isaac, and Jacob"; when I hear Valparaiso Dean Ed Gaffney remind an audience composed largely of believing Christian law teachers and theologians that "all Christians worth their salt or pepper understand that they are Jews," but that "Christians may not expect all Jews to answer the Jesus question in a way that would make them Christians"; when I realize that these expressions are not simply some off-beat law teachers talking but are mirrored in the writing of contemporary Christian theologians, I am enabled to listen to the Christian message for its own sake.[253]

What I find in it is much like that which I seek, and find, in Jewish sources. Professor Shaffer again provides a telling example: He sees, and values, in Judaism what I would most want Jews no less than Christians to see in it. Hear his description of the 1986 pastoral letter of the United States Catholic Bishops on the economy and social justice as: "based on the Hebraic understanding that human dignity is a higher value than either prosperity or individual rights, that community is a higher value than individual autonomy, and that the moral minimum for the person in a just society is not economic freedom but adequate material and personal participation in common life."[254] In all too few congrega-

tions in America today could an applicant for an appointment as
rabbi run successfully on *that* platform—nor, I am quick to note,
for bishop in Shaffer's own Church today.

It is probably because of these openings that I have noticed in
recent years the fact, alongside the fact of massive complicity in
genocide on the part of European Christians, of case after case of
heroic defiance of the Nazi regime. The story of the French village of Le Chambon is well known;[255] less so is the fact, asserted
to be so by one Jewish writer, that in Poland, a legendary bastion
of virulent anti-Semitism (before and after the period of the occupation), twenty-five hundred Christians were executed for helping Jews. Far more presumably escaped notice.[256] One of the most
affecting exhibits in the Holocaust Museum is that of "the Rescuers." From Denmark's King Christian and Sweden's Raoul
Wallenberg, through thousands of ordinary people leading ordinary lives, the acts of heroic decency ring out. Two examples
echo in my mind: one, a Polish woman, an observant Catholic,
who not only hid a Jewish woman and her daughter in her home
for several years, smuggling food to them every day in a manner
that avoided detection, but so honored their faith that she set
aside a cooking pot for their exclusive use so that they would not
violate the dietary laws; the other, a Greek Orthodox bishop,
spiritual leader of his Mediterranean island, who responded to the
Nazi commander's request that he supply a list of resident Jews
by sending him a paper with one name on it, his own.[257]

I have acknowledged that my finding salience in the stories of
the Rescuers, notwithstanding the far more numerous examples
of eager or reluctant participation in Nazi genocide, probably has
its roots in experience rather than cognition. Nonetheless, without seeking to judge or persuade those fellow Jews who cannot
draw sustenance from the deeds of the Rescuers, I recall here the
rabbinic teaching that "whoever rescues a single soul from the
children of man, Scripture credits him as though he had saved a
whole world."[258] Yes, the passage immediately goes on to say that
"if anyone destroy a single soul from the children of man, Scripture charges him as though he had destroyed a whole world," and
there were far, far more destroyers than rescuers. The task of
being able to embrace both truths is not limited to situations
where they are of equal salience, and to embrace them both is not
to deny the magnitude of that inequality.[259]

In recent years, through the profound spiritual depth and the unparalleled teaching gifts of Rebecca Kratz Mays, my teacher at the Quaker study center at Pendle Hill near Philadelphia, the opening to Christianity that I have experienced has been extended to the Gospels as well. She has in a very real sense brought me to Jesus and his ministry, not as a proselyte, but in a manner that is squarely within the grain of the rabbinic tradition: I have found in her a guide to a text that can seldom be penetrated in untutored solitude. I do not mean anything academic here, but rather the loving evocation of the responses of her students and the courageous sharing of her own encounter with the person and the words of Jesus. To have had the opportunity to see Jesus through her eyes has been a true inspiration.[260]

I hope that the text of this book has given sufficient specific content to what I have seen in Jesus. "Teacher and brother," to Pastor Niemoller; "great brother," to Martin Buber; the "Inward Teacher," to George Fox—all those terms testify to the powerful truth in the Christian idea that Jesus is a guide to the moral life in a dual sense: not only as a source of discernment of moral truth but as a source of the strength of will to follow it as well. Here we approach the frontier, the boundary between the ministry of Jesus, the first-century teacher whose life and work are recorded in the Gospels for all to draw discernment and strength from, and the mystery of Christ, who in Christian belief twice transcended the boundary between time and eternity, both God-with-us in full divine humanity and the Risen Lord who, though as a mortal he experienced death itself, dwells forever among us and beyond. For it is clear that, notwithstanding the Christian emphasis on Christ at the right hand of God, Christ as "teacher" dwells among us, and within us, as well. When George Fox preached, "Christ was come to teach his people himselfe,"[261] he did not mean only back then in biblical times, but here with us now, whenever we call upon him. To his own question, "What is the good news, the gospel?" the Dominican Thomas O'Meara answers, it is "the ongoing incarnation of Christ and his spirit in ordinary life."[262]

In one sense, it is easier for me, as a Jew, than it is for many Christians to deal with the question whether I "believe" the account of the Incarnation and Resurrection. I do not believe it, in the same sense as I do not believe the accounts of the parting of the Red Sea or the revelation at Sinai as ontological propositions, but not being a Christian, I feel no need to struggle over that lack of belief. At the same time, I do need to recognize that the sense of "heuristic truth" I have espoused with respect to Jewish narratives has salience with respect to the question of "believing in Jesus" as well. Marcus Borg observes that the Greek, Latin, and German origins of the word suggest that believing refers not to "a set of doctrines" but "to give one's heart to," to love:

> The "heart" is the self at its deepest level. *Believing*, therefore, does not consist of giving one's mental assent to something, but involves a much deeper level of one's self. Believing in Jesus . . . means to give one's heart, one's self at its deepest level, to the post-Easter Jesus who is the living Lord, the side of God turned toward us, the face of God, the Lord who is also the Spirit. . . . [It] is the movement . . . from having heard about Jesus with the hearing of the ear to being in relationship with the Spirit of Christ. For ultimately, Jesus is not simply a figure of the past, but a figure of the present.[263]

With Rabbi Hershel Matt, I see a significant difference between not believing and having to deny. For, as Rabbi Matt goes on, with respect to the central "miracles" of Jesus's birth, life, death, and resurrection:

> [T]he point is not their mere occurrence but their significance, not their outer manner but their inner meaning, not their empirical verifiability but their religious authenticity. But . . . in this realm the whole notion of affirmation or denial by one person of the faith-knowledge of another is inappropriate. . . . The most that a Jew can do . . . is to acknowledge that in the lives of countless men and women who profess Christ the power and presence of God appear to be evident.[264]

It is is not only revisionist theologians who take a non-propositional approach to the historicity of the resurrection. Conservative Catholic theologian Luke Timothy Johnson, notwithstanding his heated attacks on those associated with the Jesus Seminar, explicitly sets to one side (as Rudolf Otto did)[265] both "traditions about the empty tomb" and talk of "visions of Jesus" among his disciples. The resurrection is "historical," Johnson asserts:

> as an experience and claim of human beings, then and today, that organizes their lives and generates their activities. That is, the resurrection has a historical dimension as part of the "resurrection community" that is the Church. . . .
> Christian faith as a living religious response is simply not directed

at those historical facts about Jesus. . . . Christian faith is directed to a living person. . . . [It] is confirmed, not by the establishment of facts about the past, but by the reality of Christ's power in the present.[266]

My effort, like Buber's (in the passage at the head of this section), is to "understand" the Christian message. There is much in that message that I am at present unable to understand, much that does not (in Fox's famous term) "speak to my condition." I can say nothing, for example, about Jesus as "Son of God," or of the idea that he was "sent" by God to die for our sins.[267] My understanding of the Christian message is as propounding *moral* truth. How would our understanding of God be affected by our thinking of divinity as made manifest in the person and life of Jesus? How would human life be transformed if we lived our lives seeing humanity and divinity as interpenetrated, or—to put it less abstractly—seeing God in all with whom we deal, and in ourselves?

A wonderful passage from Albert Nolan's study of "Jesus Before Christianity" speaks eloquently to the first of these questions:

> We have seen what Jesus was like. If we now wish to treat him as our God, we would have to conclude that our God does not want to be served by us, but wants to serve us; God does not want to be given the highest possible rank and status in our society, but wants to take the lowest place and to be without any rank and status; God does not want to be feared and obeyed, but wants to be recognized in the sufferings of the poor and the weak; God is not supremely indifferent and detached, but is irrevocably committed to the liberation of humankind, for God has chosen to be identified with all people in a spirit of solidarity and compassion.[268]

The U.S. Catholic Bishops, writing of ordinary economic life, have recognized the significance of seeing God in each of us: "When we deal with each other, we should do so with the sense of awe that arises in the presence of something holy and sacred. For that is what human beings are; we are created in the image of God."[269] That, of course, is good Jewish teaching, and profoundly transformative if taken to heart. Rodger Kamenetz recounts a beautiful Hasidic account, that "before every human being comes a retinue of angels, announcing, 'Make way for an image of the Holy One, Blessed be He.' How rarely do we listen for those angels when we encounter another human being. How rarely do we see in another human being's eyes an image of everything we hold most dear."[270] For the most part we have been far readier to see the Devil than the Lord in one another.

It is also good Jewish teaching that God is infinitely forgiving, "full of compassion, slow to anger, showing mercy to thousands," but somehow it is easier to discern divine judgment than love.[271] Rabbi Nancy Fuchs-Kreimer has observed that the traditional image of God as father, or parent, need not be taken as conjuring up the image of a stern, punishing judge addressing a hapless miscreant, but that of "the unconditional, unqualified, nonnegotiable love of a parent for a child." This image "gives us the courage to face [divine] judgement . . . in the very midst of our lives. [For] in the end, . . . there is finally and simply and conclusively: love."[272]

There is a sense in which the Incarnation presents God as ratcheting the point up a long step further. Hear Thomas Merton: "[H]uman nature, identical in all men, was assumed by the Logos in the Incarnation. . . . Consequently, we have the obligation to treat every other man as Christ himself. . . ."[273]

Every other person, but oneself as well. Of the many names that Christ has borne in Christian practice, the word "Reconciler" expresses the thought best for me.[274] "Now, will you believe me?" God insists: "You are worthy, and dear to me." Yes, we are "fallen": fallible, limited in understanding and weak of will, prone to do evil; but we are not hopelessly depraved, meriting pure condemnation. The hardships, oppression, and failures of everyday life should not dominate our consciousness of what humanity is all about, for God has shared it all with us, coming among us, not as a nobleman or warrior, but as the infant child of (again, the bishops) "a displaced person and a refugee, the daughter of an oppressed people";[275] in infancy marked for death by a ruler fearful for his dynasty; enjoining his fellow humans to "love one another just as I have loved you" (John 13:34); and sharing fully in the injustice and pain of the world, even to the point of accepting for himself the painful and shameful death that is the lot of so many others. "He was in the form of God; yet . . . bearing the human likeness, sharing the human lot, he humbled himself, and was obedient, even to the point of death, death on a cross" (Philippians 2:6–8).[276] Whatever injustice and oppression human failings subject humankind to, God has shared, has taken to himself. We are thereafter forever tinged with divinity, however we fall short, and we may not allow ourselves to deny, not only among us, but within us, the presence of God.[277]

The Christian story is also a powerful expression of a most profound teaching about the meaning and value of success and failure, strength and weakness, happiness and suffering. St. Paul describes his resolve to "know nothing . . . except Jesus Christ and him crucified" (1 Corinthians 2:2). What did Paul mean by this? "God chose what is foolish in the world to shame the wise; God chose what is weak in the world to shame the strong; God chose what is low and despised in the world, things that are not, to reduce to nothing things that are . . ." (1 Corinthians 1:27–28). The prolonged (yet never complete) betrayal of this message by the post-Constantinian Church should not block its salience and centrality from our awareness, for its power to transform our daily lives and redirect our striving is truly awesome.

"Our hope had been that he would be the one to set Israel free." This simple declaration (Luke 24:21) by two disconsolate Jews walking on the road to Emmaus succinctly and poignantly captures the devastation felt when the power of empire and hierarchy so easily destroyed the hopes of liberation. But . . . "They recognized him at the breaking of bread": All it takes to bring Jesus back among us, and work the transformation of our lives, is to invite the stranger to our table and break bread. Christ appeared in the moment of the breaking of bread; as promptly, he vanished from sight, yet, and to me this is the core of the Christian message, the transformation of the travelers, once effected, endured. He remained with them, as he remains with us today. "To believe in the resurrection," in Carlos Mesters's account, is, "first and foremost, an attitude to life arising out of the discovery of a friend, alive in our lives, thanks to the power of God."[278]

Dorothy Day, a founder and for a generation the guiding spirit of the Catholic Worker movement, operated a drop-in center in New York's Lower East Side. Asked once how she was able for so many years to treat with genuine welcoming love each new derelict appearing at her door, she is said to have responded that, as each new person approached her, her effort was to remind herself that he may be Christ returned to earth.

And so he was.

5

Odyssey (Reprise): Professing Law

In the chapter after this my goal will be to express a view of law congruent with the way that this book has looked at religion, conscious of it as an expression *not of a command but of a truth*. In seeking to give voice to an understanding of God as living within as well as outside human beings, a God not thought of as the super-potentate whose law is our command and whose command is our law, I have found much greater validation within the religious tradition than I had been aware of. I still believe that the prevalent consciousness is the familiar command-and-obey, but I have come to realize how over-weighted that reading of the tradition has been, by both those who support and those who reject it. Aspects of Scripture and teachings that express a very different consciousness abound, in both Judaism and Christianity, and it is no less legitimate for me to find guidance in them than it is for others to cleave to aspects of the tradition that are congruent with their outlook. Conservative religionists fond of smugly asserting that others find in Scripture reflections of beliefs they bring to it have no special exemption from the hazard of falling prey to that temptation.[279]

Consistent with the considerations about which I wrote at the end of the introductory chapter,[280] I want to begin, however, with the way that my outlook on law has been affected by the course of my life as a lawyer and law teacher, and by the many changes, large and small, that the world has undergone since I first entered law school in September 1955. Until I entered law school, I had never met a lawyer. I was aware that I had entered a "professional school," rather than returned to the "graduate school" study of American History that I was pursuing when I was called to join the Army. In deciding, while I was in the service, not to go back to graduate school, I certainly did not have it in mind to teach law rather than history, but the practice of law was a great unknown to me, and the attraction of studying and learning law was a sufficient basis for becoming a law student, without regard to the use to which I might come to put what I learned.

This curious lack of attention to what now seems such an obvious question probably reflected my father's influence. Denied an opportunity by economic necessity to complete high school, he was a self-taught man. He read most of the books I brought home as a student, and he made clear his belief that learning was of inherent value. His lack of educational credentials kept him from a professional career, but he carried on his business as a small manufacturer with honesty and dignity. He spurned the ready availability of illegal profits during the War. He expected a fair day's work from those he employed, as from himself, but told me, more than once, that he would "never ask a man to do anything that I wouldn't do."

His one occupational regret was that he was not able to do work that he regarded as socially beneficial; had he had the chance, he would have gone into science or medicine, fields which, during the '30s and '40s, seemed fruitful outlets for such an aspiration. Whatever nascent medical or scientific inclinations I might have had were aborted in tenth grade by my first encounter with the dissection of a frog, and in any event paled in comparison to my emerging interest in history and government.

My father never pressed his own occupational priorities on me. What mattered more to him than my choice of work was the question whether I carried it on responsibly. Notwithstanding that money was never plentiful in our household, he told me, in one of the few explicit admonitions that I recall, not to put much emphasis on making a lot of money. Although privation and insecurity had played a major role in his own life, he did not transmit to me a fear of getting a toehold on an economically viable job track. I think that my motivation to study law was just that, to "study law." What use it would be, occupationally, could abide the event.

The boundaryless quality of graduate-level study of history was captured by a line used (a bit ungrammatically) as the frontispiece of a leading text, "As an Historian, every Thing is in my province,"[281] while the mindless vacuity of my military career was summarized by my anti-aircraft gun section leader's admonition,

"When you ain't got nothing to do, wipe on the gun." These experiences, coming to me in rapid succession, powered my immediate and unqualified resonance with the Columbia Law School of the 1950s. Law, I discovered, was focused on the concrete; it was problem-oriented, solution-oriented, and decision-oriented; it emphasized, and rewarded, precision in thought and expression, and a keen sense of relevance; it dealt with real-world problems, but at a level one step removed from the messiness of the real world; it was intellectually challenging, but not really hard; being able to understand law was obviously important work in the world, but one didn't need to be anyone important to master it.

Achieving justice through law appeared then to be largely a matter of thinking a problem through in a rigorous and disciplined way, fueled to be sure by being a person of good will but not heavily dependent on having a particular political stance or fighting ideological battles. Society was thought to be characterized by a fair degree of consensus, and the law (properly reformed by the application of high-level thought) reflected that consensus.

The "common law" (judge-made law) was viewed as a reasonably coherent set of decisions, whose results were often wiser than their reasoning, and a central task of legal thinking was to penetrate the conclusory and sometimes obfuscating judicial rhetoric by focusing instead on the facts and the outcomes to induce the legal rule that was in actuality being developed and applied. Legislation was to be viewed hospitably by the courts, as the voice of the sovereign people, correcting judicial errors and supplying responses beyond the capacity of courts; it was thought both desirable and possible for judges to approach the task of interpreting statutes free of their own policy preferences, and to discern and apply the "gamut of values" embodied in the legislative enactment, however they might differ from the values of individual legislators or factions.[282] The Supreme Court was effectively bringing the States into the twentieth century, and the Nation out of the McCarthyite excesses of the early '50s. Legislatures and courts listened to the voices of reason and empirical truth, provided they were the product of high-level professional skill. There was much good work to be done, but doing it was for the most part a technical process, and work well done would inevitably lead to improvements in the state of the law and the life of the community.

While many faculty members were probably not delighted that so many talented graduates went on to work in large commercial firms, the implicit message was that high-quality work done there was inherently worthwhile, serving the public interest, and in any event providing valuable training for participating in the creation of public policy in later life, through periods of government service and ongoing law-reform work within the organized bar. Columbia students were being taught—the message was at times explicit—not the nuts-and-bolts stuff of bar examinations, the focus of lesser places, but what they would need to know twenty years on, when they began to assume their rightful places of influence in professional and public life.[283]

Curious but undeniable, this celebratory set of assumptions coexisted with a casual acceptance of practices that today would seem serious indictments of the legal system. The exclusion, total or partial, of Jews from large-firm practice was taken for granted. With a single exception—one large New York firm hired both Jews and Christians in significant number—law firms were either Christian or Jewish, and the former either hired no Jews or had recently become willing to take on a carefully limited number. There were few black law students in those days, and we all knew how, a decade earlier, William T. Coleman (a generation later a member of President Ford's Cabinet), after a brilliant law school career and a year as clerk to Supreme Court Justice Felix Frankfurter, had had to go to Philadelphia to find law-firm employment. A classmate of mine, the only woman on the Law Review, sent out sixty résumés but did not receive a single interview.

Although I received job offers only from Jewish firms (despite having very high grades and being Editor-in-Chief of the Law Review), it seemed more salient to me at the time that I did get a job, well-paying by the standards of the time, and that the lawyers whose firm I joined did high-quality work, and were able and willing to teach me much. We—I did think of it as "we," not "they"—had a large labor-relations practice, a major attraction, and although it was mostly (but not entirely) on the management side, which did not correspond to my predilections, the clients on whose cases I worked were unionized firms, and the disputes were all carried on within a framework that took the

continued existence and health of a collective-bargaining relationship for granted. The opportunity to see highly fact-specific
questions from management's perspective reinforced my tendency to see disputes as arising out of a context of fundamental
consensus, and to regard the conscientious espousal of either side's
position as socially beneficial.

A few months after I began to practice law, a former teacher at
Columbia told me that the School was interested in recommend-
ing me as a law clerk to Justice John Marshall Harlan of the Supreme Court for the coming year. The following August, I began
to work at a place that truly looked and felt like a Temple of
Justice, for a man who was without question the most highly
respected Justice then sitting. Four years earlier, I had been a Private First Class, U.S. Army, and had never met a lawyer.

The day I was to start work was the day that my father died, at
the age of 55, after a two-year struggle with cancer of the esopha-
gus. (It was only later that I began to think of his death as courtesy
of the R. J. Reynolds Company.) "Do a good job in Washington," were his words to me the day before he died.

Working for a year at close hand with Justice Harlan, and as a
participant-observer in the work of the Court, was hardly a setting calculated to foster a sense of alienation from law and the
legal system. The Supreme Court, then in the early "Warren
Court" years, was deeply divided on many issues, but in the public perception had taken a series of steps upholding claims of individual protection of civil liberties and equal rights that had raised
a firestorm of criticism from the Right. This was fueled, during
those years following *Brown v. Board of Education*,[284] by its determination (as it then appeared to friends and critics alike) to delegi-
timate thoroughly the legal regime supporting white supremacy
that had characterized the southern states for two-thirds of a century.

Except on questions of racial equality, Justice Harlan was usually on the conservative side of constitutional-law issues, but to
say that is to give only a distorting portion of the story. Grandson
of another Supreme Court Justice John Marshall Harlan, Rhodes
Scholar, name partner in a highly respected Wall Street firm,
counsel to the DuPont family, in his practice as a judge he bore
eloquent witness to the impoverishment, in the years since his
death in 1971, of words like "judicial conservative" and "judicial

restraint." He had a strong sense of fair-mindedness, and a healthy skepticism about ideology that extended to that which he embraced as well as that which he found unattractive. Committed to a jurisprudence that was grounded on a fair amount of trust in those exercising power, he would readily, albeit sadly, repudiate governmental actions that seemed to him disreputable, and he was a leader on the Court in finding ways to uphold claims of individual liberties on non-constitutional grounds, forcing Congress, before it trenched on constitutional values, to say explicitly that it found such action necessary.[285]

To Harlan, the idea that judicial supremacy should be rarely invoked was not a rhetorical device for letting legislatures do what he approved of in any event. He took no pleasure in upholding, as he often would, acts of injustice, and if the means were available to set them aside without overstepping the judicial role as he conceived it, he would use them. One example from "my" year will make the point.

Much of the Supreme Court's jurisdiction is discretionary; that is, in a wide category of cases it may choose whether to consider the merits of a decision of a state or federal court, or to decline to hear it, in which event the decision appealed from stands, without either the endorsement or the disapproval of the Supreme Court. The Court received a state's petition for a writ of *certiorari*—an application for discretionary review—to the Court of Appeals for the Fifth Circuit, which heard appeals from federal courts in the southern states. The petition challenged a decision of that court, ordering the retrial or release of a convicted defendant sentenced to death. The defendant was black, and his claim was that blacks were systematically excluded from jury service, which the Supreme Court had long since held was constitutionally impermissible and would vitiate the conviction. The problem was that the state, like most jurisdictions, required such a claim to be raised initially at the trial itself, and the defendant's attorney had not done that. When a new lawyer representing the defendant in the federal-court *habeas corpus* proceeding raised the objection, the state argued that it had been waived. The Fifth Circuit held that, because it was well known that attorneys in southern communities, especially white attorneys, would not raise this claim for fear of reprisal against them and their clients, the defendant was not bound by his attorney's action, and could litigate the issue of racial exclusion in federal court.[286]

Justice Harlan could not accept that reasoning. To him, the law was that, barring seriously inadequate representation, a client was bound by his or her attorney's tactical decisions, and he would not have voted to recognize an exception for all-white juries in southern courts. Nonetheless, he readily joined the Court in denying the petition for *certiorari*. That act would leave intact the Fifth Circuit decision setting aside the conviction, but would not constitute a Supreme Court precedent approving the Court of Appeals' reasoning. He recognized the fact that racially motivated exclusion was endemic, and that informal sanctions made challenges to it most difficult. While he was "conservative" enough to believe that the legal rule should not be changed to take account of that reality, he was quite content to have the southern judges of the Court of Appeals make the change.

This judgment was fueled by his antipathy to the death penalty. Again, the idea that the death penalty was unconstitutional would never have occurred to him in 1960 (and when it did, he readily avowed its permissibility), but he viewed it with abhorrence, and certainly believed that justice was done on all counts by allowing the conviction and capital sentence to be set aside.[287]

The year of my clerkship drew on, and reinforced, the interest in Labor Law that I had brought with me to law school, and had strengthened there and in law practice. The Court, with an unusually active Labor Law docket, reversed a number of National Labor Relations Board decisions of the so-called "Eisenhower Board," decisions many of which, embodying long-sought conservative objectives, had overruled precedents of the Board established during Democratic administrations.[288] In joining most of those decisions, Justice Harlan—Republican, patrician, Wall Street lawyer that he was—illustrated the difference between his brand of conservatism and the political activism of many of his self-proclaimed conservative successors.[289]

Working then with a man who bore witness to the wisdom of the view that personal qualities were more important than political orientation, I was working at an institution that was perceived by the public as principally driven by an egalitarian agenda. This assessment was in those years largely shared by those who applauded and those who condemned such priorities. One rainy morning, the Justice's secretary came in smiling, and recounted that, when she asked the driver of the taxi she had taken that day to drive into the Court's garage, so that she would not have to climb the outside staircase in the rain, he replied, "I didn't know that they let white people into this building." In differing but mutually reinforcing ways, the experience of working at the Court and of being a Harlan clerk reinforced my tendency in those years to think of the legal system as responsive and hospitable to the claims of justice as I understood them.

Midway through the year, I accepted an invitation to teach Labor Law at the University of Pennsylvania. My decision was of a piece with what had gone before. First of all, I had not applied for teaching jobs, Pennsylvania had sought me out, and who could find wanting a system that so readily affirmed and rewarded my merit? I soon learned that the University, like the Philadelphia legal community long a bastion of religious exclusivity, was beginning to become hospitable to Jews, and the Law School, which had gingerly hired its first Jewish teacher shortly after the War ended, and one or two more in the next dozen years, was by 1959 willing to hire two in one year!

A large part of the appeal of a teaching career was my belief that, by applying critical intelligence to difficult and controversial legal issues, the law could be improved, that there was a genuine dialogue between those who exercised law-making power and those whose job it was to criticize the work product of those in power.

When asked, why Labor Law, I would probably have emphasized the excitement and controversy generated by rapidly changing judicial, administrative, and legislative involvement in the field, its combination of challenge to the intellect and engagement of strong emotions. I would not have made much of my belief, which I had as surely as I was only dimly aware of it, in the centrality of work in human life, and of the potential of the union movement to bring democratic principles and a sense of citizenship to people's work lives. It was plainly possible, it seemed to me at the time, simply to follow fairly neutral principles of good lawyering and judging to make the law increasingly consonant with my underlying values.

The early years of my teaching career validated my beliefs about law and the legal system. Within five years, having done only what I enjoyed doing, I was a full professor, with academic tenure. My writing in Labor Law was received with respect and attention by judges, administrators, and practitioners, as well as by academic colleagues at Pennsylvania and elsewhere. The "Warren Court" had shed its ambivalences and was making a relatively far-reaching attempt to place equality concerns at the center of its jurisprudence, while the judicial and administrative appointments of the Kennedy and Johnson administrations gave important penetration to those attempts from on high. My attitude toward the law and its courts was typified by the pious disapproval I registered when the folk singer Pete Seeger appeared in court for his sentencing for contempt of Congress—a prosecution and conviction for refusal to answer questions, which to me were a misguided holdover from the McCarthy era—with his guitar over his shoulder. Perhaps his conviction for contempt of Congress was wrong, I sputtered in offended outrage, but he should certainly be held in contempt of court for deliberately trying (as he was) to deny the magisterial authority of the court.

For me, the 1960s began on May 1, 1964, when Robert Kennedy, in the annual Law Day address of the Attorney General, linked the oppression of the racial caste system of the southern states with the oppression of poor people throughout the country, and proposed to ground an egalitarian response not merely in reform of the laws but in making legal representation available to people unable to buy it in the market.[290] It was from this insight that the inclusion of the Legal Services Program in the "War on Poverty" arose, launched by the enactment of the Economic Opportunity Act of 1964. Soon thereafter, I began an involvement with the cause of the representation of poor people that, with greater or lesser intensity, has for three decades remained an important part of my work.

Initially, the effort was simply carrying significantly further the prophetic underpinnings of the civil rights movement. We were seeking only to make good on the premises of the American Dream: The portal of the Supreme Court building has since its unveiling had inscribed on it the words "Equal Justice Under Law." In the political-legal climate of the mid-'60s, it seemed quite possible to combine a celebratory stance toward law and the legal system with a willingness to acknowledge the existence of long-overlooked pockets of injustice, for the act of acknowledgment came at times from the Supreme Court, the President, and Congress, as well as from academic literature, television specials, and best-selling books, and many such acts prompted quick and positive governmental and societal responses.

In 1965, I began to design and teach a course that I called Legal Control of Economic Insecurity, focusing on those unable to find, or even seek, work by which they could become economically viable and politically enfranchised. I began too to work closely with lawyers who staffed the newly opened legal services offices, and in 1967 became the first director of the Reginald Heber Smith Community Lawyer Fellowship Program, named for a leader of the organized Bar of the early twentieth century who had done much to make visible the problem of the inadequacy of legal representation of poor people. The "Reggie" Program recruited and selected outstanding young lawyers nationally to bring to legal services offices across the country the training and consciousness necessary to make their work part of an aggressive and, hopefully, far-reaching means of empowering poor people.

At the Law School, I was drawn to a new breed of student, who challenged me to question the apologies for hierarchy embedded in the law school curricula, and in what we regarded as unproblematic aspects of social life. In 1969, driving with several graduating students to a "Reggie" training program, I happened to point out the suburban home (a rather modest one, to my eyes) of one of our faculty colleagues. When I casually mentioned that it was _____'s house, one student was shocked: "How can you expect someone who lives in such luxury," he expostulated, "to be really able to understand the lives of poor people, and to judge the fairness of legal rules and institutions?" It was easy, all too easy, I was coming to understand, to dismiss a statement like that on account of its blend of naïveté and extremism, but I began to deem it more important to attend to its core of truth than to evaluate it for its failings.

Finding wisdom and justice in many such challenges, I gradually moved further and further from the presuppositions that seemed so unproblematic a few years earlier and that too many of my colleagues continued to accept. As I came to be drawn into seeing as pervasive and penetrating the injustices that characterized our legal and political system, the University and the polity came more and more to reach the limit of their willingness to respond hospitably rather than defensively or repressively. In the four years of Lyndon Johnson's elected presidency, my ability to combine a strong redistributive agenda with a basically celebratory attitude toward American law was overcome. The assassination of Bobby Kennedy on the heels of his victory in the California primary was for me a turning point. Convinced that, alone among public figures, he was a bridge between those segments of the New Deal coalition that had moved Right since the '50s and those that had moved Left, I was convinced also that he would have won the Democratic nomination and the election, and would have set the nation on a fundamentally different course from that which it has for the most part taken since his death.

I recognize, too, that, although my wife's and my separation in 1971 was due to personal factors present to some degree through many of the seventeen years of our marriage, the fact of the separation and divorce removed a brake on the changes in my outlook on the world. It seemed as if many of my friends and I had split up as well, and much that had seemed unproblematically true now appeared as grievously flawed. Lawyers and judges, even colleagues, whom I had admired now seemed obtuse at best, and often just plain evil.

In this best and worst of times, the "audience" of my work as a lawyer and teacher shifted dramatically. No longer did I think of my work as speaking sense to those in power, hoping to improve the state of the law by writing about legal problems in ways that judges, administrators, and litigants might find useful. Rather, I sought to support students and lawyers who were led to practice law on behalf of poor people, to help them resist the tendency to think themselves in the wrong profession by reason of their political values, and to help them bring to their legal work sophistication in qualities of mind and training, and dedication to making a difference in their clients' lives.

To the extent I continued to speak to power, it was directly, through participation in litigation as an avowed advocate, rather than through the indirection of "neutral" academic writing. When I was asked to succeed a departing colleague as supervisor of the Law School's first venture into clinical education—whereby students learn the work of a lawyer by actually representing people, in an academic setting—I agreed, expanding the program to cover civil as well as criminal matters. I wrote the

initial draft of the brief that led to the Supreme Court's first constitutional decision in the welfare area.[291] I prepared a report designed to persuade the National Convention of the American
Civil Liberties Union to recognize that, if it was effectively to
espouse protection of the civil liberties of the poor, it was necessary to go beyond traditional civil-liberties issues such as "midnight searches." The civil liberties of the poor will be respected, I
urged, only if they have available an adequate and comprehensive
program of income maintenance and minimum guarantees of access to housing, education, and health care.[292] When the Supreme
Court's widely noted decision in the *Bakke* case generated many
overly expansive interpretations of its impact on affirmative action
programs, I prepared a legal analysis, for the Society of American
Law Teachers, designed to aid teachers in resisting such efforts at
their schools.[293]

For the most part, efforts such as these led mostly to narrow
victories or real defeats—in some cases, to no response at all. I
saw anger not only as a healthy motivating ingredient of a useful
life as a lawyer, but as the only sensible response to the world
around us. Although I felt a bit embarrassed to hear a colleague
refer on one occasion to what I had just said at a faculty meeting
as a Jeremiad, the important question, I insisted (to myself), was
whether what I had said was true or false. My actions were a lot
less radical than my outlook—I continued to teach students, and
to a lesser extent to work on legal issues in conventional lawyer-
like ways—but I consistently found myself preferring to be challenged from the Left, which was a source of growth in my understanding and empathy, rather than by colleagues and friends in
more mainstream frames of mind, who often struck me as suffo-
catingly smug about the ability and willingness of an unjust legal
order to right itself.

The wheel turned again, as I suppose it had to, but gradually,
in response to a variety of influences on me. One factor surely
was the change in my personal life. The years following the ter-
mination of my marriage were ones that, at the time, I regarded
as happy, but which (in retrospect) plainly had an excessively tur-
bulent quality that both fed and was supported by my attitude
toward law and my work. Coming gradually, with Carolyn, to
feeling drawn to make the commitment that marriage and children meant—a state that I expected never to find myself in

again—inevitably leavened the alienated quality of my world-view, and brought more into balance the intensity of my disaffection with law, legal education, and the legal system.

I was affected, too, by the dramatic change in the legal/political climate that was triggered by the unraveling of the Watergate conspiracy. Chief Justice Burger was heard to say, as he swore in Gerald Ford as President, "The system worked," and I had to agree.[294] The nation had peacefully removed Richard Nixon from power through law, with Judge Sirica, Attorney General Richardson, Special Prosecutor Cox, the Senate Judiciary Committee, and the Supreme Court all playing critical roles.[295] In doing so, we had as a polity disgorged the man who was perhaps the most venomous representative of an entire era.[296] Those dramatic events led, shortly thereafter, to the election of Jimmy Carter, whose administration generated the hope (short-lived though it proved to be) that the conservative ascendancy of the preceding decade was a momentary detour in the national mood.

The most significant input, however, to the gradual easing of my attitude was the work, to which I briefly referred earlier, with a group of law teachers interested in making our work more expressive of our values and aspirations. The explicit focus on values, the bringing out of seldom expressed aspirations, for ourselves and for the world, that animated our choice to study law and become teachers of law, tended to "soften" what could be a rather shallow, adversarial, programmatic political stance. The emphasis on becoming aware of our own subjective experience, and on the importance and difficulty of acknowledging the need to search for meaning in our work, shifted the focus from trying to change "the law" to paying attention to the possibilities for change in local interactions with students and colleagues. The emphasis on the limiting quality of polarized ways of thinking taught me that I could avoid becoming complacent and justificatory of pervasive injustice in the legal system without allowing continuing anger at injustice to dominate my outlook. Jack Himmelstein, who developed and led the program to which I was first attracted in 1978, became a close friend and mentor, and was a colleague in several aspects of my work during the '80s. There has been little in my work and outlook over the past two decades that does not bear the mark of what I have learned from our association.

I turned my attention more to the uncovering and articulation of unacknowledged barriers to choice in teaching, studying, and practicing law, and to the dynamics of the teacher-student inter-action. It was important, but not sufficient, to retain a political consciousness that challenged the justification for hierarchy, and identified with the less powerful; it was necessary as well that the manner in which I carried on my work validated, rather than contradicted, that consciousness. I began to see teaching more as a process of *evoking* than *imparting* knowledge or skills, an ap-proach that, curiously enough, is embedded in one aspect of the etymology of the word "educate": it is derived from the Latin word *educere*, "to draw out something latent." It revolutionizes the idea of teaching to think of it as bringing out something that is in a student, rather than putting something in that the student lacks. When Socrates demonstrated in the *Meno* that the slave-boy "knew" that "the square on the diagonal of a square is double its area," to me he was demonstrating, not the latency of some forgotten prenatal knowledge, or his own ability to ask leading questions, but the latent ability to transform oneself that is consti-tutive of being human.[297]

There is somewhere a magnificent line of Albert Schweitzer's which (as best I can remember it) says that there is a physician in each of us, and the practice of medicine is the art of bringing out the physician in the sick person. From this perspective, legal education should primarily be about the exploration with students of what it would mean to assume individual responsibility for our work as lawyers, why we might want to do that, and what the barriers are to our doing it. So, having taught the subject of pro-fessional responsibility—"legal ethics"—for some time, I shifted the focus of the course away from the rapidly evolving "law of lawyering," as the subject was coming to be called, to emphasize (as I call my course) individual choice and responsibility in law practice.[298] My aim is to ask students to ask themselves what their practice will mean in their lives, rather than what others (includ-ing myself) have said it should mean, and to seek to identify and grapple explicitly with the barriers to individual choice, rather than to assume automatically that those barriers are dispositive.

Having taught several courses in aspects of "Poverty Law" for many years, I developed instead a course that I call Legal Re-sponses to Inequality, in which I attempt to use legal doctrine and theory to trigger students' realization of the subjectivity of the underlying premises that channel their own legal responses and those of judges, legislators, and academic writers. My purpose is to encourage students neither to discard their underlying values as "unprovable" nor to cling to them as constitutive of their identity, but to hold to them in genuine dialogue with others.[299]

The 1980s were for me a sobering time. First, and perhaps most fundamental, I crossed the divide of reaching, and hurtling past, my fiftieth year. I could no longer imagine myself in the first half of my life. As far as public life was concerned, the ease with which the "Reagan Revolution" was able to effect a major redistribution of wealth, and with which its evident failures simply fueled the nation's desire for more of the same, was a telling contrast with the ready eagerness of the polity to declare the rather mild redistributive measures of the '60s a failure. In the late '90s, we see ideas that were discredited a generation ago unveiled as new solutions, and, despite their indifference to every input but the punitive, criticized as "too liberal."[300] The country seems to be riding an ever-rising tide of mean-spiritedness. The Manichaean world-view that drives it is captured in these words attributed to the neo-conservative guru Irving Kristol: "So far from having ended, my cold war has increased in intensity, as sector after sector has been corrupted by the liberal ethos. . . . Now that the other 'Cold War' has ended, the real cold war has begun. We are far less prepared for this cold war, far more vulnerable to our enemy, [etc]."[301]

In this environment, rigidly conservative values appear not only to have been entrenched in the centers of political power in a manner that has created built-in barriers to reversal, but to have generated widespread support for their ideological underpinnings as well. Case after case of the exposure of obscene misuse of private and public authority for private gain, often at astronomic levels of profit, seem no longer to have even passing impact on the persistent belief in "the market" and the profit motive as a mechanism for generating and distributing wealth. While I deeply admire those who continue to struggle against all this in the public forum, including their law practices, I have difficulty joining with them.

It is this response to the prevailing environment that has in large measure been responsible for my no longer teaching Labor Law.

The national agenda, at both the legislative and the judicial levels, in both the professional and the public arenas, has moved too far from what to me are fairly debatable issues. The last decade has seen the accelerating decline in the role of collective bargaining; the equation with the public good of the continuing abolition of jobs, reductions in wage levels, and erosion of job security; the acquiescence in and legitimation of the apparently limitless escalation of compensation and stock-market profits for people whose major talent is their rapacity; and the proliferation of half-hearted ventures like early warning of plant closings, unpaid family leaves, and protection against arbitrary dismissals that are almost immediately seen as "going too far." I have unbounded admiration for teaching colleagues who continue to struggle against this tide, most especially Clyde Summers, Jack Getman, and Karl Klare, whose careers continue to be eloquent testimony to what academic acumen can accomplish when yoked to a deep and enduring commitment to bringing the democratic ideal to the workplace and our "private" lives.[302] The truth is, however, that I no longer have heart for teaching the subject.

Closer yet to home for me was the experience, from 1982 until 1988, of guiding the development of an entire rethinking of the law school curriculum at the newly founded City University of New York Law School. I had resigned my professorship at Pennsylvania in 1982, when Charles R. Halpern, a leading public-interest lawyer and a good friend appointed as the nascent school's founding dean, invited me to join him, not merely in starting a law school, but in committing ourselves to structure every aspect of it—the selection of faculty and students, and the administration of the school in areas such as governance and "placement" as well as the content, teaching methods, and evaluation system used in the courses—in response to a consciously chosen and articulated vision of legal education and practice. The account of our vision is too complex even to summarize; for me, it was encapsulated by the motto we chose for the school: Law in the Service of Human Needs.[303]

In one sense, the CUNY experiment has been a great success. The far-reaching changes that we introduced in the educational program have survived to some substantial degree. The School has by now graduated more than one thousand lawyers a very significant number of whom are practicing law, in public or pri-

vate positions, with a commitment to the representation of ordinary people and to seeking a legal career that has meaning for
them. But I learned how powerful the forces of the traditional
consciousness of education are, both in the ways in which the
world outside the enclave that was the Law School impinged
upon our freedom of action within it, and also in the ways in
which we had internalized some aspects of that consciousness and
"imposed" it on ourselves. I found, too, that we were unable, in
the years that I was there, to create an environment that supported
our joint efforts, free of the hostility, suspicion, and divisiveness
that have always characterized the Left. Berthold Brecht said it
well, and too truly:

> Even anger against injustice
> Makes the voice grow harsh. Alas, we
> Who wished to lay the foundations of kindness
> Could not ourselves be kind.[304]

Personal, professional, and political experience in the last decade and a half, then, have conspired to leave me ill-suited to pursue programmatic efforts at change with energy and confidence.
This evolution in my outlook on the world has surely contributed
to my receptivity to the reflective quality of spirituality, and to its
focus on the immediate and local, on "being" rather than
"doing."

Still the wheel turns, however. As the quality of American public life has become increasingly poisonous, it has been my turn to
religion itself that, most recently, has moved me back to seeking,
and has helped me to identify, a way of working as a law teacher
that a bit more fully serves values that are important to me. The
experience of being given a paid leave to write this book heightened my long-festering concern that I devote far too little of my
work as a lawyer and teacher of law to resisting the pervasive
injustice of the world. Yet, for many months, I was blocked from
finding a means of implementing this concern that was true to
my current life situation and outlook. When I turned my focus to
my teaching itself, rather than to seeking some variety of practice-
oriented legal work, however, I found that (in classic Quaker parlance) the "way opened" to me to discern the outlines of a new
course, in what law schools call a clinical setting, focused on the
representation of refugees and migrants. The motivation for that
choice was, at bottom, religious.

When I say that, I do not mean a "divine command," but an experience of strong resonance between what I find within myself and what I am learning from my increasing openness to the teaching of the religious tradition. Scripture admonishes us to this effect: "The alien who dwells among you, you shall not wrong, for you were aliens in the land of Egypt" (Exodus 22:21). More than merely abstaining from doing wrong, however, we are enjoined to imitate God, who "loves the strangers, giving them food and clothing. You shall also love the stranger, for you were strangers in the land of Egypt" (Deuteronomy 10:18–19).

Although this reminder of the significance of slavery and liberation is repeated many times in the Hebrew Scriptures, the Torah and the Prophets, and the Gospels as well, can support other aims of work in law, too. And the most recent surge in hostility to the alien and the stranger—food and clothing may still lawfully be sold to aliens, but a job is more problematic[305]—is echoed in the venom with which the current political atmosphere addresses all too many other issues. My coming to recognize a desire to turn specifically to the law of the migrant is grounded in a recognition of my own identity.

My grandparents left czarist Ukraine for a land that may not have been openheartedly welcoming—after all, they were "new immigrants," who, I read in school forty years later, were a less desirable set of folks than the older, Western European stock[306]—but that did admit them, without requiring that they document sufficiently grievous particular acts of persecution, untainted by "economic" motives; a land characterized, to be sure, by pervasive anti-Semitism, but for the most part not of a physically lethal sort, and embedded in social rather than legal norms; and a land not at all paved with gold as they had heard, but one that, over time, allowed them and their children and grandchildren to share in its abundance.[307]

I can no longer approach this work with the heavily instrumental mindset so characteristic of political causes: Although my students represent individual applicants for asylum and aid lawyers engaging in litigation and other work on behalf of immigrants, I do not judge the value of our work by our ability (with others) to "stop Proposition 187," establish dramatic new constitutional constraints on legislative xenophobia, or change the political climate measurably. My hope is that, in the work that my students and I do, we will spend some time "being with" a few of those who are now being reviled and denied the share in the nation that my grandparents were given; that we will learn something of what they have to teach us, about themselves, the lands that they have left, and the global social, political, and economic forces that have given us a world of refugees; most of all, perhaps, that my students will learn from the opportunity to see the law, and the world, as their clients experience it.

It is an oft-told story, which I first heard told with respect to the Catholic Worker house of Dorothy Day on the Lower East Side in New York, providing hospitality year after year to thousands of destitute people. Asked, "Do you think that all of your efforts have been effective?" one of their number answered, "We have not tried to be effective. We have tried to be faithful."

To what will I be trying to be faithful? In working on behalf of refugees seeking to remain in the country, I will be honoring my grandparents, and expressing my gratitude to them and to my country for saving me from an early death in a Soviet or Nazi prison camp, and for much else. In working to resist "English only" legislation, I will be honoring my father, who, though born here, entered first grade knowing no English. Deuteronomy reminds me to identify myself in these words: "A wandering Aramean was my father." He lived in Egypt as an alien, and came to a land flowing with milk and honey. I am a lawyer and a teacher, with rare opportunities to choose how I carry on my work. So now I seek a place to bring a portion of the ongoing "fruit of the ground" that I have been given.[308]

6

The Consciousness of Religion and the Consciousness of Law

> But this is the covenant that I will make with the house of Israel after those days, says the Lord: I will put my law within them, and I will write it on their hearts; and I will be their God, and they shall be my people. No longer need they teach one another, neighbor or brother, to know the Lord; all of them, high and low alike, will know me. . . .
>
> —JEREMIAH 31:33–34

Moses's final charge to the Israelites for the most part speaks in the language of commandments and obedience, of divinely ordained reward and punishment, a central passage admonishing the people in terms plainly worded as an injunction: "You shall love the Lord your God with all your heart, and with all your soul, and with all your might. Keep these words that I am commanding you today in your heart" (Deuteronomy 6:5–6).[309] Yet he spoke as well in words that have a very different ring, in words that ground the prophecy of Jeremiah. The commandment to "turn to the Lord your God with all your heart and with all your soul," Moses reassured us, "surely, . . . is not too hard, nor is it too far away": "It is not in heaven, that you should say, 'Who will go up to heaven for us, and get it for us so that we may hear it and observe it?' Neither is it beyond the sea, that you should say, 'Who will cross to the other side of the sea for us, and get it for us so that we may hear it and observe it?' No, the word is very near to you; it is in your mouth and in your heart for you to observe" (Deuteronomy 30:10–14).

By "the word," I understand, Torah. Drawing on the rabbinic teaching that "God consulted the Torah and created the world," Susan Handleman finds in the Jewish tradition a basis for regarding Torah as "a blueprint for the architecture of creation; . . . not simply . . . a set of prescriptive laws, but the primordial design of the world."[310] But if the word is in our hearts, the template that exists in the world, by which the world and its moral order came to be created, mirrors that within each person. It may have been given *to* us from outside, but in Jeremiah's sense of being implanted *within* us, of being an attribute of our creation.

The term "the Word" (now capitalized) appears most famously in the opening lines of the Gospel of John, and it is striking to me that Protestant theologian John Cobb says of it what Handleman says of Torah. Handleman understands rabbinic teaching to name Torah as "the Wisdom that preexists the world,"[311] while Cobb proposes that, "despite the predominance of 'Word' in the tradition, we speak today of 'Wisdom', the Wisdom that is present everywhere and at all times."[312] Law professor Richard Stith attributes to St. Thomas Aquinas the teaching that "the eternal law is part of the very being of God, rather than something merely willed by Him for arbitrary or contingent reasons."[313]

Though Torah be thought so transcendent as to pre-exist creation itself, our understanding of it is nonetheless transformed by thinking of Torah as Wisdom, written in our hearts. The translator of the Soncino edition of the Book of Jeremiah interprets the prophecy that God will put the law on the hearts of the people in these words: "I will no longer be something external to them, but so deeply ingrained in their consciousness as to be part of them."[314] "Obedience" then becomes an active, creative practice, in which we listen "for," not only "to," God. In "submitting" to the will of God, we first search for the voice to which we will submit. Discernment of it requires our fullest creative participation, and to obey is not so much to yield our will to a superior force as to align our actions with that which is within us, that which is most holy, most our birthright as both creature and co-creator.

I believe that a strikingly parallel interaction exists with respect to the way we think about law in the civic arena. One of the most famous epigrams describing the nature of law is by Justice Holmes: "The common law is not a brooding omnipresence in the sky, but the articulate voice of some sovereign or quasi-sovereign that can be identified."[315] The enduring debate between the positivism of such thoughts and the natural law tradition[316] should not make us lose sight of a salient commonality. Both an "omnipresence" (religious or secular) and a "sovereign or quasi-sovereign" are characterized by an entire otherness.

They arise from outside us and constrain our choices. This view, it has been observed, is reflected in both religion and law:

> In the Western theological tradition, God is lawgiver, as well as enforcer, of a legal and/or moral code. Western political tradition mimics this concept of deity. . . . The Bible assumes that God and God's demands existed prior to creation. . . . The government is based on a system of law that develops a significance independent of its creators and obligates. The legal system, although open to influence, functions as an institution apart from its citizens, just as a transcendent God is open to supplication and prayer, but is ultimately separate from the creatures who were created.[317]

A consciousness of law as an expression—albeit a partial and distorted one—not of a command but of a truth is cognizant of three characteristics that law has (along, of course, with others, in some cases inconsistent with these). First, it is within as well as outside us, an aspect of our being; in that respect, it is ontological, it "is" written in our hearts. Writing of Catholic teaching, Joseph Boyle observes:

> [M]oral norms are not, on the Catholic conception, arbitrary impositions by God. They are not tests set up to make life difficult, but the demands of our own rational natures. According to natural law theory, morality is a participation by rational creatures in God's providence so that they may guide their lives to what is genuinely good. . . . Thus, the reason which provides the basis for moral norms is a person's own reason, not something alien or imposed.[318]

Second, law is normative as well; because there is much to draw us away from that which is within us, we are enjoined to write it in our hearts as an ongoing not simply a past act, to remain aligned with the terms of our being. "You shall teach [these words] diligently to your children, and shall talk of them when you sit in your house, and when you walk by the way, when you lie down and when you rise up" (Deuteronomy 6:6–7). Third, both its content and the mode of discerning that content are described by the enigmatic term "wisdom."[319]

In seeking to give intelligible content to the implications for law of the religious consciousness I have sought to express, I want to avoid being drawn more into an analysis of law and contending approaches to it than is consistent with the tenor of this book. What follows, then, is more evocative than comprehensive, more pointed toward than definitively articulated and defended. In this chapter, by "law" or "enacted law" I will ordinarily mean the rules of conduct promulgated by the civic authorities; when I want to refer to what in this book I have at times called "the will of God" or (in secular terms) the norms of moral truth, I will speak of "the moral law."

I will begin by simply asserting, without seeking to justify, my belief in the truth of a proposition about the relation of law, morality, and obligation that has been debated since the dawn of philosophy, and which is central to what follows: *The moral law, and only the moral law, obliges.*[320]

It is, I hope, clear that by obligation I do not have reference either to a command or to a threat. Rather, the source of the obligation is ontological; it is an aspect of what we are as human beings. C. S. Lewis has put the matter in terms whose central meaning I find apt (allowing for his fondness for the dangerous word "obedience"): "God is to be obeyed because of what He is in Himself. If you ask why we should obey God, in the last resort the answer is, 'I am.' To know God is to know that our obedience is due to Him."[321]

As humans, then, we are under an obligation to do what morality requires and to abjure what it forbids. Enacted law sometimes reflects the moral law, sometimes violates it, and often does neither. Not infrequently, it overlaps the moral law, going at times further and at times not so far in what it asks of us. There is an obligation to follow the law only when it reflects the moral law. When it does not, we may follow it out of prudence or feelings of solidarity, except that, where the law violates the moral law, our obligation is to refuse to follow it.

As I have sought to explore fully above, to assert all this is in no way to assert that one knows what the requirements of morality are, whether in general terms or in a specific situation. We may therefore decide to follow the law because we allow ourselves to be guided by the enactor's discernment of what morality requires, provided that we justifiably believe that the law's enactment reflects a moral judgment and have no sufficient reason to believe that judgment wrong. In any case, our "obedience" to the moral law is bound up with the success of our efforts to discern its content. We act wrongfully if we obey a voice wrongly claiming to speak, or wrongly perceived by us to speak, in the voice of God.

From this highly contestable base, I find that the religious consciousness to which I have given voice in this book has a number of significant implications for one's stance toward enacted law. The first is that the process of following the moral law becomes a matter more of *assuming responsibility* than of practicing obedience.

Assuming Responsibility

> Israel is the people that is to see and understand the action of God in everything that happens and to make a fitting reply. So it is in the New Testament also. The God to whom Jesus points is not the commander who gives laws but the doer of small and of mighty deeds, the creator of sparrows and clothier of lilies, the ultimate giver of blindness and sight, the ruler whose rule is hidden in the manifold activities of plural agencies but is yet visible to those who know how to interpret the signs of the times.
>
> —H. Richard Niebuhr[322]

Responsibility has in common with obedience the quality of a required response: an admonition may not simply be shrugged off.[323] But the responsible response is far more textured than the simply obedient; judgment, insight, a wise discretion—in short, wisdom—play as much of a role as conformity to rule. Miriam Starhawk, a practitioner and expositor of Goddess religion, writes of the obligation to act justly, "not as a written code or set of rules imposed from without. Instead, justice is an inner sense that each act brings about consequences that must be faced responsibly."[324]

Keeping the law written in our hearts means more than following the rules wholeheartedly; it entails acting as a co-creator of the law by which we are governed, giving it meaning in myriad applications by bringing to bear the qualities of moral imagination with which we are equipped.

This concept is not some lessened sense of obligation, a soft means of avoidance; indeed, in some contexts it can be more demanding than a rote obedience, for, as the next section will explore, it presumes fidelity to a moral norm that may be only partially expressed. More fundamentally, however, it is not to be compared on a quantitative scale at all.

A discussion by medical ethicist Albert Jonsen provides a specific factual context that will illuminate the inquiry.[325] He postulates a complaint by students at a Catholic seminary that the detailed rules of the institution are "repressive, paternalistic, and detrimental to maturity." In response, the director tells them that the bells signaling each activity in the daily order will be turned off, and the "constant checking" discontinued. "You can be responsible," the director says. "It is now up to you to follow the daily order and fulfill your duties on your own."

This response is immediately challenged as misunderstanding the meaning of responsibility. It is not, the students assert, "following the rules without being reminded. . . . It means letting us design our own order and way of living here, an order which we find suitable for living together as human beings and as brothers in Christ and suitable for doing the job we are here for, acquiring the skills necessary to be effective priests."

Jonsen comments on the "quite different views of responsibility" at work in this interaction: The director does understand the responsible person not merely as one who is accountable for his or her observation of the rules, but "as one who has appropriated the existing law, who has made it his own, who obeys it on his own initiative and recognizance." To the students, however, the responsible person is one who not only "appropriates the law, but who partakes in [its] creation." "He creates the law, makes himself responsible *for* the law, not out of a pure, totally uncommitted freedom but in view of the distinct task to which he commits himself."

The director finds in this approach an insufficient recognition of the fact that the regulations "are God's will for you." The seminarians in reply would characterize the rules and regulations as God's will (only) in the sense that "God wills us to use our freedom and intelligence to work toward the accomplishment of the job he has given us. His will is really that the job be done."

This process of "creating" the very rule that is being applied does not displace the rule, but goes on in interaction with it. It is not simply "a generalized admonition to act in a conscientious, considered, committed" way. "[F]irst and foremost it commands that the total moral order—the structure of rules, values and agent—be taken seriously. [The moral agent] is not only ruled, but ruler. He engages himself to bring into effective reality the norms and values which he accepts. This requires that he accept the task of understanding them, of bringing them to clarity of conception, of cultivating them and criticizing them."

Again, it is a serious misunderstanding or distortion to see this approach as more "permissive" than the traditional one. I will examine in the next section how the idea of responsibility, of what Jonsen terms the appropriation of a moral norm, may constrain discretion where the "rule" appears to leave it untouched. As Jonsen observes, "the complexity of [human] problems far surpasses the utility of . . . rules. This seems to leave vast areas of human endeavor without moral principle, and when an ethic which has emphasized rules has nothing to say, it appears to approve 'laissez faire'." But, he objects:

> The principle of responsibility requires that the responsible man, salesman, general, politician, or physician carry the spirit of the ethical principles which they adopt into the areas where no clear rules exist. He is asked to reflect upon the fundamental values which he espouses in the light of the actual facts of his work. In this context he must be moral entrepreneur, bearing the responsibility of devising procedures which will, even if remotely, reflect the general stance which he takes toward human life.

At bottom, I believe that a major prop of the widespread reluctance to view this concept of responsibility as seriously "law-abiding" is the difficulty it presents in judging whether an agent has met the norm in question. Responsibility is normally *imposed* on people, not *assumed* by them, in religion and in law. Marcus Borg has vividly described the "conventional wisdom" of traditional religion in terms that resonate graphically with this characteristic of law. He speaks of "the Christian life [in this consciousness] as a life of requirements," a world of "judging" and "anxious striving."[326] To proceed from the insight that the law "is" written in our hearts is to move the role of passing judgment off center-stage, not, I insist, to remove it entirely, but to refuse to allow the desire to facilitate judging questions of compliance to play so primary a shaping role in describing what is rightful conduct.

I can illustrate this thought with a rather routine professional-discipline case that arose some years ago in Ohio. An attorney had caused an accident resulting in the death of one young person and serious injury to two others. Pleading guilty to involuntary manslaughter and driving while intoxicated, he received a six-month jail sentence, a three-year suspension of his driver's license, and a suspended three-year prison sentence; he was suspended indefinitely from law practice by the Supreme Court of Ohio by reason of these felony convictions. Two years later his application for reinstatement of his professional license came before the court.

The hearing had produced a wide array of support for his over-all character and fitness as an attorney. He said that he recognized the danger of his being an alcoholic (his father had been in recovery for several years), and testified that he now had no more than an occasional drink—"a glass of wine with my wife" and house guests—for social reasons and "to prove to myself . . . that I can stop." His probation supervisor regarded him as a "budding alcoholic," with "very little insight into his potential alcoholism."

The court held, first, that an eighteen-month suspension was appropriate as a sanction in light of the loss of life caused by his drinking. It noted, however, that it viewed its responsibility as going beyond the imposition of a sanction, speaking of the increasing "opportunities" existing to assist attorneys and judges to become free of alcohol or drug dependence. "[T]he disciplinary process of this court can and should be viewed as a potential for recovery as well as a procedure for the imposition of sanctions."

In light of this analysis, the court ordered the former attorney placed on five years' probation, with the assistance of the State Bar Association's Lawyers Assistance Committee, a body that works to rehabilitate "impaired lawyers," and concluded that his readmission and later status would be partially determined by his compliance with the terms of his probation. One of those terms was that during his probation he abstain totally from use of alcohol.[327]

Note that, without detracting from its perceived need to impose a punitive sanction and a total ban on drinking during the period of his probation, the court saw as among its functions assisting the former attorney to actualize his own desire to become free of his addiction. The court's recognition of the likely presence of self-delusion and weakness of will in the attorney's consciousness did not lead it to refuse to credit the simultaneous presence of a genuine desire to do right. Most of his probationary period would be served with his license restored, and the reliance on the Bar Committee indicates that the probationary period was meant to do more than pressure the attorney to comply with professional norms as a means to achieve reinstatement. By the court's disposition, responsible behavior was being facilitated as well as demanded.[328]

The ready assumption that the law exists to coerce people into acting as they should, or to punish those who do not, needs to be leavened with the recognition that the moral law "is" in our hearts. It exists within us, alongside much that cuts us off from it. We see the function and the possibilities of legal regulation more broadly when we act on that dual recognition.

Educational theorist Nel Noddings, writing about the emerging tendency to relegate seriously ill people to "high-tech" home health care in the charge of relatives, and the resultant posing of the question to what extent the giving of such care should be deemed an obligation, argues that "we should put aside the notion of moral obligation in favor of one of moral support."[329] She vividly recounts the poignant difficulties, physical and emotional, that care providers often face, and argues for policy formulation from a different premise from the reflexively available one of the imposition of responsibility through the setting of standards and sanctions:

> To insist today that individuals have a moral obligation to care for their children, siblings, or parents invites a debate among those obligated, and renewed attention to the individual rights of agents and victims. Worse, such insistence overlooks the fact that many, perhaps most, people want to care for their loved ones. They need help, not legal coercion or preaching, to do so. Collective obligation has to be aimed not at direct action but at the social conditions that make it possible for people to care for one another.

Nodding's assertions are needlessly polarized; she speaks of "help, not legal coercion," "aimed not at direct action but at the social conditions." Both may appropriately play a role; the central point is the desirable *primacy* of a legal response that is built on a recognition of the inward desire of the agent to do what is right, and that acknowledges a public responsibility to ease some of the very real barriers to acting on that desire. That insight, I believe, is strongly supported by the view of the relation between human beings and the moral law that I have set forth here. As was recognized by the decision of the Ohio Supreme Court, weakness of will, and just plain wrongheadedness and immorality, can be constrained by the power of the law where it need be, while yet recognizing the distorted character of such a response as a total response.

As I will develop in the final section of this chapter, the public avowal of a norm, which is often contained in legal regulation, can have powerful heuristic force in establishing the existence of an obligation. The next step, however, in "implementing" that expression of a norm is to apprehend and take account of the impediments existing in people's private and social lives that limit their capacity and willingness to act consistent with it. The *first* response of the law should be to act to remove or lessen the force of relevant impediments. It is not a foolish "pollyanna-like" mindset to insist on keeping in the forefront of our minds that most people have within them the desire to act rightfully, residing along with influences—arising from within their personalities and from outside as well—that may move them powerfully in other directions.

The kind of deep-rooted punitive spirit that is simply not interested in helping "sinners" to become better persons, a spirit that characterizes so many political initiatives today, is based on a Manichaean understanding of the world, which views the law as "written on the hearts" only of the elect, however defined—and the rest be damned.[330] There is much in the religious tradition that manifests and legitimates such a view. There is, however, no less that reflects and supports a very different view, a most significant instantiation of which I would like now to recall.

FEELING THE WEIGHT

> Just then a lawyer stood up to test Jesus. "Teacher," he said, "what must I do to inherit eternal life?" He said to him, "What is written in the law? What do you read there?" He answered, "you shall love the Lord your God with all your heart, and with all your soul, and with all your strength, and with all your mind; and your neighbor as yourself." And he said to him, "You have given the right answer; do this, and you will live."
>
> But wanting to justify himself, he asked Jesus, "And who is my neighbor?"
>
> —LUKE 10:25–29

Here we meet a very lawyerly lawyer indeed. All admonitions
have parameters, and all statutes require the definition of terms.
That I must love my "neighbor" suggests that I need not love
any other. I need to know, then, whether my "neighbors" are,
for example, those who live adjacent to my home, the residents
(the citizens?) of my community, or all people of my ethnic or
religious affiliation. If I am "law-abiding," I will conscientiously
ask myself what is the likely authoritative answer, and perhaps
turn to a wise or learned person, a "teacher" of the law, for guidance. The premise of this action, however, is that the law operates
to limit my will, that apart from the rule I am free to do as I
please.

Jesus's response to the request to define neighbor, to delimit it,
to demark its boundary, is to do something quite different. He
recounts the Parable of the Good Samaritan, and asks, "Which of
these three, do you think, was a neighbor to the man who fell
into the hands of the robbers," his fellow countrymen who (perhaps for good reason) did not tarry to give aid, or the Samaritan
who bandaged his wounds, cared for his animals, and took him
to an inn? "The one who showed him mercy," answered the
lawyer, to which Jesus responded, "Go and do likewise."

One establishes with another the relation of a neighbor (and
thereby entitles him or her to be shown love) by showing the
very love that one is bound to show a neighbor: No first-year law
student could get by with such a circular answer, for on such an
answer, there is no obligation to love anyone. By choosing not to
love one, I exclude him or her from the circle of those whom I
am enjoined to love. This is a "law" applicable to no one.

Or to everyone. What Jesus teaches the lawyer is to start from
a different premise. Yes, we are "obliged" to love one another,
but the obligation is not a constraint on our will, to be accepted
only if within the scope of the mandate. Rather, the obligation is
to recognize and take the *opportunity* that our being gives us to
love the other. We can expand the range of this power to embrace
all with whom we come in contact, transcending boundaries of
ethnicity and religion and overflowing the day-to-day "important" priorities that divert us (as they did the priest and the Levite)
from responding to another's need. The opportunity to "define"
the term by our conduct, which by the consciousness of the lawyer's question allows us to deprive it of much normative force,

and indeed to see in it a legitimation of indifference to those not closest to us, allows us also to expand its scope as we will. Embracing wholeheartedly the norm expressed by the law, expanding its reach, expands thereby our congruence with the contours of our creation.[331]

The central question, however, is whether we are to regard ourselves as *obliged* to "expand our congruence with the contours of our creation." Jesus ends his teaching with the admonition, "Go and do likewise." Recalling that he told the story in the first place as an answer to the lawyer's lawyerly question, we can understand him to mean that the lawyer should not ask questions that seek to learn how circumscribed his response may be; rather, he should embrace the norm wholeheartedly, seeing it not as a limitation on his being but as a manifestation of it.

In the rabbinic tradition, the question has been much discussed whether there is an obligation to aspire, a duty to reach beyond duty. The question is a tricky one, because in Jewish law many actions that the Anglo-American legal tradition clearly understands as not required—taking action to rescue one in peril of his or her life, for example—are legal imperatives.[332] More broadly, there is a general obligation to go "beyond the line of the law," which is regarded as itself part of the law: "You must do what is right and good" (Deuteronomy 6:18); "You shall walk in His ways" (Deuteronomy 28:9). Observes Rabbi Aharon Lichtenstein, we are "commanded to aspire."[333]

The critical difference between duty and aspiration is not their obligatory character, which both share, nor the presence of a sanction, although that does mark a distinction (see note 360, below). The central point is the lesser generalizability of the content of aspiration. Aspiration is necessarily more contextual and less rule-bound, more responsive directly to the agent's underlying moral sensibility. This is not an invitation to exonerating rationalization. Rather, Rabbi Lichtenstein recounts: "[O]ne of its principal modes entails the extension of individual [laws] by (1) refusal to avail oneself of personal exemptions; (2) disregard of technicalities when they exclude from a law situations that morally and substantially are clearly governed by it; and (3) enlarging the scope of a law by applying it to circumstances beyond its legal pale but nevertheless sufficiently similar to share a specific telos."[334]

The process has much in common with what Quakers call "feeling the weight" of a moral concern. The task is not simply to judge whether one is obligated by the contours of a particular rule of conduct, but rather to allow the concern to weigh on our conscience a while longer, to count the "moral costs" of the action or inaction that we are about to decide is the right course to take, to act informed by a "genuine reluctance to bring about [an] injury."[335] In that process, the most important task is to open our eyes, to maintain an expanded awareness of consequences, to take in rather than shut out the suffering of others that may be involved, to hold at bay the pressures to let other legitimate priorities lead us too quickly to accept a justificatory response. The Vietnamese monk Thich Nhat Hanh expresses a relevant Buddhist Precept in these terms: "Do not avoid contact with suffering or close your eyes before suffering. Do not lose awareness of the existence of suffering in the life of the world. Find ways to be with those who are suffering by all means, including personal contact and visits, images, sound. By such means, awaken yourself and others to the reality of suffering in the world."[336]

In none of these versions is there in the obligation to aspire, to "be with" suffering or the weight of a concern, a polarized insistence on settling for nothing short of (posthumous) sainthood. Few of us are called upon to emulate St. Francis, or to martyr ourselves for another. We are each called upon, however, to stretch a bit beyond our comfort level, to reach for a degree of virtue-going-beyond-duty that for each one is at least a modest degree beyond our own norm. Enacted law probably cannot, but in any event should not, seek to express or enforce such an admonition, but I believe that it is nonetheless part of the moral obligation of a person.

For example, Charles Fried (academic philosopher, former U.S. Solicitor General, now a state-court judge) is surely right when he asserts that "we recognize an authorization to take the interests of particular persons [especially friends and relatives] more seriously and to give them priority over the interests of the wider collectivity."[337] Although Fried may justifiably infer from this premise that "one who provides an expensive education for his own children surely cannot be blamed because he does not use these resources to alleviate famine or save lives in some distant land," the "surely" bespeaks a polarizing tendency that can easily outrun the moral foundations of the premise. By contrast, legal philosopher Richard Wasserstrom, while accepting the same premise as Fried's, cautions against taking "the rightness of parental preference so for granted" that we not examine specific instances of it critically, expressing the view that in our society "the *degree* of parental preference is far too extensive to be morally justified."[338]

Obviously, the point at which each person exceeds morally acceptable favoring of those near to him or her does not allow for precise calibration, even by the individual involved, certainly by public law. That is one reason why prohibitory regulation is inappropriate. Such measures as progressive taxation and redistributive spending policies, however, which burden somewhat the ability of wealthy persons to favor their families "excessively" may be justified by the moral principle that Wasserstrom expresses. Beyond that, the "duty to aspire" speaks primarily to the individual, and can be applied by him or her only in an examination of conscience. The idea that the choice is between limitless self-aggrandizement and giving away all one has to feed the hungry is a perniciously false polarization of the question.[339]

There is more to be learned, however, from Jesus's responses than the obligatory quality of aspiration. The lawyer's questions are portrayed as illicitly motivated. He expresses not honest moral perplexity, a desire for moral guidance, but an attempt first to "test" Jesus, then to "justify" himself, presumably to justify his reluctance to take in and find meaning in the admonition to love God and neighbor. Yet, Jesus ignores these signs of delict and, in telling him the parable, and then asking what he has learned from it ("Which was a neighbor to the man?"), responds instead to the undisclosed aspect of the lawyer that is congruent with what Jesus wants him to be, which coexisted with his moral failings. This aspect Jesus saw as latent in one whom he might have regarded simply as a sinner or an adversary. The tone of the lawyer's final statement is responsive and reflective; he has been moved and changed, despite (what appeared to be) himself.

Jesus is not only speaking to us, as individuals, about love and obligation. He is also saying something to us, as members of the body politic, about the ways in which we can, in the name of law, address those among us whose conduct we wish to affect by law.

ENACTED LAW

> Abraham should have replied to this supposedly divine
> voice as follows: "That I ought not to kill my good son
> is absolutely certain. But that you who appear to me are
> in fact God is something of which I am not certain and
> of which I can never become certain, even if your voice
> should thunder down from the visible heavens."
>
> —IMMANUEL KANT[340]

> CREON: But tell me thou—and let thy speech be
>   brief—
>   The edict hadst thou heard, which this
>   forbade?
> ANTIGONE: I could not choose but hear what all men
>   heard.
> CREON: And didst thou dare to disobey the law?
> ANTIGONE: Nowise from Zeus, methought, this edict
>   came
>   Nor Justice, that abides among the gods
>   In Hades, who ordained this law for men.
>
> —SOPHOCLES[341]

The eloquence of Antigone's response to her government should
not lead us to forget that, as a result of it, she was buried alive.
Creon had (in Holmes's terms) an "articulate voice" indeed, and
the consequences of defying the command of the sovereign might
well lead one to feel "obliged" to obey enacted law. The idea of
law (enacted law) as command certainly fits with our intuition.

The British philosopher H. L. A. Hart distinguishes between
that which we feel obliged to do and that which we have an
obligation to do. Forking over a wallet (to use his paradigmatic
example) to a person who credibly says, "Your money or your
life," is for most of us what we would feel obliged to do, but one
would not say that a robbery victim normally has an obligation to
surrender his or her wallet.[342] I say "normally" because if we
change the context a bit, the issue becomes more complex: "Your
money or *her* life," an innocent stranger. Some would say that
here there is obligation as well as incentive. Others might disagree, on the ground that there is no duty to rescue another from
even the peril of death when one has done nothing to cause it.

The agreement underlying that difference of view is that to speak of obligation is to speak of morality, not merely prudence.[343]

Enacted law is certainly the command of the sovereign,[344] but that is not the end of the matter. Although a command might make one feel obliged, it is insufficient to cause one to *be* obliged, it does not alone give rise to an obligation. For me, the analogy to religion is profound. Recall that, although I do not accept the binding authority of Torah as an expression (irrespective of its content) of God's will, I do embrace its heuristic value as a means of my coming to know God's will, and to develop my capacity and willingness to follow it.[345] Enacted law too will often have heuristic salience. Removing its obligatory character as command uncovers, rather than sweeps away, its heuristic character.

Much enacted law is meant to reflect moral insights, and not infrequently does so with substantial accuracy. As my law school colleague Heidi Hurd puts it: "Democratic results may . . . function as heuristic guides to right action. If we think that the majority of individuals is more likely to be right than we are about what behavior is morally required . . . , then we have every reason to take the majority's opinion as *evidence* of the content of morality."[346] We are obligated, I believe, always to seek to know the good (God's will), and the fact that a norm has been enacted into law counsels against our simply disregarding it merely because prudence may allow that response. Our obligation is to inquire as to the existence and scope of a moral norm that the enacted law might bring into focus.

The law-making process itself is often part of that heuristic. The political events that led to the abolition of slavery, woman suffrage, and the civil rights legislation of a generation ago each made us as a polity, and many of us as individuals, aware of moral truths that many did not apprehend previously. Moreover, the embodiment of the anti-discrimination principle in statutory text was itself a powerful heuristic, which may well have contributed at least as much as enforcement patterns to changing the national climate. This power has three aspects: First, the legislative delegitimation of discrimination served epistemically to crystallize realization of the injustice of long-accepted practices. It also served to encourage (to en-courage) those who, although perhaps tacitly recognizing the wrongfulness of discriminatory acts, allowed them to pass unchallenged in local settings (including their own actions) rather than set themselves apart from their neighbors, but now found disavowals not only right but acceptable.[347] Finally, it was the teaching function of the Civil Rights Act of 1964 as applied to race, religion, and sex that led many to see as wrongful much societally imposed disadvantage grounded on age, physical condition, and sexual orientation.

At the same time as we need to be open to the heuristic that might be embedded in enacted laws, especially those to which we are not instinctively drawn, we need to be wary about the tendency to give them too much normative power. I find the quotation from Kant that opens this section stunning because in it he so clearly (albeit hypothetically) retains his moral compass in the face of an experience of the voice of God, reflexively questioning that experience because it lacks congruence with his reading of that compass. For too many of us, influential human voices too readily "de-magnetize" our moral compass, and the challenge is to distinguish authentic humility from the desire not to stand against the tide of prevailing opinion.

The most dramatic question, although happily not the most common one in a democratic society, arises when there is a direct conflict between moral obligation and enacted law, when the law requires what morality forbids, or forbids what the moral law requires. The problem with which this book began, the conflict between conscription and conscientious objection to participation in war or service in the military, is a well-known example. In approaching such issues, two clarifications should be borne in mind.

First, our thinking is channeled, in some ways distorted, by the fact that enacted law itself at times protects individual freedom of conscience. So, Daniel Seeger's conviction was reversed according to enacted law, for the Constitution (whatever its natural-law grounding may have been) is "higher law" in a positivist sense. Under our legal system, it (or, more precisely, an authoritative judicial interpretation and application of it) trumps the actions of the legislative and executive branches.

Second, many claims made under the free-speech and related protections embodied in the First and Fourteenth Amendments are claims of a legal right to be free of specific restraints of enacted law, for example, to march in protest despite a local ordinance forbidding it. Normally, this is not a direct clash, for typically what is asserted is a right to march, not an obligation to march. That assertion raises only a question of interpretation of enacted law. Only for one who avows an obligation (whether grounded in religion or not) to "stand with" asserted victims of injustice or oppression, as by marching in protest, is the direct clash present.

My response to the problem of the direct clash, the problem of *Antigone*, is as simple to state as it is difficult to live by: Our obligation being grounded only in the moral law, we are obliged to violate enacted law if necessary, even where the legal claim based on freedom of conscience will be rejected. (The qualification, "if necessary," should not be quickly passed over. The words that Robert Bolt spoke on behalf of Sir Thomas More [who ultimately did surrender his life rather than take a false oath] make the point simply: "Our natural business lies in escaping."[348])

That the government follows legitimate procedures in passing on a claim of moral right is not dispositive. And while a proper humility about one's capacity to discern the content of moral truth counsels against simply ignoring the teaching of one's political community (assuming that the law in question can be thought to reflect a community judgment about morality), ultimately each of us is obligated to judge as best we can whether the polity has rightly discerned the will of God.

The more complex question is as to the meaning and content of an obligation of this sort. My answer is that one is obliged to "feel the weight" of it, to consider conscientiously and as free of rationalization as possible, what course of action to take. We are all, I believe, "commanded to aspire," but there is no procrustean bed into which we must all fit. Each of us is called upon to stretch ourselves some significant amount; to what plateau varies with (in Quaker terms) the Light that each one has.

Again, a specific context will be helpful. For me (being long past the age of conscription), the most salient example I can think of—and one I fervently hope never to have to face—is a repeated request by a relative or close friend, who is suffering from an extremely painful or disabling illness or injury, and whose condition is either terminal or irreversible, for aid in ending his or her life. Depending on the manner and extent of "aid" that is necessary in light of my friend's condition, for me to accede to the

request might be assistance in suicide or murder (both of which I
will presume for present purposes would be a felony).

I am convinced that killing or assistance in suicide in those
circumstances would not be a wrongful act. Albert Jonsen has
noted the "deeply rooted tendency in the ethical animal to can-
onize rules." He cautions:

> Even quite properly moral rules can become detached from the
> values they once protected and promoted, and which are their rai-
> son d'être. "Thou shalt not steal" has, in human history, justified
> the death or mutilation of the starving man who dared snatch bread
> from the prince's table. Put less picturesquely, it has prevented land
> reform, just taxation, fair wages. There is something about the
> definiteness and specificity of a rule which attracts and assuages the
> human conscience.[349]

Even as a matter of enacted law, and certainly as a matter of
moral norm, the supposedly categorical prohibition on killing is,
in truth, not wholly categorical. As my law school colleague
Michael Moore wisely notes:

> [M]oral norms must have exceptions implicit in them to have any
> moral plausibility. To be morally plausible, "thou shalt not kill"
> must be taken to be an elliptical reference to a much more compli-
> cated norm: "Don't kill, unless in self-defense, to protect your fam-
> ily, to aid in a just war lawfully declared, to execute those deserving
> of the death penalty such as Adolph Eichmann . . . ," etc.[350]

Now, each of Moore's postulated exceptions, although it may
be an accurate description of enacted law, is contested terrain as a
matter of morality. By my lights, his (and the law's) exceptions
are unjustifiably broad, but the case I have hypothesized presents
an instance that calls for an additional exception. Catholic philosopher Joseph Boyle distinguishes between "prohibitions" and
"foundations" of moral imperatives. Recognizing the "essential
role" of moral prohibitions, "including absolute or non-defeasible
prohibitions," he understands Catholic teaching to recognize that
"prohibitions are not foundational." He reads Aquinas as proceeding, even when considering prohibitions as basic as those
against killing and stealing, by deriving "reasoned justifications
for specific moral prohibitions." All moral precepts, Aquinas assertedly maintained, "are derived from more fundamental moral
principles."[351]

In my judgment, the moral imperative that underlies the general prohibition on killing is the obligation not to treat any person solely as a means to one's own ends. It is for that reason that it is impermissible to kill an innocent person for a greater good, such as prevention of the death of several others.

That norm is not violated in the case I have put. Rather, to *refuse* such a request can constitute a refusal to acknowledge its author as an end in himself or herself. For the truth is that most of the reasons for the refusal to act are self-serving—the fear of exposure and prosecution, or the reluctance to do the act, which is understandable but hardly involves the same order of travail as that which the dying person is experiencing—and the presence of a close family or friendship bond makes it far more difficult to say that there is no obligation because to refuse is not to "do" anything. What I would be refusing to do would be to give necessary aid to one with whom I have a special relationship, and who is seeking to carry out a most basic act of self-definition.

At the Zen Buddhist farm that we visit (see pp. 18–19, above), my wife and I attended a discussion by a physician of the impact on her work of the Buddhist Precepts, principally the one that says "a disciple of the Buddha does not take life." She recounted an experience in the hospital one night, where a terminally ill patient who had several times removed the tubes that were keeping him alive, only to have a staff member come in "too soon" and reimplant them, told her that he was going to try again after midnight that night. He asked her not to enter his room to check on him until morning, and to try to arrange things so that no nurse entered either. She said that she felt obligated to refuse this request.

Carolyn (who is a nurse) responded to this story by saying: "If I had done as you did, I would think that I *had* taken his life." And (bearing in mind the difference between the doctor-patient relation and a bond of love or friendship) I cannot discern a critical moral difference arising from the fact that the doctor in this story was not being asked to "do" anything, whereas in the case I have hypothesized some affirmative act on my part would be required. I recognize that my belief is (apparently) flatly contrary to Jewish law.[352] Here, no amount of respectful attention to that teaching has overcome my conviction that not only would it not violate a moral norm to accede to the request in question, it might be wrongful to refuse to do so.[353]

I acknowledge too the illegality of such an action under enacted law, and for present purposes acknowledge even the justifiability of such a law, for a legislature may reasonably be wary, out of fear of abuse, of attempting to define in abstract terms the scope of a justification for active participation in suicide. My law school colleague Seth Kreimer has succinctly summarized the difficult policy question:

> Assisted suicide presents our society with a fearsome dilemma. Forbidding active assistance leaves some citizens with the prospect of being trapped in agony or indignity from which they could be delivered by a death they desire. But permitting such assistance risks the unwilling or manipulated death of the most vulnerable members of society, and the erosion of the normative structure that encourages them, their families, and their doctors to choose life. . . . [T]he State must choose between preventing deliverance from suffering, and acquiescing in the risk of what all would concede is murder.
>
> The current prohibitions against assisted suicide and euthanasia sacrifice the autonomy and dignity of some citizens for the safety and support of others. Its elimination would reverse the terms of the sacrifice but would not avert the tragic choice.[354]

This reasoning makes it clear, I believe, why my obligation to follow the moral law is unaffected by a legislative choice to maintain the prohibition. "Living a moral life," says Herbert Fingarette, is a matter of "responding to particular human beings," and I cannot justifiably do harm to a specific person (especially one with whom I have a close relationship, and in a face-to-face encounter) on the ground that it might be good for society as a whole for other people in future situations to continue to be discouraged from acting similarly in morally different circumstances.[355]

By my statement of obligation, I intend two implications: First, it is extremely difficult, perhaps impossible, for anyone but me to judge whether it actually would be wrong for me to refuse the request. The elements that go into that judgment—the details of the relationship, the condition of the person making the request, exactly what act I would be called upon to do, and (because I too am entitled to be treated, even by one in extreme circumstances, as an end in myself and not merely a means to his or her concededly compelling ends) my honestly measured aversion to doing it—are too textured and subtle, too individuated, to warrant making a general pronouncement. It is not that wrongfulness depends on subjective opinion; in my view, it does not. But discerning accurately the rightness or wrongness of the act depends on knowledge to which only I may have sufficient access.

Second, even to say that I am obligated to accede to the request (if such is my answer) is not the end of the matter. I may have counter-obligations—if, for example, I honestly believe that I am likely to be subject to prosecution and that others (especially my minor children) would suffer harms that I have a responsibility to prevent if I reasonably can. More broadly, it is a central aspect of human freedom that we can choose to do wrong, that we can disobey God's will; and it is a central teaching of religion that at times we will.[356] I might decide that, right or wrong, I simply "cannot" do the act, whether out of fear, reluctance, or uncertainty. In a sense, in such a case I will have breached an obligation; in another sense, if I can honestly say that I have genuinely "aspired," I have fulfilled it, even if in outcome I have failed.

A far more common set of difficulties arises because the moral principles underlying enacted law often have contours that vary significantly from the legal norm enacted. The task in such cases is to extract a relevant moral principle, to which the law has given partial expression. Following it may call for more than, or less than, compliance with the law. The challenge is to approach the statute as a heuristic, listening for the moral truth (partially) embodied within it.

It is often said that a major function of the law is to solve "coordination" problems. For example, it is not inherently immoral to drive on one side of the road or another, but it is necessary for us all to drive on the same side, and the law (in this country) specifies the right side. We are said to be obligated to respect the lawmaker's solution.

I agree, but not because legislatures may justifiably solve coordination problems. That a law is "justified" is a matter of political theory, and is insufficient, in my view, to ground obligation. The applicable moral principle is to avoid endangering others by overweighting one's own interests, including the interest in not being bothered to pay attention to danger to others. Plainly, it is wrongful to drive on the side of the road on which I can expect to encounter cars driven by people who have reason to feel secure in the belief that they will not suddenly encounter a car heading right for them. I do not, on the other hand, have an obligation to resist the urge to drive down the middle of a long, flat, curveless, deserted country road in full daylight, as long as I move over in plenty of time to avoid seen and unseen dangers. (Doing such an act habitually may make it increasingly likely that I will lose too much of the capacity to judge when it can be safely done; it is a moral defect to overestimate one's ability to deal with moral hazards). Understand that I do *not* assert that lack of obligation, which is a moral concept only, should get anywhere in court should a police helicopter happen by. The fact that the law goes (a bit) further than morality requires does not create a moral right to act contrary to the law, for as a matter of governance all but the most extreme libertarian would agree that the interest in driving as I hypothesize in this rather improbable example is exceedingly trivial.

It is probably far more common for enacted law to fall short of what moral conduct requires. Recall Aharon Lichtenstein's observation that the "duty to aspire" may call on one to expand the reach of a norm beyond its terms, by acts such as "disregard of technicalities when they exclude from a law situations that morally and substantially are clearly governed by it."[357] An example is the limitation on the prohibition of employment discrimination contained in the Civil Rights Act of 1964 by reason of its application only to establishments with more than fifteen employees.[358] Whether an employer with fewer employees is obligated to abjure discriminatory conduct turns, in my judgment, on two questions: whether the enacted prohibition reflects a moral truth, that the forbidden conduct is wrongful, and, if so, whether the exemption itself also reflects a relevant moral judgment or is (in Lichtenstein's term) a "technicality."

The answer to the first question, as far as it applies to the core of the statutory prohibition, is, I believe, plainly, yes. As to the second, it is likely that the exemption of smaller employers reflected a legislative reluctance to impose on them the record-keeping and related requirements and burdens of the statute, more than it did the idea that countervailing considerations of privacy or autonomy came into play (as might be the case, for example, with the rental of a room or apartment in a small owner-occupied building).[359] An employer with fewer than fifteen employers would, on this rationale, be free to take advantage of the exemption with regard to enforcement matters, but obligated not to engage in purposeful discrimination forbidden by the Act.[360]

Another example concerns the speed limit, which in some specific circumstances is much too high (as it is elsewhere too low). The notion that one need not account morally for dangerous *lawful* conduct is a pernicious by-product of collapsing morality into law in seeking the sources of obligation. Worse yet is the effect of the tendency to regard "the law" as expressed wholly in sanctions and other enforcement patterns.[361] A widely held ethic asserts that there is no binding norm, there is only a sanction constituting a disincentive to non-compliance. I am therefore allowed, not only to drive up to 55 (or 65) mph, notwithstanding the evident dangerousness occasioned (in a particular instance) by conditions of traffic, weather, the vehicle, or myself, but am similarly "entitled" to go 65 (or 75) mph where the police have more or less openly acknowledged that they don't stop anyone going less than that (or, to ratchet it up a bit more, where I know that no police have me in sight).[362] The moral imperative, however, is not to disregard or under-weight the danger that our actions cause others; statutory or police permissions that do not speak to that are irrelevant to the existence of that imperative.[363]

It is true that, in deciding what conduct violates such a moral imperative, we may sensibly draw guidance from the judgments of others, and if we believe in good faith that we actually have adequate reason to take either the setting of the speed limit or changes in enforcement patterns as indicative of judgments about danger, we are warranted in viewing them as reliable heuristics, as long as we do so conscientiously, that is, not as an easy rationalization for justification of self-regarding conduct.

The idea that lawful conduct is rightful conduct is a source of much grievous wrong. We begin with the sensible idea that, in a polity committed to a very substantial degree of individual freedom, the fact that an act is widely believed to be immoral does not suffice, even among those who share the belief, to support the enactment of a law prohibiting it. Many issues of wise statesmanship go into that latter decision. The experience with Prohibition is probably the major historical case in point; today there are many who believe that abortion is wrong in many (or even all) circumstances but on grounds of overall wise governance oppose its criminalization, even oppose denying government financial assistance to women seeking abortions (especially those that are medically indicated) but unable to pay for them.[364] Beyond that factor, however, in many cases what is at work in the failure of enacted law to forbid that which is wrong is something a lot less admirable than "wise statesmanship." The political process allows those with ready access to it to insulate themselves from regulation, regardless of the objective "merits" of their case.

Although it should therefore be clear that the fact of legality is not dispositive, and may even be wholly neutral, with respect to morality, our political commitment to a "laissez-faire" baseline is strong enough that the claim that one "has a right" to do whatever the law allows is frequently taken to settle the moral question with the legal. This logical non sequitur has sufficient ideological force that it is invoked even when the failure of an enacted law to proscribe the conduct in question is not the deliberate decision of the enacting authority, but can be achieved only through imaginative and aggressive initiatives.[365]

A particularly lurid example appeared in the newspapers not long ago. A person described as a "billionaire investor," who had spent much of his career (and made much of his non-inherited money) in Michigan, moved with his family in 1989 to Sarasota, Florida, assertedly in order to "take advantage of lower tax rates." This was unquestionably lawful, and most might say within his moral rights as well. I would probably agree, provided that the Floridian (or Sarasotan) definition of residency was sufficiently demanding to prevent one from establishing residence there without a genuine change of domicile. (I recall reading some years ago that former President Ford was one of a large number of wealthy individuals making up the "5–29" club, who each year regularly resided in California one day short of the half-year that would have subjected them to its residents' tax).

Lower local taxes proved insufficiently attractive, however, for this billionaire, and in 1994 he enabled himself to escape all federal income taxes by renouncing his American citizenship and becoming a citizen and resident of the Caribbean island country of Belize. Again, a perfectly lawful act, although here I have no difficulty saying that it was plainly wrong. Wholly apart from the question whether there is an independent obligation not to divest oneself of all responsibility to pay some semblance of one's fair share of taxes, the renunciation of American citizenship for such an unworthy reason is a disreputable act.

All this is mere prologue, however. Our beset billionaire's wife and children apparently did not follow him to Belize, and were he to spend more than one month a year visiting them in Sarasota he would lose his tax exemption. The news account was that Belize had asked our State Department for permission to open a new diplomatic office in Sarasota, to be headed by . . . none other. From this strategic location, he would assertedly help Belize (which already has an office in Miami) to finance and "possibly" operate a consulate in New York.[366]

The State Department was reported to be "not enthusiastic," but it seems clear to me that no moral consequences would have flowed from any decision it may have made to overcome that reaction and approve the venture. Nor would it be conclusive that neither Congress nor the state or local legislatures has seen fit to redraw the legal parameters of their tax laws to keep such fish as this in their net.

Although this story probably has more analogues in the lives of wealthy people (and their tax advisers and lobbyists) than most of us realize,[367] the broader point implicates less dramatic, yet more pervasive, aspects of everyday life. Many of them involve the widely held principle that we have no obligation to respond to the need of others, apart from (immediate) family and those whose need we have caused. (Of course, the owner of a large manufacturing company who moves away from the community that has made it possible for him or her to operate profitably for many years most assuredly does cause to be in need many of those left behind—employees, customers, suppliers, fellow taxpayers and other citizens.) This principle of non-responsibility is deeply rooted in our legal/political ethic, and for many is a matter of morality as well. Nonetheless, it is a principle that is strongly rejected by central strains in the religious tradition, in Judaism, Christianity, Islam, and Eastern religions as well. I have found, in ways that are a principal focus of Chapter 4, religious language, symbols, and practices to be of great heuristic value in aiding me not to let my own moral judgment be anesthetized or intimidated by that of the prevalent moral environment. Federal Judge Martha Vazquez paid tribute to her Catholic education as leading her and her classmates to see their religion as a process by which "we begin to see our place in society as affecting the lives of others, a process by which we feel a responsibility towards the weak, the defenseless, a process by which we are in tune with our conscience."[368] And my law school colleague Seth Kreimer, writing of "The Responsibilities of the Jewish Lawyer," invokes a norm that speaks forcefully to lawyer and lay person alike: "Our tradition teaches us that we are not entitled to keep all of the proceeds of our good fortune. We have a specific obligation to those who . . . are at the opposite end of the social spectrum."[369]

Our life situation affects that of others; such success as we have in life reflects our good fortune along with our desert; our responsibility is toward those in need: To allow these simple truths to play a shaping role in our everyday lives is neither self-righteous nor triumphalist. That I am not and cannot be certain of the truth of my moral perceptions, that I cannot prove to you that you should share them, does not require me to act as if I do not have them. Humility, openness, and respect for difference are real and important virtues. They do not warrant the insistence that we have no values whatever, that our values represent nothing more than our "doing our own thing," which it is inappropriate to adhere to when they differ from prevalent ones.

The teaching of enacted law can move us toward what is right, but toward what is wrong as well. *Vox populi, vox Dei* may (or may not) be a metaphorical shorthand statement of good political philosophy. Taken as a sure guide to moral truth, however, it is idolatry, making of the law a graven image. What Norman Beck wrote about the authority of Scripture (p. 87, above) can be said with equal truth about enacted law, substituting the word "political" for "scriptural" or "religious": "Subscription to the significant authority of [political] traditions and of institutions is appropriate and essential in order that there may be proper accountability within a [political] community. Subscription to them as infallible and ultimate authority, however, is idolatrous."[370]

CODA

O how may I ever express that secret word
O how can I say He is not like this, and He is like that?
If I say that He is within me, the universe is ashamed:
If I say that He is without me, it is falsehood.
He makes the inner and the outer worlds to be indivisibly one;
The conscious and the unconscious, both are His footstools.
He is neither manifest nor hidden; He is neither revealed nor unrevealed:
There are no words to that which He is.

KABIR[371]

With what shall I come before the Lord,
    and bow myself before God on high?
Shall I come before him with burnt offerings,
    with calves a year old?
Will the Lord be pleased with thousands of rams,
    with ten thousands of rivers of oil?
Shall I give my firstborn for my transgression,
    the fruit of my body for the sin of my soul?
He has told you, O mortal, what is good;
    and what does the Lord require of you
    but to do justice,
    and to love kindness,
and to walk humbly with your God?

MICAH 6:8

We have seen what Jesus was like. If we now wish to treat him as our God, we would have to conclude that our God does not want to be served by us, but wants to serve us; God does not want to be given the highest possible rank and status in our society, but wants to take the lowest place and to be without any rank and status; God does not want to be feared and obeyed, but wants to be recognized in the sufferings of the poor and the weak; God is not supremely indifferent and detached, but is irrevocably committed to the liberation of humankind, for God has chosen to be identified with all people in a spirit of solidarity and compassion.

ALBERT NOLAN[372]

NOTES

1. The factual description in the text, and the quotations that follow, are taken from the judicial opinions in *United States v. Seeger*, 326 F.2d 846 (2d Cir. 1964), and 163 U.S. 65 (1965).

2. The extent to which the obligation to act rationally is or gives rise to a *moral* obligation is a matter of much dispute among philosophers. For an analysis of differing views on this question and the related one of the extent to which the actor's beliefs about a question of moral judgment are relevant, see Philippa Foot, "Does Moral Subjectivism Rest on a Mistake?" *Oxford Journal of Legal Studies*, 15 (1995), 1–14.

3. Scriptural translations are for most part those of the New Revised Standard Version, but I have used others for all or part of some passages, where I have preferred the sense or the aesthetics of the other rendition.

4. Daniel Maguire, *The Moral Core of Judaism and Christianity: Reclaiming the Revolution* (Minneapolis: Fortress Press, 1993), p. 42.

5. My law teacher colleague Tom Shaffer points out that the word "metaphysical" is often used with an undertone of sarcasm, to suggest subliminally the inherent incompatibility of claims about the nature of Reality with respectable intellectual work. I do not have any such connotation in mind. Metaphysics is not paraphysics. For a discussion of the attitude that Shaffer has in mind, see p. 60, below.

6. Some widely noted examples of current critique are Stephen L. Carter, *The Culture of Disbelief: How American Law and Politics Trivializes Religious Devotion* (New York: Basic Books, 1993); Kent Greenawalt, *Religious Convictions and Political Choice* (New York: Oxford University Press, 1988); Michael J. Perry, *Morality, Politics, and Law* (New York: Oxford University Press, 1988); Michael J. Perry, *Love and Power: The Role of Religion and Morality in American Politics* (New York: Oxford University Press, 1991); Garry Wills, *Under God: Religion and American Politics* (New York; Simon & Schuster, 1990).

Much of this writing, including that hospitable to a greater role for religiously grounded priorities in setting public policy, is not about the religious experience at all, but rather about what law teacher David Smolin terms "the application of a secular philosophy . . . which simply takes religion and politics as a subject of investigation." David M.

Smolin, "Cracks in the Mirrored Prison: An Evangelical Critique of Secularist Academic and Judicial Myths Regarding the Relationship of Religion and American Politics," *Loyola of Los Angeles Law Review*, 29 (1996), 1507.

7. James Boyd White, "What Can a Lawyer Learn from Literature?" *Harvard Law Review*, 102 (1989), 2017–2047. One instance of an analysis that acknowledges the relevance of the author's own life experience to his policy views, and begins with a description of that experience, is Sanford Levinson's "Some Reflections on Multiculturalism, 'Equal Concern and Respect,' and the Establishment of the First Amendment," *University of Richmond Law Review*, 27 (1993) 489–506.

8. Poet Kathleen Norris, speaking of her craft, has described her stance in ways that resonate with the objective here. Poets, she asserts, "speak with no authority but that which the reader is willing to grant them. Our task is not to convince but to suggest, evoke, explore." Kathleen Norris, The *Cloister Walk* (New York: Riverhead Books, 1997), p. 37.

9. Warren Lehman, "The Pursuit of a Client's Interest," *Michigan Law Review*, 77 (1979), 1078–1098.

10. *Franz Rosenzweig: His Life and Thought*, ed. Nahum N. Glatzer (New York: Schocken Books, 1953), p. 179.

11. See Oliver Wendell Holmes, Jr., *The Common Law*, ed. Mark DeWolfe Howe (Cambridge, Mass.: The Belknap Press of Harvard University Press, 1963), p. 5.

12. John B. Cobb, Jr., "Toward a Christocentric Catholic Theology," in *Toward a Universal Theology of Religion*, ed. Leonard Swidler (Maryknoll, N.Y.: Orbis Books, 1987), p. 89.

13. The Bund, a fraternal benefit society of the sort that many immigrant ethnic and religious groups had formed, was during the '30s strongly pro-Nazi and anti-Semitic in its public face. Smith and Coughlin, two enormously popular figures, combined a form of populism, and fierce hostility to the New Deal, with a viciously militant anti-Semitism. See Leo P. Ribuffo, *The Old Christian Right: The Protestant Far Right from the Great Depression to the Cold War* (Philadelphia: Temple University Press, 1983); Glen Jeansonne, *Gerald L. K. Smith: Minister of Hate* (New Haven, Conn.: Yale University Press, 1988); John Roy Carlson, *Under Cover: My Four Years in the Nazi Underworld of America* (New York: E. P. Dutton, 1943), pp. 54–69, 304–336. For a brief account, see Arthur M. Schlesinger., Jr, *The Politics of Upheaval* (Boston: Houghton Mifflin, 1960), pp. 16–28, 64–65, 550–559. *The Brooklyn Tablet* was the official newspaper of the Roman Catholic Diocese of Brooklyn, and was similarly explicitly and vigorously hostile to the "Jewish influence" in American life. See Leonard Dinnerstein, *Antisemitism in America* (New York: Oxford University Press, 1994), pp. 114, 121–122.

14. President Roosevelt's 1941 State of the Union Message, largely devoted to the rearmament program designed to aid the Allies in their resistance to the advance of Nazi armed forces in Europe, spoke of a world "founded upon four essential human freedoms": Freedom of Speech and Religion, and Freedom from Want and Fear. *The State of the Union Messages of the Presidents, 1790–1966*, 3 vols. (New York: Chelsea House, 1966), 3:2855–2860.

Jesse Owens, the black Olympic track star, was seen to push Nazi racism down Hitler's throat by winning four gold medals in the Berlin games in 1936. The dramatic story about Hitler's leaving the stadium to avoid receiving him as victor was apparently more legend than fact—see William J. Baker, *Jesse Owens: An American Life* (New York: The Free Press, 1986), pp. 89–106—but it was taken as true during my childhood. (What was true, but kept from public notice in those days, was the complicity of the American Olympic Committee in removing two Jewish members of the team from competition in the 400-meter relay finals. See ibid., pp. 103–105.) Joe Louis, the Brown Bomber, was heavyweight champion of the world. His achievements too took on global political significance when he knocked out the German champion, Max Schmeling. For a stirring account of another Louis fight, as told through the eyes of an eight-year-old black girl in the prewar rural South, see Maya Angelou, *I Know Why the Caged Bird Sings* (New York: Bantam Books, 1971), pp. 111–115.

Hank Greenberg, the Hall of Fame Detroit first baseman of the '30s, was one of the few Jewish ballplayers in the Major Leagues. There is a complete listing of Jewish Major League players and their records in the appendix to Peter C. Bjarkman, "Six-Pointed Diamonds and the Ultimate Shiksa: Baseball and the American-Jewish Immigrant Experience," in *Cooperstown Symposium on Baseball and the American Culture*, ed. Alvin L. Hall (Westport, Conn.: Meckler, 1991), p. 338.

Nicolo Sacco and Bartolomeo Vanzetti, and Tom Mooney, were political radicals of the '20s, ethnically Italian and Irish, respectively, who were convicted of crimes in notorious trials of the period. See Sidney Lens, *Radicalism in America* (New York: Thomas Y. Crowell, 1969), pp. 249–251, 279–281. Sidney Hillman, a Jewish immigrant from Eastern Europe, was a labor leader, a founder of the CIO, and an influential adviser to President Roosevelt during the Second World War. The fact that one with his political views, labor-union background, religion, and immigrant status was near the center of political power unleashed enormous hostility. See Steve Fraser, *Labor Will Rule: Sidney Hillman and the Rise of American Labor* (New York: The Free Press, 1991), pp. 526–530.

15. The practice of girls becoming *bat mitzvah* was literally unheard of in the world of my childhood.

16. This is how I have always understood the story. *The Encyclopedia of Religion* attributes to "Hindu mythology" a version that reverses things a bit: "the earth rests on the back of elephants, which rest, in turn, on the back of a huge tortoise." Manabu Waida, "Elephants," in *The Encyclopedia of Religion*, ed. Mircea Eliade, 15 vols. (New York: Macmillan, 1987), 5:82.

17. Paul Mendes-Flohr, *Divided Passions: Jewish Intellectuals and the Experience of Modernity* (Detroit: Wayne State University Press, 1991), p. 418.

18. See the brief summary in Lucy S. Dawidowicz, *The War Against the Jews, 1933–1945* (Toronto: Bantam Books, 1986), pp. 357–359.

19. Wendell L. Willkie, *One World* (New York: Simon & Schuster, 1943).

20. For published fruits of this work, see Elizabeth Dvorkin, Jack Himmelstein, and Howard Lesnick, *Becoming a Lawyer: A Humanistic Perspective on Legal Education and Professionalism* (St. Paul, Minn.: West Publishing Company, 1981), and a symposium of essays, published under the title, "Reassessing Law Schooling: The Sterling Forest Group," *New York University Law Review*, 53 (1978), 561–591.

21. *Faith and Practice*, the Quaker handbook published by London Yearly Meeting (London: Headley Brothers, Ltd, 1960), attributes a statement much like this to William Penn. See Extract 183.

22. Sydney Carter, "George Fox," in *Rise Up Singing*. Ed. Peter Blood and Annie Patterson (Bethlehem, Penn.: Sing Out Corp., 1988), p. 42.

23. On the response of Pope Pius and the Vatican to the Nazis' program of genocide, see the detailed, country-by-country study by John F. Morley, *Vatican Diplomacy and the Jews During the Holocaust, 1939–43* (New York: KTAV Publishing House, 1980), and the summary of the Pope's role and responsibility, ibid., pp. 207–209. The Legion of Decency was a Catholic organization that monitored motion pictures for immorality, which as far as I was aware translated wholly into relatively mild departures from traditional notions of reticence and propriety regarding sex. Its "C" rating ("Condemned") was something that the industry tried mightily to avoid. Francis Cardinal Spellman, archbishop of New York, was the quintessence of pre-conciliar Catholicism: conservative in national and global politics, fiercely parochial in religion, and a skilled and aggressive practitioner of behind-the-scenes political influence in the City. For an excellent biography, see John Cooney, *The American Pope: The Life and Times of Francis Cardinal Spellman* (New York: Times Books, 1984).

Bing Crosby? As the saying goes, you had to have been there—to have seen his "priest" movies and experienced his caroling *"Adeste Fide-*

lis" (the Latin rite, no "O Come All Ye Faithful" for Bing)—to know why I include him. In retrospect, I understand the Crosby phenomenon as part of the emergence of the Catholic community from the "ghetto-ization" of traditional American anti-Catholicism, and an egalitarian development. To a Jewish teen-ager in Cardinal Spellman's New York, however, that perspective was far beyond reach.

24. For a detailed description of a few illustrative events during the Second World War, see Cooney, *American Pope*, pp. 133–145. Some of the broader story is told in a book that appeared (to great controversy over its wide-ranging critique of the role of the Catholic clergy) during my teen-age years: Paul Blanshard's *American Freedom and Catholic Power* (Boston: Beacon Press, 1949). See pp. 244–261 for the author's account of the Vatican's role in international politics during the period from 1922 to 1949.

25. On the tradition of anti-Semitism, see p. 102, below. On the social teachings of Pope Paul VI, see Donal Dorr, *Option for the Poor: A Hundred Years of Vatican Social Teaching* (Maryknoll, N.Y.: Orbis Books, 1983), pp. 139–206. For the major documents, see David J. O'Brien and Thomas A. Shannon, *Catholic Social Thought: The Documentary Heritage* (Maryknoll, N.Y.: Orbis Books, 1992), pp. 238–345. For a skeptical assessment from a conservative perspective, see Michael Novak, *Freedom with Justice: Catholic Social Thought and Liberal Institutions* (San Francisco: Harper & Row, 1984), pp. 133–148.

In public memory, these important teachings have been eclipsed by the decision of Paul VI to reaffirm, over the advice of a broad spectrum of Catholic opinion, the rigid disapproval of every use of "artificial" methods of contraception. The encyclical *Humanae Vitae*, while praised by theological and political conservatives, is widely regarded as the single most powerful source of disaffection among the laity. (For the story of the struggle that preceded the issuance of *Humanae Vitae*, see Robert McClory, *The Turning Point: The Inside Story of the Papal Birth Control Commission* . . . [New York: Crossroad, 1995]). Theologian Rosemary Radford Ruether characterizes it as "perhaps one of the greatest moral disasters of the Roman Catholic Church" ("Watershed for Faithful Catholics," *Conscience: A Journal of Prochoice Catholic Opinion* [Winter 1993–94], 31). See also the eloquent essay by Father Owen O'Sullivan, "The Silent Schism," *Cross Currents* (Winter 1994–95), 518–526; and a symposium issue of *Conscience: A Journal of Prochoice Catholic Opinion*, 18, No. 2 (Summer 1997).

26. Rodger Kamenetz, *The Jew in the Lotus: A Poet's Rediscovery of Jewish Identity in Buddhist India* (San Francisco: HarperSanFrancisco, 1994), pp. 250–251.

27. A friend has recounted an analogous reaction to her first Quaker

Meeting. She read, on the card that often is posted outside the Meeting-house explaining Quaker Worship to newcomers, the line: "Meeting begins when the first attender sits down, and silently turns his or her mind to God." For her, coming from a Catholic background, where it was very clear who was (and who was not) authorized to open the service, this idea was a dramatic witness to the Quaker testimony on equality, more telling perhaps than the fact that there is no clergy, be-cause the authority to begin Meeting is not shared only by officers or elders.

28. Most of this learning has been experiential, but one book that has supported it is Lawrence Kushner's *Honey from the Rock: Ten Gates of Jewish Mysticism* (San Francisco: Harper & Row, 1983).

29. Kamenetz, *Jew in the Lotus*, p. 251.

30. H. Richard Niebuhr, *The Responsible Self: An Essay in Christian Moral Philosophy* (New York: Harper & Row, 1963), p. 43.

31. Mircea Eliade, Preface, in *The Encyclopedia of Religion*, ed. Mircea Eliade. 15 vols. (New York: Macmillan, 1987), 1:xi.

32. Martin Buber, *Eclipse of God: Studies in the Relation Between Reli-gion and Philosophy* (New York: Harper, 1952), p. 7. For Buber's re-sponse, see pp. 7–9.

33. Thich Nhat Hanh, *Being Peace* (Berkeley, Calif.: Parallax Press, 1987), p. 89.

34. For a description of the shift over several centuries in the mean-ing of belief toward "intellectual assent" rather than "approval and trust," see James Turner, *Without God, Without Creed: The Origin of Un-belief in America* (Baltimore: The Johns Hopkins University Press, 1985), p. 24. A contemporary example of an unalloyed avowal of a proposi-tional meaning of religious belief is Article VI of the Articles of Affirma-tion and Denial of the Chicago Statement on Biblical Hermeneutics, issued by the International Council on Biblical Inerrancy in 1982: "We affirm that the Bible expresses God's truth in propositional statements. . . . We further affirm that a statement is true if it represents matters as they really are, but is an error if it misrepresents the facts." International Council on Biblical Inerrancy, *Hermeneutics, Inerrancy, and the Bible*, ed. Earl D. Radmacher and Robert D. Preus (Grand Rapids, Mich.: Aca-demic Books/Zondervan, 1984), pp. 881, 882.

35. See Rabbi Joseph H. Hertz, *The Authorised Daily Prayer Book*, rev. ed. (New York: Bloch Publishing, 1961), p. 209n5. On the title of the king of Persia, see Edwin M. Yamauchi, *Persia and the Bible* (Grand Rapids, Mich.: Baker Book House, 1990), p. 71.

36. Rabbi Joseph Soloveitchik attributes to Rabbi Akiba the teach-ing that, at Sinai, God "bent down the heavens, lowering them to the top of the mountain." Joseph B. Soloveitchik, *Halakhic Man* (Philadel-

phia: Jewish Publication Society of America, 1983), p. 45. The description of Mary is that of the Second Draft of a proposed Pastoral Letter of the U.S. Catholic Bishops; see the National Conference of Catholic Bishops, "One in Christ Jesus: A Pastoral Response to the Concerns of Women for Church and Society," in *Origins: Catholic News Documentary Service*, April 5, 1990, para. 137.

37. Being a Jew, I set aside the question whether Christians and Muslims, who are in a significant sense descended theologically (if for the most part not biologically) from Moses and the biblical "Israelite community," are to hear the admonition as addressed to them. It surely embraces all Jews.

38. See note 60.

39. Jewish theologian Neil Gillman has written profoundly, in my judgment, of the process of change in the interpretation of Torah from one generation to another, and of the manner in which he finds such evolution provided for in Talmudic understanding of divine revelation itself. See his *Sacred Fragments: Recovering Theology for the Modern Jew* (Philadelphia: Jewish Publication Society of America, 1990), pp. xxiv–xxv.

40. This passage appears in Rabbi Lamm's contribution to a remarkable symposium, "The State of Jewish Belief" in *Commentary*, August 1966, p. 110.

Compare the reference, by Jesuit theologian Avery Dulles, to the "rather credulous attitude toward the supernatural" of a "prescientific age," which read the Bible "in a naïvely literalistic way." Rejected officially by the Catholic Church in favor of an "historical-critical approach" only since 1943, the traditional view is still held to "by fundamentalists inside and outside the Catholic fold." Avery Dulles, "*Sensus Fidelium* [The Sense of the Faithful]," *America*, November 1, 1986, p. 242.

41. *The Midrash on Psalms* I, trans. William G. Braude (New Haven, Conn.: Yale University Press, 1959), p. 345. Compare the statement of the U.S. Catholic Bishops, in discussing the use of male imagery for God, that the reason God has no gender is that God is "pure spirit." "One in Christ Jesus," para. 135. For a strikingly similar statement from the other end of the Christian spectrum, a service of a group of rural Southern members of a snake-handling sect, see Dennis Covington, *Salvation on Sand Mountain: Snake Handling and Redemption in Southern Appalachia* (Reading, Mass.: Addison-Wesley, 1995), p. 16: "'This God we worship, he's a living God'. *Amen.* 'God ain't no white-bearded old man up in the sky. He's a spirit'. *Amen. Thank God.* 'He's a spirit. He ain't got no body'. *Amen. Thank God.* 'The only body he's got is us.' *Amen.*"

I should note that the translation, "God answered him with a voice," which I have quoted, is at variance with the New Revised Standard and many other contemporary Christian translations, "God would answer him in thunder"; see *The Complete Parallel Bible* (New York: Oxford University Press, 1993), pp. 152–153.

42. Robert Bolt, *A Man for All Seasons* (New York: Random House, 1962); Nikos Kazantzakis, *God's Pauper: St. Francis of Assisi*, trans. Peter A. Bien (London and Boston: Faber, 1975).

43. Michael Lerner, *Jewish Renewal: A Path to Healing and Transformation* (New York: G. P. Putnam's Sons, 1994), p. 77. I find a not dissimilar thought in the account of the Resurrection given by a conservative Catholic theologian, Luke Timothy Johnson; see his *The Real Jesus: The Misguided Quest for the Historical Jesus and the Truth of the Traditional Gospels* (San Francisco: HarperSanFrancisco, 1996), pp. 135–138, and generally chap. 6.

44. See Karen Armstrong's discussion of a similar quality of the central figures of Greek tragedy: *A History of God: The 4000-Year Quest of Judaism, Christianity, and Islam* (New York: Alfred A. Knopf, 1993), p. 37. I do not recall the source of the Piercy line, and have been unable to locate it.

45. Compare Ronald Goetz's review of William Dean's *The Religious Critic in American Culture* in *Theology Today*, 52 (1995), 414, criticizing, as "not significantly different from atheism," the view that "some projections [specifically, the experience of the sacred] take on a life of their own" through a "critical social process."

46. My law school colleague Heidi Hurd has been my guide, through her writing and in conversation, to an extensive philosophical literature that distinguishes two sorts of authority. Content-dependent claims are "heuristic guides to detecting the existence and probable truth" of reasons to act in a certain way, reasons of which we may have been unaware until the claim gives us "a better reason to think that the premises [grounding that action] are true." Content-independent claims, such as the request of a friend, the instruction (to a child) of a parent, or—in traditional religion—the command of God, supply in themselves reasons to believe that did not exist before their utterance. They derive their influence from their source rather than their content, and are of dispositive character or not depending on other factors. See Heidi Hurd, "Challenging Authority," *Yale Law Journal*, 100 (1991), 1615–16.

47. See the discussion of the gap between justified belief and knowledge in the section on "Discernment" in Chapter 4, p. 88–89.

48. Dorothy Soelle, with Shirley A. Cloyes, *To Work and to Love: A Theology of Creation* (Philadelphia: Fortress Press, 1984), p. 42.

49. The first quotation is from Rabbi Heschel's essay "No Religion

Is an Island," in *No Religion Is an Island: Abraham Joshua Heschel and Interreligious Dialogue*, ed. Harold Kasimow and Byron L. Sherwin (Maryknoll, N.Y.: Orbis Books, 1991), p. 9; the second, his *The Sabbath* (Cleveland: World Publishing Co., 1963) (published with *The Earth Is the Lord's*), p. 75.

Rudolf Otto wrote of the "clear overplus of meaning" that the word "holy" has, beyond "the consummation of moral goodness." *The Idea of the Holy*, trans. John W. Harvey (London: Oxford University Press, 1972), p. 5.

50. Ibid., p. 110.

51. Maguire, *Moral Core of Judaism and Christianity*, p. 39.

52. Maguire goes on to articulate the converse relation as well. Morality is aided in "taking root" by religion. "Morality is compelling, obligatory, and noble because it embodies something of the awe-inspiring sacred." Ibid., p. 40. I develop this relation too more fully below; see pp. 79–82.

53. Otto, *Idea of the Holy*, pp. 8–40.

54. Mircea Eliade, *The Sacred and the Profane: The Nature of Religion*, trans. Willard R. Trask (New York: Harcourt, Brace, 1959), p. 10.

55. Samuel H. Weintraub, "The Spiritual Ecology of Kashrut," *The Reconstructionist*, Winter 1991–1992, p. 13.

56. Maguire, *Moral Core of Judaism and Christianity*, p. 33. Note the author's linking of purity with "caring in all life." Christian writers, even those committed to a radical revision of the traditional hostile Christian understanding of the Judaism of Jesus's day, often tend to view the prevalent Jewish belief-system of that time as having dichotomized purity and compassion, upholding the first over the other, and Jesus as continuing that dichotomization but reversing values, upholding compassion at the expense of purity. See, for example, Marcus J. Borg, *Meeting Jesus Again for the First Time: The Historical Jesus and the Heart of Contemporary Faith* (San Francisco: HarperSanFrancisco, 1994), pp. 50–58. There is a movement in contemporary Judaism, of which the Weintraub article, in note 55, above, is an example, to seek to integrate the two aspects of holiness.

57. Abraham Joshua Heschel, *Man Is Not Alone* (New York: Farrar, Straus, & Giroux, 1951), chap. 2. Compare this passage from Rabbi Rami Shapiro's rendition of the third-century *Ethics of the Fathers*:

> Wonder is the heart of life.
>> beating in the breast of the living.
> Do not imagine that you merit wonder—
>> only dare to encounter it.

Rami M. Shapiro, *Wisdom of the Jewish Sages: A Modern Reading of* Pirke Avot (New York: Bell Tower, 1993), p. 102. For a good brief discussion of Heschel's term, see Gillman, *Sacred Fragments*, pp. 131–132.

58. *The Empty Chair: Finding Hope and Joy—Timeless Wisdom from a Hasidic Master, Rebbe Nachman of Breslav*, ed. Moshe Mykoff (Woodstock, Vt.: Jewish Lights Publishing, 1994), p. 59 (R. Nachman); Soloveitchik, *Halakhic Man*, p. 46; Harold M. Schulweis, *For Those Who Can't Believe: Overcoming the Obstacles to Faith* (New York: HarperCollins, 1994), pp. 56–57. Karen Armstrong asserts that "the essential paradox at the heart of the religious quest is that the sacred manifests itself in the profane, the absolute in the relative, the eternal in the temporal." *Jerusalem: One City, Three Faiths* (New York: Ballantine Books, 1996), p. 147.

59. Richard Stith, "Images, Spirituality, and Law," *Journal of Law and Religion*, 10 (1993–1994), 42n34.

60. William Blake, "Auguries of Innocence," in *Blake's Poetry and Designs*, ed. Mary Lynn Johnson and John Ernest Grant (New York: W. W. Norton, 1979), p. 209.

Jewish theologian Daniel Matt has eloquently, albeit in prose and in many more words, expressed a like idea: "Divinity pervades the universe: sparks in every single thing, energy latent in each subatomic particle. We can raise the sparks, restoring the world to God. We become aware that whatever we do or see or touch or imagine is part of the oneness, a pattern of energy. Religion is transformed from a list of do's and don'ts into a spiritual adventure. The simplest, most mundane activity becomes an opportunity to expand awareness, to exercise compassion.

"God is not some separate being up there. She is right here, in the bark of a tree, in a friend's voice, in a stranger's eye. The world is teeming with God. Since God is in everything, one can serve God through everything, by raising the sparks. In looking for the spark, we discover that what is ordinary is spectacular. The holy deed is doing what needs to be done.

"God is not somewhere else, hidden from us, but rather, right here, hidden from us. Enslaved by our routines, we rush from one chore to the next, from event to event, rarely allowing ourselves to pause and open. Our sense of wonder has shriveled, victimized by our pace of life. How, then, can we find God? A clue is provided by one of the many names of *Shekhinah*. She is called ocean, well, garden, apple orchard. She is also called *zot*, which means simply 'this.' God is right here, in this very moment, fresh and unexpected, taking you by surprise. God is this." "Beyond the Personal God," *The Reconstructionist,* Spring 1994, p. 46. The *Shekhinah* is the divine presence, manifested as feminine, from a word signifying dwelling within, hence denoting the immanent aspect of God.

61. Abraham Joshua Heschel, *God in Search of Man: A Philosophy of Judaism* (New York: Harper & Row, 1955), p. 49.

62. Vanessa Ochs, *Words on Fire: One Woman's Journey into the Sacred* (San Diego: Harcourt Brace Jovanovich, 1990), p. 5.

63. Heschel, *God in Search of Man*, p. 75.

64. This line is inscribed on a wall commemorating Penn's life, near Second and Market Streets in Philadelphia. A slightly different version of the statement appears in London Yearly Meeting, *Faith and Practice*, Extract 183.

65. *The Babylonian Talmud*, ed. Isidore Epstein (London: The Soncino Press, 1935), Seder Nezikin IV, Tractate Aboth, III:6, p. 30. The first three words are bracketed in the original, to signify that they have been added by the translator. I have substituted "one or more" for the text's "ten," based on the remainder of the passage, which explains why "the same applies" even if there are five, then four, then three, two and, finally, one. On the *Shekhinah*, see note 60, above.

This passage is strikingly similar to a famous Christian Scripture, Matthew 18:20: "When two or three are gathered together in my name, there am I in the midst of them." It should come as no surprise that the thought has long since occurred to others; see the examination by a Catholic theologian, expert in the period, of the likely origins of both passages, who concludes that "there is reasonable probability that some literary relationship exists," and that the most probable one is that the Gospel passage is "based on a Jewish tradition and not vice versa." Joseph Sievers, "Where Two or Three . . . : The Rabbinic Concept of *Shekhinah* and Matthew 18:20," in *The Jewish Roots of Christian Liturgy*, ed. Eugene J. Fisher (New York: Paulist Press, 1990), p. 53.

66. Judith Plaskow, *Standing Again at Sinai: Judaism from a Feminist Perspective* (New York: Harper & Row, 1990), p. 157.

67. Harold S. Kushner, *When Children Ask About God* (New York: Schocken Books, 1989), p. 23. Protestant theologian Carter Heyward says it this way: "God is 'no one' but is rather a transpersonal spirit, power in relation, which depends upon humanity for making good/ making justice/making love/making God incarnate in the world. To do so is to undo evil. The doing of good and the undoing of evil is a human act, a human responsibility. God is our power to do this." Carter Heyward, *The Redemption of God: A Theology of Mutual Relation* (Washington, D.C.: University Press of America, 1982), p. 159.

Jesse Holmes, a Quaker teacher of the interwar period, expressed a similar thought in somewhat different words: "God means to us just that unifying influence which makes men long for a brotherly world; and our whole religion is built on the assumption of God as the Chief Imperative of human existence. To us God is . . . the name of certain common experiences of mankind by which they are bound together into unity." Jesse Holmes, "To the Scientifically-Minded," *Friends Journal*, June 1992, p. 23 (reprint of an essay first published in 1928).

Carmelite priest Carlos Mesters says it this way: "Where is God? Where can I find God? The answer is that God enters human life and is discovered wherever human beings are trying to be faithful to themselves and others, wherever they are looking for an absolute value and trying to live it." Carlos Mesters, *God, Where Are You? Rediscovering the Bible* (Maryknoll, N.Y.: Orbis Books, 1995), pp. 25–26.

68. Quoted in Armstrong, *History of God*, p. 199.

69. Cheri, *That Which You Are Seeking Is Causing You to Seek* (1990). The Introduction begins: "If we didn't already know the experience of what we're looking for, we would never look. It simply wouldn't occur to us. . . . We know we are separate, but separate from what? We feel alone, isolated, abandoned—but what are we missing? What have we lost?" (The book, which does not disclose the author's last name, is published by the Center for the Practice of Zen Buddhist Meditation in Mountain View, California.)

Rabbi Zalman Schachter-Salomi teaches that God calls to us, not from the past, or even the present, but from the future. As Michael Lerner ascribes the thought to Reb Zalman: "It is as if God is the voice of what could and ought to be, calling us from the future and moving us toward the fulfillment of our possibilities. *Jewish Renewal*, p. 36.

70. White, "What Can a Lawyer Learn from Literature?" 2016–18.

71. Kurt Bendall and Frederick Ferre, *Exploring the Logic of Faith: A Dialogue on the Relation of Modern Philosophy to Christian Faith* (New York: Association Press, 1962), p. 52.

Chapter 1, "Paradise: Myth or Reality?" in Mesters, *God, Where Are You?* applies this approach to the story of the Fall: "The biblical author was not thinking primarily of what had taken place in the distant past; he was thinking of what was going on around him, and perhaps even within himself. . . . He wants everyone to wake up to their personal responsibilities, to tackle the roots of evil in themselves" (p. 14).

Rabbi Heschel may have had a similar idea in mind when he said that scriptural words "must neither be taken literally or figuratively but *responsively.*" *God in Search of Man*, p. 182.

Biblical scholar John Dominic Crossan, asked in an interview whether Jesus was "virginally conceived," answered, yes; he responded to the question, "what does your answer mean?" with an account of the Greek story that Augustus was born as a result of Apollo's impregnating his mother as she slept. Everyone in the ancient world, Crossan asserted, whether they believed that story "literally or symbolically, . . . took it very seriously. Augustus had established peace in the Roman world. Augustus was divine."

As for Jesus, looking at the story "as a historian," he does not accept it as historical. Yet, he goes on, "As a Christian, I believe the Jesus story, not the Augustus story, because the story means, 'Where do I find God?' I do not find God in a Palatine palace with imperial pomp. I find God in a stable at Bethlehem with a peasant kid.

"I would be willing to argue, though it's harder to prove this, that that's what it meant for Luke, too. That if you really pinned him back and asked, 'Now is this biology we're talking about? Could we check this with doctors?' he'd probably be disgusted. I don't know if he could understand the question. . . . Luke knows what he's up against. The options are Augustus or Jesus. It had nothing to do with biology. It has to do with where you find God." James Halstead, "The Orthodox Unorthodoxy of John Dominic Crossan: An Interview," *Cross Currents,* 45 (1995–1996), 519–520.

72. Heschel, *Man Is Not Alone,* pp. 5–6. Neil Gillman introduces in these words a brief, eloquent expression of this concept of truth as applied to expressions of "a reality that lies behind or beyond human experience": "Their truth lies in their ability to reveal unanticipated dimensions of meaning in our lives, to grip our emotions, to inspire us to act in certain ways and strive for certain goals, and most important, to lend infinite meaning to our lives in the here and now." *Sacred Fragments,* p. 271; see also pp. 271–272. To like effect, see Dennis Hamm, "Burning Bush, Barren Fig Tree," *America,* March 7, 1998, p. 31: "our human experience of God is always somehow distinct from God."

That this approach is no latter-day heresy, see R. H. Snape, "Rabbinical and Early Christian Ethics," in *A Rabbinic Anthology,* ed. C. G. Montefiore and H. M. Loewe (Cleveland: World Publishing Co., 1963), p. 620: "Clement of Alexandria, at the beginning of the third century, implies throughout the existence of a double meaning in Scripture, and holds that the primary sense is only for babes in religion. His great successor Origen defended the method against the philosopher Celsus: 'Are the Greeks alone at liberty to convey a philosophical meaning in a secret covering?'"

73. Quoted in *Faith and Practice,* the Quaker handbook published by London Yearly Meeting, Extract 200.

74. Richard J. Niebanck, *By What Authority? The Making and Use of Social Statements* (New York: Lutheran Church in America, Division for Mission in North America, 1977), p. 10. The author criticizes "the equating of the literal word of Scripture with divine revelation," as an "unbiblical rationalism which treats the Scriptures as a sourcebook of propositional truth." Ibid., pp. 16–17.

The heterodox (to some, heretic) Episcopal Bishop John Shelby Spong has expressed the matter in terms much like those I have quoted in these paragraphs: "It is not the human description of the reality of God that is important and must be protected. Human descriptions, no matter how deeply sanctified by the passage of time, are not reality. . . . [R]eality itself . . . can only be pointed to; it can never be captured by human words." John Shelby Spong, *Liberating the Gospels: Reading the Bible with Jewish Eyes* (San Francisco: HarperSanFrancisco, 1996), p. 300. His book is a radical reconstruction of the Gospel story, viewing all but Jesus's life and death as efforts by the first (Jewish) Christians to find "the means to process this experience [the 'primal experience of Easter'] adequately." Ibid., p. 308.

75. See *A Hebrew and English Lexicon of the Old Testament*, ed. Francis Brown et al. (Chicago: Moody Press, 1973), pp. 434–435.

Martin Buber flatly calls "law" a "mis-translation": "In the Hebrew Bible Torah does not mean law, but direction, instruction, information." God is repeatedly called "not law-giver but teacher." Martin Buber, *Two Types of Faith*, trans. Norman P. Goldhawk (London: Routledge & Paul, 1951), pp. 56–57. Rabbi Heschel deems the Greek rendering of Torah as "nomos," translated as "law," a "fatal and momentous error." Scripture, he asserts, was "considered as teaching"; "the Torah is primarily *divine ways* rather than *divine laws*." Heschel, *God in Search of Man*, pp. 325, 288. See also Susan Handelman, "*Emunah*: The Craft of Faith," *Cross Currents*, Fall 1992, pp. 301, 303: translation as law is "very inaccurate and misleading"; Torah is "not simply a set of stories *about* the world, or a set of prescriptive laws, but the primordial design of the world."

76. Thomas L. Shaffer, "Judges as Prophets," *Texas Law Review*, 67 (1989), 1337.

77. See p. 4, above.

78. See Shaffer, "Judges as Prophets," 1337.

79. Maguire, *Moral Core of Judaism and Christianity*, p. 33.

80. See the entries in *Hebrew and English Lexicon of the Old Testament*, ed. Brown et al., p. 761. Abraham Joshua Heschel recounts this as the view of "some scholars," noting that others question the etymological relation between the two words. *God in Search of Man*, pp. 58, 59n7.

81. As a corrective to the common belief that God as "presence" is a lesser sort of deity than the traditional personal God of most believers, I cannot do better than refer to Rudolf Otto's marvelous essay "The Supra-Personal in the Numinous," Appendix V to *Idea of the Holy*. Compare p. 101.

For a defense of the "common belief" by a Christian analytic philosopher, see William P. Alston, "Realism and the Christian Faith," *International Journal for the Philosophy of Religion*, 38 (1995), esp. 45–47.

82. Compare the slightly different rendition attributed to St. Teresa by Andrew Harvey, *The Essential Mystics: The Soul's Journey into Truth* (San Francisco: HarperSanFrancisco, 1996), p. 206.

83. Schulweis, *For Those Who Can't Believe*, p. 61. To the same effect, see Jeffrey K. Salkin, *Being God's Partner* (Woodstock, Vt.: Jewish Lights Publishing, 1994), pp. 96–97. Rabbi Salkin quotes a hasidic saying, "Human beings are God's language." Ibid., p. 95.

Compare Neil Gillman's discussion of the views of Mordecai Kaplan, founder of Reconstructionism, in *Sacred Fragments*, pp. 18–19, 48–49.

84. *Babylonian Talmud*, ed. Isidore Epstein (London: The Soncino Press, 1935), Seder Nezikin III, Tractate Sanhedrin 98a, p. 664.

85. Compare Rabbi Harold Kushner's briefer, milder catalogue: *When Children Ask About God*, pp. 4–5.

86. To cite sufficient historical examples to document the indictment would be to write another book. Let Martin Luther's response to a peasant rebellion whose grievances he had acknowledged to be justified stand for millennia of similar instances: "[A]nyone who is killed fighting on the side of the rulers may be a true martyr in the eyes of God. . . . On the other hand, anyone who perishes on the peasants' side is an eternal firebrand of hell, for he bears the sword against God's word and is disobedient to him." Quoted in Merold Westphal, *Suspicion and Faith: The Religious Uses of Modern Atheism* (Grand Rapids, Mich.: W. B. Eerdmans, 1993; repr. New York: Fordham University Press, 1998), p. 177.

87. Roberto Unger, *Knowledge and Politics* (New York: The Free Press, 1975), p. 232.

88. Westphal, *Suspicion and Faith*, p. 175n11. Being a Christian, Westphal has naturally used Christian examples to illustrate his point. There are certainly Jewish ones, and I believe—albeit with the most fragmentary knowledge—Muslim ones as well. Indeed, the failing is not a product only of theistic belief-systems. Thai Buddhist Sulak Sivarska's indictment of his own tradition has a familiar ring: "Buddhism, as practiced in most Asian countries today, serves mainly to legitimize dictatorial regimes and multinational corporations." Sulak Sivarska, *Seeds of Peace: A Buddhist Vision for Renewing Society* (Berkeley, Calif.: Parallax Press, 1992), p. 68.

89. Merold Westphal has espoused "the hermeneutics of suspicion," the thesis that "from a religious point of view the atheism of Freud, Marx, and Nietzsche should be taken seriously as a stimulus to self-examination rather than refuted as an error." *Suspicion and Faith*, p. x. He notes that opposition to religion on moral rather than epistemological grounds "cannot be refuted by arguing for the truth of religious beliefs, for what suspicion attacks is the *function* of religious beliefs." Ibid., p. 152.

Daniel Maguire sees religions as (in the words of the title to his first chapter) "an unlikely savior." *Moral Core of Judaism and Christianity*, p. 1.

Christianity, he asserts, is largely "lost in its doctrinal and ecclesial constructs and trapped in tangential moral concerns," while an "overly segregated Judaism has defaulted on the universalist dream of Isaiah." Yet he describes in passionate terms how both religions were "moral revolutions of classical proportions," which can find the "rescue" they need by attention to their roots. The quoted passages appear on pp. 3, 4, ix.

90. Martha Nussbaum, *Love's Knowledge: Essays on Philosophy and Literature* (New York: Oxford University Press, 1990), p. 3. See also, to similar effect but speaking of "narrative" ethics rather than literature, James M. Gustafson, "Moral Discourse About Medicine: A Variety of Forms," *Journal of Medicine and Philosophy*, 15 (1990), 137.

91. James Boyd White, "Response to Roger Cramton's Article," *Journal of Legal Education*, 37 (1987), 533.

92. Sallie McFague, *Speaking in Parables: A Study in Metaphor and Theology* (Philadelphia: Fortress Press, 1975), p. 45.

Jesus also taught by way of aphorisms, "short, memorable sayings, great 'one-liners.' . . . The aphorisms and parables of Jesus function in a particular way: they are invitational forms of speech. Jesus used them to invite his hearers to see something they might not otherwise see." Borg, *Meeting Jesus Again for the First Time*, p. 70. See also the discussion, pp. 70–75.

93. Bendall and Ferre, *Exploring the Logic of Faith*, pp. 65–66. (For the parable of the lost sheep, see Luke 15:4–7.) See also Don Cupitt, *Taking Leave of God* (New York: Crossroad, 1981), p. 54: "[T]o believe in God is simply to declare an intention to be loyal to religious values whatever happens."

94. Borg, *Meeting Jesus Again for the First Time*, p. 74.

95. National Conference of Catholic Bishops, *Economic Justice for All: Pastoral Letter on Catholic Social Teaching and the U.S. Economy* (Washington, D.C.: U.S. Catholic Conference, 1986), p. 166. Catholic writer Henri Nouwen sees in the Eucharist "a movement, the movement from resentment to gratitude, that is, from a hardened heart to a grateful heart." Henri J. M. Nouwen, *With Burning Hearts: A Meditation on the Eucharistic Life* (Maryknoll, N.Y.: Orbis Books, 1994), p. 13.

96. James A. Gustafson, *Theology and Christian Ethics* (Philadelphia: United Church Press, 1974), pp. 169–170. Mordecai Kaplan has written in a similar vein of the human ability to transcend the tension between faith and doubt, and between the awareness of evil and the awareness of goodness in the world. Mordecai A. Kaplan, *The Future of the American Jew* (New York: Macmillan, 1948), pp. 235–236.

97. Emily Fowler Hartigan, "The Power of Language Beyond Words: Law as Invitation," *Harvard Civil Rights–Civil Liberties Law Review*, 26 (1991), 89.

98. Michael Moore, "Moral Reality," *Wisconsin Law Review* (1982), 1064. Martha Nussbaum, speaking of what she terms "abstract values"—"ethical standards that are independent of a particular culture"—admonishes us that "we should not forget the liberating role that such value-talk can play, in asserting the claims of the powerless to a form of life more in keeping with human dignity and personhood." Martha C. Nussbaum, "Valuing Values: A Case for Reasoned Commitment," *Yale Journal of Law and the Humanities*, 6 (1994), 214.

99. Moore, "Moral Reality," 1062.

100. Hartigan, "Power of Language Beyond Words," 83.

101. Bolt, "A Man for All Seasons," pp. 52–53.

102. Otto, *Idea of the Holy*, Appendix XII. The quotations in the following paragraphs are from the few pages of this essay, which begins at p. 222. Job's affirmation is at 19:25.

103. Buber, *Two Types of Faith*, pp. 7–8. See note 34, above.

104. Nussbaum, *Love's Knowledge*, p. 265n7.

105. Marcus Borg emphasizes a distinction between resurrection and resuscitation: "Resuscitation intrinsically involves something happening to a corpse: A dead person comes back to life, resumes the life that he or she had before, and will die again. Whatever the resurrection of Jesus was, it wasn't that. Instead, resurrection means entry into another kind or mode of existence, one beyond life and death, beyond time and space. A resurrected person will not die again. Resurrection need not involve something happening to a corpse." Marcus J. Borg, "The Historian, the Christian, and Jesus," *Theology Today*, April 1995, p. 11.

106. Otto, *Idea of the Holy*, p. 224.

107. Frederick J. Streng, "Truth," in *The Encyclopedia of Religion*, ed. Mircea Eliade, 15 vols. (New York: Macmillan, 1987), 15:65.

108. Hartigan, "Power of Language Beyond Words," 86.

109. Martin Buber, *I and Thou*, trans. Walter Kaufmann (New York: Charles Scribner's Sons, 1970), p. 57.

110. Hartigan, "Power of Language Beyond Words," 82.

111. Mesters, *God, Where Are You?* p. 27.

112. Moore, "Moral Reality," 1116.

113. Otto's concept of "divination" is not "based on the authority and testimony of others," but is a firsthand experience, "the unconstrained recognition and inward acknowledgment that comes from deep within the soul, stirred spontaneously, apart from all conceptual theory." He regards it as cognition, a mode of knowing, but "not the result of logical compulsion; it does not follow from clearly conceived premises; it is an immediate, underivable judgement of pure recognition, and it follows a premise that defies exposition and springs directly from an irreducible feeling of the truth." See *Idea of the Holy*, chaps. 18–19; the

quoted passages are at pp. 145, 162, 170. Compare Martha Nussbaum's description of a "cataleptic condition," p. 45, above.

114. As quoted in the Reconstructionist prayer book, *Kol HaNeshama* (New York: The Reconstructionist Press, 1994), p. 489.

In all the translations of Scripture that I consulted, the passage quoted by Rabbi Heschel is rendered with a very different sense, "Abraham remained standing. . . ." I went to my law school colleague Leo Levin, as I have with other queries on many occasions (always to find the breadth of his learning and the depth of his wisdom matched only by the rigor of his modesty), to inquire about the compatibility of Heschel's version with the Hebrew text. In a forty-minute session of Torah study for which I will always be grateful, he shared with me the rabbinic teaching on the passage, which led him to conclude that Heschel's reading was permissible "as homiletics."

115. Otto, *Idea of the Holy*, Appendix VIII, pp. 210, 212.

116. Compare Leonard Swidler's "Interreligious and Interideological Dialogue: The Matrix for All Systematic Reflection Today," in *Toward a Universal Theology of Religion*, ed. Leonard W. Swidler (Maryknoll, N.Y.: Orbis Books, 1987), p. 5, with Paul J. Griffiths's "Why We Need Interreligious Polemics," *First Things*, June–July 1994, p. 31.

117. Griffiths, "Why We Need Interreligious Polemics," 31.

118. Ibid., 36.

119. McFague, *Speaking in Parables*, pp. 39, 28, 58n.

120. Andrew Harvey recounts a conversation in India with a Westerner who had taken up Buddhist practice. To the question "Have you become a Buddhist?" he got this reply: "[T]ruth is a living intensity transmitted from person to person, a living experience, not a set of practices or even philosophical positions. I revere Buddhism; I meditate in Buddhist ways; but I would not call myself a Buddhist or a Hindu." *A Journey in Ladakh* (Boston: Houghton Mifflin, 1983), p. 136.

A textured examination of the question of "worship in common" is Lawrence A. Hoffman, "Jewish-Christian Services—Babel or Mixed Multitude?" *Cross Currents*, Spring 1990, p. 5–17, and responses to it, ibid., pp. 18–33.

Compare, with Griffiths's *a priori* dismissal of interreligious practices as "almost always the adumbrating of vacuous claims upon which, it is supposed, all religious persons can agree" ("Why We Need Interreligious Polemics," 33), the powerful first-person account by a South African theologian of the celebration of the inauguration of Nelson Mandela as president. Along with indigenous African religious leaders, there were present "a Hindu priest, a Muslim imam, a Jewish rabbi, a Christian bishop, each praying according to his particular tradition's insight rather than some deist prayer addressed 'to whom it may concern'." John W.

de Gruchy, "Waving the Flag," *Christian Century*, June 15–22, 1994, p. 597.

121. Peter Elbow, "The Uses of Binary Thinking," *Journal of Advanced Composition*, (1993), 59. An eloquent rejection, on theological as well as historical grounds, of the desirability of seeking "common denominators" is a classic essay by a preeminent and widely revered Orthodox rabbi of the last two generations, Joseph B. Soloveitchik's "Confrontation," *Tradition: A Journal of Orthodox Thought*, 5 (1964), 18–25: "Standardization of practices, equalization of dogmatic certitudes, and the waiving of eschatological claims spell the end of the vibrant and great faith experience of any religious community."

122. It is a special danger for believing Christians to expound the teachings of Jesus by means of a contrast with an understanding of the "Old Testament" that too uncritically takes the Gospel accounts at face value, describing a Judaism that "the Jews" would not recognize. Jewish morality and law then become a reified foil for the main message, rather than being taken or rejected on their own terms. For what to me is a mild instance of falling prey to this danger, see Mesters, *God, Where Are You?* pp. 168–173.

For a powerful critique of the danger, from within the Protestant tradition of "salvation by faith," see Borg, *Meeting Jesus Again for the First Time*, pp. 78–80.

123. See George Eliot, *Adam Bede*, Everyman edition (New York: Charles E. Tuttle, 1994), pp. 283–95; *Romola* (New York: E. P. Dutton, 1956), pp. 347–355.

124. See, for example, Carter, *Culture of Disbelief*, pp. 11–12, 57, referring critically to the decision of the U.S. Court of Appeals in *Roberts v. Madigan*, 921 F.2d 1047 (10th Cir. 1990). This criticism is all the more surprising in light of Professor Carter's recognition, in another context, of the special "lurking danger" in public proclamation of the faith claims of "large and influential Christian denominations." *Culture of Disbelief*, p. 91.

An especially distressing manifestation of this obtuseness is the complaint of law professor Richard Stith that the law would support one who was sufficiently "hypersensitive, if not small-hearted," to protest his hometown's practice of having a live Nativity scene on the courthouse grounds, which he blandly describes as "entertaining for the whole town [!], especially the children." He contrasts with this probable judicial response the fact that no legal remedy would be available to redress the offense felt by some over the replacement of a revered war memorial several years earlier with a sculpture that probably did not reflect the taste of a majority of the townspeople. Richard Stith, "Why the Taint to Religion? The Interplay of Chance and Reason," *Brigham Young Uni-*

versity Law Review, 1993, 469. If I am wrong to presume that there were some Jewish children—to say nothing of yet more exotic variants— living in Valparaiso, Indiana, and wrong to presume also that the history of Indiana embodies no heritage of denigration (and worse) visited on those whose aesthetics run more toward war memorials than avant-garde sculpture, I concede Professor Stith's point. (I will leave it to a co-religionist to comment on an understanding of the Nativity scene as "entertainment.")

125. For the decision, see *North Carolina Civil Liberties Union Legal Foundation v. Constangy*, 947 F.2d 1145 (4th Cir. 1991). The text of the prayer was certainly modest and pertinent: "O Lord, our God, our Father in Heaven, we pray this morning that you will place your divine guiding hand on this courtroom and that with your mighty outstretched arm you will protect the innocent, give justice to those who have been harmed and mercy to us all. Let truth be heard and wisdom be reflected in the light of your presence with us here today. Amen."

I do not contend that either the reasoning of the court's opinion, rooted as is typically the case in the arcane legalisms of church–state jurisprudence, or the plaintiff's objections would have responded as I suggest to a different judicial manner of personal prayer.

126. The Jesuit Order of the Roman Catholic Church—surely one of the worst offenders over the centuries—has done this with a clarity and vigor that I find powerfully moving. Speaking, for example, with reference to its missionary activities among "indigenous cultures," the 34th General Congregation of the Society of Jesus acknowledged its prior failure to recognize that "aggression and coercion have no place in the preaching of the Gospel of freedom," and its failures in "contributing to the alienation of the very people we wanted to serve," in remaining "foreign presences" in the cultures they resided among, in failing to "discover . . . the depth, transcendence and values" of other cultures, and in "allowing the cultures of poor or indigenous communities to be destroyed." "Interim Documents of General Congregation 34 of the Society of Jesus," §1.1.2, ¶ 12, *National Jesuit News*, April 1995. See, to similar effect, the Statement of U.S. Catholic Bishops on Native Americans, "1992: A Time for Remembering, Reconciling, and Recommitting Ourselves as a People," *Origins: Catholic News Documentary Service*, January 9, 1992, pp. 493, 495–499.

For a polar action, see Rev. Richard John Neuhaus's characteristically sneering response to President Clinton's omission of the date from his 1994 Thanksgiving proclamation. Neuhaus speculates (persuasively, in my view) that the White House omitted the date to avoid repeating the traditional "in the year of Our Lord," and that it was thought that the term "likely offended somebody's sense of what is appropriate in this 'pluralistic' [*sic*] society." Asking, "What about the Muslims, the Californicating New Agers, the Buddhists, the Confucianists, and the ACLU-ists?," Neuhaus spins out some familiar, but hardly relevant, ideas about pluralism's being rooted in "particularity" and the "celebration of difference," and dismisses the White House action as "a dispiriting mix of the banal and the mendacious." "The Public Square." *First Things*, February 1995, p. 66. One can only wonder what it would take for Neuhaus to acknowledge a distinction between celebrating difference and celebrating Mass.

127. For a stunning example of the willingness of some Christians not to leave the Gospels unaltered, see the rendition of a group called Priests for Equality, *The Inclusive New Testament* (1994). Acknowledging that "the very sound of the word 'Jew' rings negatively when it is hurled as an epithet, . . . where the texts use the word 'Jew' indiscriminately—and especially in places where the early church's polemic against non-messianic Jews was especially virulent—we particularize the text by substituting *Temple authorities* or *Jewish people*." See *The Inclusive New Testament* (Brentwood, Md.: Priests for Equality, 1994), p. xxvi. This is as part of a wide-ranging revision of the ways in which "those whom society has marginalized" are referred to in the Gospels. Ibid.; see also, pp. xxii–xxv. See also *Faith Without Prejudice: Rebuilding Christian Attitudes Toward Judaism*, ed. Eugene J. Fisher (New York: Crossroad, 1993), pp. 59–61; John M. Oesterreicher, *The New Encounter Between Christians and Jews* (New York: Philosophical Library, 1986), p. 142, adducing historical-theological bases for his conclusion that "the Johannine use of the expression 'the Jews' may be a literary device. . . ."

At Purim, the liturgy is the recitation of the Book of Esther, celebrating the deliverance of the Jews from a genocidal plot by Haman, the king's minister. After they were saved, the Jews of the region took revenge on "those who hated them," killing 75,000 in one day (Esther 9:16). Reconstructionist Rabbi Arthur Waskow, stunned by the realization that it was not a coincidence that the 1994 massacre of Muslims at prayer in Hebron by the Israeli settler Abraham Goldstein occurred at Purim, proposes liturgical innovations, such as recitation of the "troubling verses . . . in the wailing melody of the Book of Lamentations, lest anyone think that these verses are a call to wanton murder." Arthur Waskow, "Out of the Tomb of Abraham," *Tikkun*, March–April 1995, p. 37.

See also n. 243, below, for the powerful recognition, by Catholic theologian Sister Mary C. Boys, of the need for Christians to "reclaim" the Cross itself. And, for a critique of the ways in which the juxtaposition of passages from the Hebrew and Christian Scriptures in the Catholic lectionary affect Catholic perceptions of Judaism, see Mark A. Smith,

"Jews and Judaism in the Catholic Lectionary,"in *Fireball and the Lotus: Emerging Spirituality from Ancient Roots*, ed. Ron Miller and Jim Kenney (Santa Fe, N.M.: Bear & Co., 1987), p. 56.

128. Bishops' Committee on the Liturgy, "God's Mercy Endures Forever: Guidelines on the Presentation of Jews and Judaism in Catholic Preaching (1988)," in *Faith Without Prejudice: Rebuilding Christian Attitudes Toward Judaism*, ed. Eugene J. Fisher (New York: Crossroad, 1993), para. 28, p. 183. See Barbara Balzac Thompson, *Passover Seder: Ritual and Menu for an Observance by Christians* (Minneapolis: Augsburg Publishing House, 1984) for a book by a convert from Judaism, designed to "help Christians experience the meaning of the Jewish Seder," and expressing similar sentiments (p. 3).

129. Quoted in *Faith and Practice*, Extract 222.

130. I find some of this tendency, along with passages that are free of it, in Michael Lerner's discussion of what Jews can learn from Jesus. See *Jewish Renewal*, pp. 141–142, especially the description of Jesus as a "sometimes insightful teacher" and the suggestion that Jews "freed of the legacy of anti-Semitism" will find that they can "occasionally glean[] some useful lessons" from reading the Christian Scriptures (p. 142).

131. A Jewish maxim expresses that profoundly orienting idea in words that repay sustained serious attention: "Let not a man taste anything until he pronounces a benediction. . . . He that gets enjoyment out of this world without a benediction, behold, he has defrauded [the Lord]." *Babylonian Talmud* (London: The Soncino Press, 1961), Order Zera'im, Tractate Berakhoth 158. A classic story, revealing the consciousness of which I have spoken in a lighter vein, is of the two Jewish women who meet every day in the park with their young children. On leaving on a Tuesday, one says to the other: "If I live so long, I'll see you tomorrow. If not, Thursday."

132. Douglas V. Steere, *Where Words Come From: An Interpretation of the Ground and Practice of Quaker Worship and Ministry*, unpaginated introduction (London: Friends Home Service Committee, 1968).

133. *Final Harvest: Emily Dickinson's Poems*, ed. Thomas H. Johnson (Boston: Little, Brown, 1961), p. 248.

134. Personal correspondence, January 1995. The assertion that philosophy begins in wonder we owe to Socrates; see Plato, *Theatetus* 155d, in *The Collected Dialogues of Plato*, ed. Edith Hamilton and Huntington Cairns (Princeton, N.J.: Princeton University Press, 1961), p. 860.

135. For two eloquent challenges to the prevalent view, see Josef Pieper, "The Philosophical Act," in *Leisure: The Basis of Culture*, trans. Alexander Dru (New York: Pantheon Books, 1952), pp. 127–46 ("wonder as decisively and exclusively human," ibid., p. 137); and Andrew Louth, *Discerning the Mystery: An Essay on the Nature of Theology*

(Oxford: Clarendon, 1983), pp. 66–70 (discussing the complementary realms of mystery and problem-solving).

136. *The Portable Walt Whitman*, ed. Malcolm Crowley (New York: The Viking Press, 1974), p. 214.

137. For a valuable attempt to integrate religious and secular spirituality, in a world-view or consciousness that blurs the distinction and a program that seeks to enable the two "sides" to hear their commonality, see Charlotte Spretnak, *The Spiritual Dimension of Green Politics* (Santa Fe, N.M.: Bear & Co., 1986). She writes: "My own working definition of spirituality is that it is the focusing of human awareness on the subtle aspects of existence, a practice that reveals to us profound interconnectedness. . . . The experience of union with the One has been called God consciousness, cosmic consciousness, knowing the One mind, and so forth. It is the core experience common to the sages of all the great religions and has been expressed in the rapture of Christian saints as well as the simple words of a *haiku* poem. . . . Such experiential, rather than merely intellectual, awareness of the profound connectedness is what I hold to be the true meaning of being in 'a state of grace.' Awe at the intricate wonders of creation and celebration of the cosmic unfolding are the roots of worship" (pp. 41–42).

My former colleague Patricia Williams has written a memoir that is certainly more accurately termed secular than religious, but which is, most fundamentally, spiritual. Patricia J. Williams, *The Alchemy of Race and Rights: Diary of a Law Professor* (Cambridge, Mass.: Harvard University Press, 1991).

138. See Jo Ann Robinson, *A. J. Muste, Pacifist and Prophet: His Relation to the Society of Friends* (Wallingford, Penn.: Pendle Hill Publications, 1981), p. 3; *The Way of Response: Martin Buber—Selections from His Writings*, ed. Nahum N. Glatzer (New York: Schocken Books, 1966), p. 158; Robert N. Bellah, *The Broken Covenant: American Civil Religion in Time of Trial* (New York: Seabury Press, 1975), pp. 137–138.

Writing in the heyday of anti-communism for Dorothy Day's newspaper, *The Catholic Worker*, Robert Ludlow referred to "our Communist brethren" as ones "many of whom burn yet with a zeal for righteousness, a love for the oppressed, a desire to see justice achieved." Robert Ludlow, "Revolution and Compassion," in Thomas C. Cornell et al., *A Penny a Copy: Readings from* The Catholic Worker (Maryknoll, N.Y.: Orbis Books, 1995), p. 65. See also Westphal, *Suspicion and Faith*, p. 142. Quoting a classic avowal by Marx of his aversion to religion, Westphal terms his atheism "Promethean," "at its heart . . . the moral claim of humanism. In other words, it does not deny God for lack of evidence; it detests the gods for their treatment of humans." And political scientist Robert C. Tucker sees Marx as a religious (but not a philosophical) moralist, one who is "obsessed with a moral vision of reality, a vision of the world as an arena of conflict between good and evil forces," the presence of which has "such overwhelming immediacy . . . that ethical inquiry [seems] pointless or even perverse." *Philosophy and Myth in Karl Marx*, 2nd ed. (Cambridge: Cambridge University Press, 1972), pp. 21–22. To Tucker, "the religious essence of Marxism is superficially obscured by Marx's rejection of the traditional religions" (p. 22).

139. Cornel West, *The Ethical Dimensions of Marxist Thought* (New York: Monthly Review Press, 1991), pp. xxvii–xxviii. A "purely secular society," Richard Rubenstein observes, "lacks a sense of the tragic. It has yet to know what even the most archaic religions comprehended: that all human projects are destined to falter and fail. For technical society, failure is an incident to be overcome by further effort facilitated by the replacement of older units of manpower with newer units. For the human person, failure is of the very essence." Richard L. Rubenstein, *After Auschwitz: History, Theology, and Contemporary Judaism* (Baltimore: The Johns Hopkins University Press, 1992), p. 27.

140. See p. 34, above.

141. Hartigan, "Power of Language Beyond Words," 84.

142. Yosef Wineberg, *Lessons in Tanya: The Tanya of R. Shneur Zalman of Liadi* (Brooklyn, N.Y.: Kehot, 1987), p. 830.

143. The passage by James Gustafson, quoted above at pp. 51–52, expresses this far better than I can.

144. I briefly develop the idea that "being of service to others, although it is an obligation, is an opportunity and not a burden," in the context of law practice, in "Why Pro Bono in Law Schools," *Law and Inequality: A Journal of Theory and Practice*, 13 (1994), 25–38.

145. Mortimer Adler, *Truth in Religion: The Plurality of Religions and the Unity of Truth* (New York: Macmillan, 1990). The references and quotations in this paragraph appear on pp. 25 and 29.

146. Elizabeth A. Johnson, "Trinity: To Let the Symbol Sing Again," *Theology Today*, 54 (1997), 300.

147. Paul E. Dinter, "Christ's Body as Male and Female," *Cross Currents*, Fall 1994, pp. 391–92.

148. Sallie McFague regards it as one of the "major tasks" of contemporary theology "to struggle with metaphorical precision." *Speaking in Parables*, p. 87. Her book is a remarkable attempt to carry on that struggle.

149. Nussbaum, *Love's Knowledge*, pp. 41, 285.

150. Harvey, *Journey in Ladakh*, pp. 165, 161. "Rinpoche" is a title, signifying a spiritual leader; the word means "diamond." Thuksey is the name given the Rinpoche by the Ladakhi community, meaning "whose heart is a sun." Ibid., p. 124.

Bioethicist Ronald A. Carson writes of the need to integrate "Sensibility and Rationality in Bioethics," *Hastings Center Report*, May–June 1994, p. 23: "Propositional discourse distills . . . ideas from the unruly abundance of deep feelings about life and death, suffering and healing, and argues their merits. Some such simplifying impulse is an indispensible prerequisite to an orderly engagement with [a] welter of emotion and opinion. . . . But as propositional discourse has become the predominant mode of analysis, the link between sensibility and rationality has been severed. . . . [T]he imagination is the joint expression of the emotions and the intellect. . . . Narrative discourse, using the figurative language of fiction, drama, and poetry is an alternative mode of knowing and naming, sorting and sifting through experience. It asks of experience not, is it true, but, what does it mean? Whereas the organizing impulse of propositional discourse is to bring rational order to experience, narrative discourse is driven by the desire to discern meaning through metaphorical approximation and refinement."

151. Norman Lamm, *Torah Umadda: The Encounter of Religious Learning and Worldly Knowledge in the Jewish Tradition* (Northvale, N.J.: J. Aronson, 1990), pp. 1–2.

152. Soloveitchik, *Halakhic Man*, pp. 33–34.

153. For a recognition of this view of Torah by two contemporary Protestant theologians, writing against the background of the long-standing Protestant distortions of Jewish "legalism," see Dennis E. Owen and Barry Mesch, "Protestants, Jews and the Law," *Christian Century*, June 6–13, 1984, pp. 601–604.

154. Emily Fowler Hartigan, "From Righteousness to Beauty: Reflections on *Poethics* and *Justice as Translation*," *Tulane Law Review*, 67 (1992), 458; Gustafson, "Moral Discourse About Medicine," 137.

Karen Armstrong attributes to Petrarch the characterization of theology as "poetry concerning God," "effective not because it 'proved' anything but because it penetrated the heart." *History of God*, p. 5.

155. "Keep these words which I am commanding you this day upon your heart. . . . Bind them as a sign upon your hand, fix them as frontlets upon your forehead . . ." (Deuteronomy 6:6–8).

"Then he took a loaf of bread, and when he had given thanks, he broke it and gave it to them, saying, 'This is my body, which is given for you. Do this in remembrance of me'" (John 22:19).

156. For a sophisticated analysis of "acts of faith" as "an indwelling rather than an affirmation," see Michael Polanyi, *Personal Knowledge: Toward a Post-Critical Philosophy* (Chicago: The University of Chicago Press, 1958), p. 28 and surrounding pages. Quaker Nancy Bieber has described in these terms the significance of a Catholic friend's practice of attending Mass daily: "The repeated acting out of her faith did more

than simply allow her to be counted among the faithful. . . . It continually strengthened her commitment to the church community and to Christ." *Communion for a Quaker* (Wallingford, Penn.: Pendle Hill Publications, 1997), p. 4.

157. "This is the meaning of Muslim: one who has accepted through free choice to conform his will to the Divine Will." Seyyed Hossein Nasr, *Ideal and Realities of Islam*, 2nd ed. (London: George Allen & Unwin, 1975), p. 26.

158. Lerner, *Jewish Renewal*, pp. 45, 48.

159. See ibid., pp. 48–49. For an eloquent critique, from within the Orthodox tradition, of the view that the "ideal religious personality" is one who "empties himself of any independent moral sense or critical judgment," see Eugene Korn, "*Tselem Elokim* [Image of God] and the Dialectic of Jewish Morality," *Tradition*, 31 (1997), 8.

Reinhold Niebuhr has written of the need to "convict the believers when faith is not fruitful of justice." *Man's Nature and His Communities* (New York: Charles Scribner's Sons, 1965), p. 27. My law school colleague William Ewald discusses the significance of this insight as it is manifested in the thought of Immanuel Kant. To Kant, he states, "the concept of the Good is logically prior to the concept of the Divinity. You can never tell that an order comes from God unless you are first able to test it by some independent criterion of morality; for you might, after all, be having an auditory hallucination, or even hearing the voice of the Devil. . . . The only way to tell for sure that you are hearing the authentic voice of God is to test it by its conformity to the moral law." William Ewald, "Comparative Jurisprudence (I): What Was It Like to Try a Rat?" *University of Pennsylvania Law Review*, 143 (1995), 1999.

Ewald supports this point by quoting an arresting response by Kant to the story of the *Akedah*. Abraham, Kant asserts, "should have replied to this supposedly divine voice as follows": "That I ought not to kill my good son is absolutely certain. But that you who appear to me are in fact God is something of which I am not certain and of which I can never become certain, even if your voice should thunder down from the visible heavens." Ibid. (Ewald's translation).

Eugene Korn, in the article quoted above in this note, makes a wonderfully similar observation (p. 16): "Even if God himself appears to visit us at night and whisper in our ears to commit an immoral act, it is not God talking, but Moloch."

160. Lerner, *Jewish Renewal*, pp. 47, 58–59.

161. See Shalom Spiegel, *The Last Trial: On the Legends and Lore of the Command to Abraham to Offer Isaac as a Sacrifice—The Akedah*, trans. Judah Goldin (New York: Behrman House, 1979). The central theme of this towering work of scholarship and devotion is expressed by the translator

in these words: "Isaac is the paradigm of whom? Not of the survivor of the ordeal, but of everyone who paid for the Sanctification of the Name with his life." It combines (in Goldin's words) industry, sensitivity, and literary style (pp. xix–xx) in a way that makes the book impossible for me to describe adequately; it can only be read.

162. Douglas V. Steere, *Traveling In*, ed. E. Glenn Hinson (Wallingford, Penn.: Pendle Hill Publications, 1995), pp. 23–24.

163. See Plato, *Apology*, pp. 3, 25–26 (Socrates's defense to the jury), and *Crito* (the death of Socrates); Louis Finkelstein, *Akiba: Scholar, Saint, and Martyr* (Cleveland: World; Philadelphia: Jewish Publication Society of America, 1962), pp. 276–77; T. S. Eliot, *Murder in the Cathedral* (New York: Harcourt, Brace, 1935), pp. 69–70, 73–74; Bolt, *Man for All Seasons*, pp. 92–94; London Yearly Meeting, *Faith and Practice*, Extract 33 (Mary Dyer); Martin Luther King Jr., "I See the Promised Land," in *I Have A Dream: Writings and Speeches That Changed the World*, ed. James Melvin Washington (San Francisco: HarperSanFrancisco, 1992), pp. 202–203 (speech delivered in Memphis, Tennessee, April 3, 1968).

164. See p. 27, and note 35, above.

165. Herman Melville, *Moby-Dick*, ed. Howard Mumford Jones (New York: W. W. Norton, 1967), p. 51.

166. Bolt, *Man for All Seasons*, p. 81.

167. Quaker scholar Douglas Gwyn describes in these words the way that George Fox's experience of Christ affected him: "Crucial to this transformation was the experience of God's alluring love, creating in Fox a *desire* to know God's will and a *power* to obey it. This personal commitment to God's will rose up in place of an outwardly transmitted code of Christian moral obligation. Standing in the light of his inward teacher, . . . Fox came to experience the divine command less in a strict *imperative* sense than as a *cohortative*: 'thou shalt' became 'let us!' *Apocalypse of the Word: The Life and Message of George Fox* (Richmond, Ind.: Friends United Press 1986), p. 64.

168. See p. 1, above.

169. Sophocles, *Antigone*, in *Anthology of Greek Drama*, ed. Charles A. Robinson, Jr. (New York: Holt, Rinehart and Winston, 1968), p. 115.

170. Nancy Fuchs-Kreimer, "God as 'Fuehrer,' " *Reconstructionism Today*, Autumn 1993, p. 13.

171. *Mahzor for Rosh Hashanah and Yom Kippur: A Prayer Book for the Days of Awe*, ed. Rabbi Jules Harlow (New York: Rabbinical Assembly, 1978), p. 258. The most eloquent scriptural expression of this thought of which I am aware is (despite its coming from a morally problematic source) Judges 8:22–23: "Then the Israelites said to Gideon, 'Rule over us, and your son and grandson also; for you have delivered us out of the hand of Midian.' Gideon said to them, 'I will not rule over you, and my son will not rule over you; the Lord will rule over you.'"

172. Clifford Geertz, *Islam Observed: Religious Development in Morocco and Indonesia* (New Haven, Conn.: Yale University Press, 1968), p. 110.

173. Helen Thomas Flexner, recounting "A Quaker Childhood," tells of her father remonstrating with her mother for continuing to give food to beggars, even though her acts encougaged more and more to come to their door: "Do show a little common sense. . . . Thee does not sufficiently consider the consequences of what thee is doing." She answered: "Christ commanded us to give to him that asketh. He did not tell us to take thought for the consequences in this world. Had Jesus what thee calls common sense, James?" Helen Thomas Flexner, "Had Jesus What Thee Calls Common Sense, James?" in *A Quaker Reader*, ed. Jessamyn West (New York: The Viking Press, 1962), p. 414.

174. An extremely powerful account of the way in which his direct experience of the continuing presence of Christ in his prison cell enabled him to resist Nazi oppression, at great cost, is Emil Fuchs's *Christ in Catastrophe* (Wallingford, Penn.: Pendle Hill Publications, 1996).

175. C. S. Lewis, *Surprised by Joy: The Shape of My Early Life* (New York: Harcourt, Brace, 1956), pp. 231–32.

176. "When God called to Jonah, 'Go at once to Nineveh, that great city, and cry out against it,' he promptly found a ship bound for Tarshish, paid the fare, and went aboard to journey with them to Tarshish, away from the Lord." Jonah 1:2–3. The humanistic psychologist Abraham Maslow has written a profound account of "The Jonah Complex," the impulse to run from what he decribes (in his secular, psychological terminology) as our impulse toward actualizing more of our potentialities. See his *The Farther Reaches of Human Nature* (New York: The Viking Press, 1971), p. 35.

177. I have found extremely helpful the discussion of "The Concept of God" in Rebecca Alpert and Jacob Staub's *Exploring Judaism: A Reconstructionist Approach* (New York: Reconstructionist Press, 1985), chap. 3.

178. For a discussion, see A. Cohen, *Everyman's Talmud* (New York; E. P. Dutton, 1949), pp. 88–93. The "evil impulse" is described as "the fermenting ingredient that stirs up evil elements in man's nature which, unless suppressed, overrule the finer instincts and result in wicked actions" (p. 88).

179. Otto, *Idea of the Holy*, p. 20 and note 1 (emphasis omitted). With a characteristic assurance that I cannot match, Otto asserts his own belief that it is "manifestly borne out by experience" th*t the "feeling-element" which he calls the numinous "indubitably has reference to an object outside the self." This "feeling," he concludes, "must be posited as a primary datum of consciousness." Ibid.

Although she plainly rejects any such assertion, Martha Nussbaum's view is not as sharply different as might at first appear. Speaking of the norms of the moral law, she says: "We picture them *as if* they stood outside of us, even though *in a sense* we are well aware that they stand within us." "Valuing Values," 212 (emphasis added). It is not our metaphysical assignment of a "location" within or outside us that is critical, but the sense (quoting Kant) of "ever-increasing awe" with which a person experiences "the starry sky above me and the moral law within me." By language of transcendence, we "express our wish to be bound" by the moral law, "even when we wish to do otherwise." Ibid. I find the terms "secular" and "religious" equally insufficient to capture her stance.

180. Bendall and Ferre, *Exploring the Logic of Faith*, p. 57. For a statement of Freud's that expresses the view ascribed to him in the text, see Westphal, *Suspicion and Faith*, p. 54.

181. *Selected Papers of Bertrand Russell*, 2nd ed. (New York: The Modern Library, 1955), pp. 1, 5, 14. Compare the section "Questioning Transnaturalism" in Alpert and Staub, *Exploring Judaism*, pp. 22–23.

182. This assumption characterizes traditional religion as well. See, for example, Goetz's critique in his review of William Dean's *Religious Critic in American Culture*, 414.

183. Kushner, *When Children Ask About* God, pp. 60, 56. He adds: "In Hebrew we read from right to left, and perhaps in theology we ought to read from right to left also. When we see a statement like 'God is good, God is forgiving,' let us not take it as a description of a person named God who lives in Heaven. Read it backwards: goodness is godly, forgiveness is godly" (p. 98).

Gordon Kaufman writes of the need to "de-reify" God-language: "[D]evotion to the 'creator/lord' today should be understood as consisting in the attempt to live in rapport with the movements of life and history that provide the actual context of our human existence; it is to attempt to be in tune with what we discern as the nature of things. . . ." Gordon D. Kaufman, "Reconstructing the Concept of God: De-Reifying the Anthropomorphisms," in *The Making and Remaking of Christian Doctrine*, ed. Sarah Coakley and David A. Pailin (Oxford: Clarendon Press, 1993), p. 102.

184. "There are two Torahs. One is revealed, and one is hidden. The revealed Torah is the source of authority. The hidden Torah is the source of inspiration." Ari Elon, *From Jerusalem to the Edge of Heaven* (Philadelphia: Jewish Publication Society, 1995), p. 59.

185. "The Testimony of Margaret Fox," in *The Works of George Fox* I (1831; repr. New York: AMS Press, 1975), p. 50.

186. *The Midrash Rabbah*. I. *Genesis*, ed. H. Freedman, 3rd ed. (London: The Soncino Press, 1983), p. 1 and notes 1 and 4. See the account in Handelman, "*Emunah*," 302–303. To like effect, see *The Midrash Rab-*

bah. III. *Exodus*, trans. S. M. Lehrman, ed. H. Freedman and Maurice Simon (London: The Soncino Press, 1983), p. 356: "This is what God said to Israel: 'Prior to My creation of the world, I prepared the Torah'."

187. According to Neil Gillman, modern Judaism is divided between those who affirm and those who deny a "tight congruence between what God wants us to know of God's will and what the Torah tells us about God's will." Neil Gillman, "Authority and Parameters in Jewish Decision-Making," *The Reconstructionist*, Fall 1994, p. 73. It may be that the rabbinic tradition has been able at times to avoid or transcend this dichotomy through what Susan Handelman terms "very aggressive modes of interpretation": "There is no simple literal fundamentalism here. Indeed, to some, these interpretations may appear a bit outrageous. For the rabbis make odd and anachronistic juxtapositions of verses; they break up the flow of the narrative, atomize verses and words, fragment the canon and collapse time." "*Emunah*," 304.

188. Buber, *I and Thou*, p. 143.

189. Regarding Moses, Michael Lerner writes that, even if "we hold to the language of the Orthodox tradition, in which Moses received the Torah directly from God, we can say that the human receptor, Moses, was himself a severely limited being whose record of God's message reflected his inevitable human limitations." *Jewish Renewal*, p. 32. As for Peter, the "rock," I hope it is not inappropriate for me to note that, if I read the account correctly, Peter (who denied Jesus three times) on one occasion spoke words in which Jesus heard the voice of Satan. Matthew 16:23; Mark 8:33.

190. David Luban, "A Theological Argument Against Theopolitics," *Report from the Institute for Philosophy and Public Policy*, 16 (1996), 13.

191. Robert N. Bellah, "At Home and Not at Home: Religious Pluralism and Religious Truth," *Christian Century*, April 19, 1995, p. 425.

192. "It is obvious that our individual consciousness always plays a role in our understanding of religious phenomena. No text has a voice; we are forced to understand every word we read through our critical faculties. In the end, it is human authorities who must always judge if a particular halakhic rule applies to a specific set of circumstances." Korn, "*Tselem Elokim* [Image of God] and the Dialectic of Jewish Morality," 16–17.

193. Adler, *Truth in Religion*, p. 29.

194. Wolfhart Pannenberg, "Christianity and the West: Ambiguous Past, Uncertain Future," *First Things*, December 1994, pp. 18, 19. Even James Madison may be cited (albeit in a rather different context) in support of this position: "When the Almighty himself condescends to address mankind in their own language, his meaning, luminous as it must be, is rendered dim and doubtful by the cloudy medium through

which it is communicated." *The Federalist Papers*, No. 37, ed. Clinton Rossiter (New York: Penguin Books, 1961), p. 229.

195. Norman Beck, *Mature Christianity: The Recognition and Repudiation of the Anti-Jewish Polemic of the New Testament* (Selinsgrove, Pa.: Susquehanna University Press/Associated University Presses, 1985), p. 33. Neil Gillman makes a similarly grounded argument against "the assumption that God's nature can be conveyed in a literal way." *Sacred Fragments*, p. 80.

196. Erling Jorstad, *The Politics of Moralism: The New Christian Right in American Life* (Minneapolis: Augsburg Publishing House, 1981), p. 9.

197. Compare the assertion attributed to Rabbi Mordecai Kaplan, "One's discovery of religious truth is God's revelation of it, since the very process of that discovery implies the activity of God." Quoted in Ellen M. Umansky, "Creative Adjustment and Other Kaplanian Principles of Change," *The Reconstructionist*, Fall 1995, p. 32.

198. Avery Dulles, s.j., "The Challenge of the Catechism," *First Things*, January 1995, p. 46. For a very different view, from within the Catholic tradition, of the "deposit of faith," see the quotation from Wolfhart Pannenberg, p. 86, above, and Paul Dinter, "Christ's Body as Male and Female," pp. 395–396.

A light-hearted essay by James Neuchterlein, "Some of My Best Friends," *First Things*, December 1994, pp. 7–8, powerfully illustrates the ingrained tendency of conservative religion to polarize views and demonize the "other." He writes of the "revelatory" realization that he had transcended the consciousness of his Lutheran boyhood, when the Catholic Church was "the great satan, the Antichrist." Now, "the religious world . . . was no longer Protestants vs. Catholics, but orthodox Christians vs. religious liberals." Some things change, some remain.

A more serious manifestation of this Manichaean tendency of religious conservatives comes from Father Neuhaus himself. In the midst of carrying on one of his favorite activities, confidently lecturing Jews on just what does and does not constitute anti-Semitism, he quotes Norman Podhoretz for the observation that "conservatives don't hate Jews. 'They hate liberals. As it happens, most Jews are liberals.'" Richard John Neuhaus, "Anti-Semitism and Our Common Future," *First Things*, June–July 1995, p. 60. The less fundamental point in this invocation of Podhoretz is to imagine how Neuhaus—who certainly does *not* allow others to decide who is and who isn't anti-Catholic—would react were someone to say that "liberals don't hate Catholics. They hate conservatives, and as it happens most Catholics are conservative." The more fundamental problem, acknowledging that it is not for me to remind a Christian cleric of his office, is that hate-mongering (literally), propagated against *any* person or group, is one thing coming from a publicist, and something else coming from a priest. Neuhaus professes to be both, but I would have hoped that the spiritual anchor of the one would have proven more impervious to the corrosive acid of the other.

199. For a carefully reasoned, and to me wholly persuasive, explanation of the existence of the gap, see Jeffrey Stout, *Ethic After Babel: The Languages of Morals and Their Discontents* (Boston: Beacon Press, 1988), chaps. 1–2, esp. pp. 22–28.

200. John Rawls, *A Theory of Justice* (Cambridge, Mass.: The Belknap Press of Harvard University Press, 1971), p. 20.

201. For a brief lucid description and justification of the process, see Martha Nussbaum, "Sophistry About Conventions," in *Love's Knowledge*, pp. 220, 222–224, 226.

202. Rawls, *Theory of Justice*, p. 46.

203. Sidney Callahan, "The Role of Emotion in Ethical Decisionmaking," *Hastings Center Report*, 18 (June–July 1988), 12.

204. Michael Moore, "Choice, Character, and Excuse," *Social Philosophy and Policy*, 7 (1990), 30.

205. Callahan, "Role of Emotion in Ethical Decisionmaking," 12. For a marshaling of the methods of analytic philosophy to support the claim that "a deficiency of this or that emotional reaction . . . may be traced to some moral failing or human short-coming," see Gabriele Taylor, "Justifying the Emotions," *Mind*, 84 (1975), 390.

206. Mary Rose O'Reilley, *The Peaceable Classroom* (Portsmouth, N.H.: Boynton, 1993), p. 82.

207. H. Susannah Heschel, "My Father," in *No Religion Is an Island: Abraham Joshua Heschel and Interreligious Dialogue*, ed. Harold Kasimow and Bryon L. Sherwin (Maryknoll, N.Y.: Orbis Books, 1991), p, 36.

208. Maguire, *Moral Core of Judaism and Christianity*, p. 171.

209. Gerald Postema, "Moral Responsibility in Professional Ethics," *New York University Law Review*, 55 (1980), 68–70.

210. Nussbaum, *Love's Knowledge*, 65–66. See also her reliance on what she terms the "recognition of tragedy" in moral choice to ground the importance of allowing the "losing option to exert a moral claim." "Valuing Values," 213–14. That claim may lead us to make "reparations," to devote "particular care to that area of our lives at other times," or to "seek to remake the world in such a way that such conflicts more rarely arise." Ibid.

211. For a fascinating account, by a Japanese professor who has practiced Zen and studied Quakerism, of the differing ways in which the two traditions respond to the tension between the need for unbroken silence and the need for ministry through speech and action, see Teruyasu Tamura, *A Zen Buddhist Encounters Quakerism* (Wallingford, Penn.: Pendle Hill Publications, 1992).

212. Frank Bianco, *Voices of Silence: Lives of the Trappists Today* (Garden City, N.Y.: Doubleday Anchor, 1992), p. 84.

213. Quoted in London Yearly Meeting, *Faith and Practice*, Extract 5.

214. The phrase is Emily Hartigan's; see note 52, above.

215. Thomas J. O'Meara, *Fundamentalism: A Catholic Perspective* (New York: Paulist Press, 1990), p. 82.

216. Thomas Merton, *The Wisdom of the Desert* (New York: New Directions, 1960), p. 6.

217. Ronald M. Green, *Religious Reason: The Rational and Moral Basis of Religious Belief* (New York: Oxford University Press, 1978), p. 136.

218. See *Rabbinic Anthology*, ed. Montefiore and Loewe, pp. 349, 347.

219. It is part of the story that religiously grounded precepts and rituals are often thought of as constituting, not merely as enabling, communion with the Divine. Matthew Berke attributes approvingly to both Jewish and Catholic thought the belief that "morality involves not just an ultimate ideal or aim but a system of specific rules and prohibitions that help keep life on a straight path to its ultimate good; . . . these rules, taken as a whole over the long run, not only lead to, but themselves constitute, a good life." Matthew Berke, "A Jewish Appreciation of Catholic Social Teaching," in *Catholicism, Liberalism and Communitarianism*, ed. Kenneth Grasso et al. (Lanham, Md.: Rowman & Littlefield, 1995), p. 239.

220. Heschel, *God in Search of Man*, pp. 343–46.

221. Arthur Green and Barry W. Holtz, *Your Word Is Fire: The Hasidic Masters and Contemplative Prayer* (Woodstock, Vt.: Jewish Lights Publications, 1993), p. 6. Hasidism, the authors assert, arose as a means of offsetting this "mechanizing" tendency. My sense is that, over the decades since its advent two hundred years ago, it has gone through periods of resolving and falling prey to the problem that it arose to avoid.

222. Frank S. Alexander, "Speaking Theologically," *Emory Law Journal*, 42 (1993), 1091.

223. Bellah, *Broken Covenant*, p. 84.

224. Nancy Bieber's pamphlet "Communion for a Quaker" is a sophisticated expression of her awareness of both aspects of this polarity.

225. Maguire, *Moral Core of Judaism and Christianity*, p. 13.

226. Abraham Joshua Heschel, "On Prayer," in *Moral Grandeur and Spiritual Audacity*, ed. H. Susannah Heschel. New York: Farrar, Straus & Giroux, 1996), p. 263.

227. Heidi M. Hurd, "Interpreting Authorities," in *Law and Interpretation: Essays in Legal Philosophy*, ed. Andrei Marmor (New York: Oxford University Press, 1995), p. 427. A discussion of Reconstructionist Judaism speaks in these words of the idea that "the past has a vote, but not a veto": "When a particular Jewish value or custom is found wanting . . . ,

it is our obligation as Jews to find a means to reconstruct it—to adopt innovative practices or find new meanings in old ones. That the past has a vote means that we must struggle to hear the voices of our ancestors. What did this custom or that idea mean to them? How did they see the presence of God in it? How can we retain or regain its importance in our own lives? That the past does not have a veto means that we must struggle to hear our own voices as distinct from theirs. What might this custom or that idea mean to us today?" Alpert and Staub, *Exploring Judaism*, pp. 30–31. Although written about customs and values, this idea has salience for me with respect to Scripture and liturgy as well.

For a brief essay, sensitively applying this stance to a number of specific issues in contemporary Judaism, ranging from the dietary laws and the prohibition on wearing wool with linen, to capital punishment and gay unions, see Tikva Frymer-Kensky, "Toward a Liberal Theory of Halakha," *Tikkun*, July–August 1995, p. 42.

228. See Abraham R. Besdin, *Reflections of the Rav: Lessons in Jewish Thought Adapted from Lectures of Rabbi Joseph B. Soloveitchik* (Jerusalem: World Zionist Organization, Department for Torah Education and Culture in the Diaspora, 1979), pp. 23–29, for a carefully nuanced exposition of the relation between "faith convictions" and "moral directives," in the context of the "unclear, incomplete, enigmatic, half-told, and half-concealed" account in Genesis of the Creation.

229. The story is recounted in Rabbi Nosson Scherman, *The Complete ArtScroll Machzor: Rosh Hashanah* (Brooklyn, N.Y.: Mesorah Publications, 1985), p. 480n.

230. *High Holiday Prayer Book*, ed. Rabbi Morris Silverman (Hartford, Conn.: Prayer Book Press, 1939), pp. 147–148.

231. *On Wings of Awe*, ed. Richard Levy (Washington, D.C.: B'nai B'rith Hillel Foundations, 1985), p. 333.

232. Msgr. John M. Oesterreicher, writing of the unembarrassed anthropomorphism of the "sacred writers" of the Hebrew Scriptures, observes: "What a difference between saying: 'His power offers safety,' and 'Beneath His arms there is safety.' The first informs, the second inspires." *New Encounter Between Christians and Jews*, p. 35.

Protestant theologian Tremper Longman makes a related claim with respect to Scripture generally: "The Old Testament does more than inform readers' intellect with facts about God and history. It also arouses emotions, appeals to the will, and stimulates the imagination. It does so not only through its content but also by self-consciousness about its form of expression." Tremper Longman III, "The Literature of the Old Testament," in *A Complete Literary Guide to the Bible*, ed. Leland Ryken and Tremper Longman III (Grand Rapids, Mich.: Zondervan, 1993), p. 97.

233. Nor is the incompatibility clear. The rabbinic tradition has struggled for centuries with the task of reconciling the several portions of the text. In addition, the traditional English translation suggests a meaning that may vary from the Hebrew, which (I am told) asserts that repentance, prayer, and righteousness avert, not "the severe decree," but "the severity of the decree." That change, focusing on the impact of the acts and consciousness of the worshipper, integrates the revised version somewhat more than does the standard English version, which of course Orthodox worshippers never hear themselves saying.

The point is broader than the single example. Orthodox Jews may be better able to carry on the struggle with "difficult texts" by reason of the circumstance that they are at once committed to the canonical quality of the text, and therefore not free to disregard or alter it, and also able to develop their understanding of a passage without filtering it through an English translation. Hebrew is a very different language from English, with fewer words, each far richer in its layered nuances, and the letters themselves of profound semantic import. See Marcia Prager, *The Path of Blessing* (New York: Bell Tower, 1998). The Hebrew text, inviolate in Orthodoxy, calls for and has called forth a succession of lifetimes of *midrashim*, of interpretation.

234. Hertz, *Authorised Daily Prayer Book*, p. 271.

235. See p. 41, above. Reinhold Niebuhr has spoken critically of faith that is "belief in propositions which may be historically dubious, though the symbols are the bearers of the meaning of the mystery of human existence. *Man's Nature and His Communities*, p. 27.

236. Bendall and Ferre, *Exploring the Logic of Faith*, p. 65.

237. Buber, *Two Types of Faith*, p. 12.

238. There are by now many surveys of the record of Christian anti-Semitism, including its grounding in Christian theology. See, e.g., Edward H. Flannery, *The Anguish of the Jews: Twenty-three Centuries of Anti-Semitism* (New York: Macmillan, 1965); Rosemary Radford Ruether, *Faith and Fratricide: The Theological Roots of Anti-Semitism* (New York: Seabury Press, 1974); Marc Saperstein, *Moments of Crisis in Jewish-Christian Relations* (London: SCM Press, 1989); Rosemary Radford Ruether, "Anti-Semitism and Christian Theology," in *Auschwitz: Beginning of a New Era? Reflections on the Holocaust*, ed. Eva Fleischner (New York: KTAV Publishing Co., 1977), pp. 79–92 and responses to her essay, pp. 93–107.

It will hardly trivialize the record, however, to set forth a single example, the core of Martin Luther's response to his own question, "What then shall we Christians do with this damned, rejected race of Jews?" "First, their synagogues or churches should be set on fire, and whatever does not burn up should be covered or spread over with dirt so that no one may ever be able to see a cinder or stone of it. Secondly, their homes should likewise be broken down and destroyed. Thirdly, they should be deprived of their prayer-books and Talmuds in which such idolatry, lies, cursing, and blasphemy are taught. Fourthly, their rabbis must be forbidden under threat of death to teach any more. Fifthly, [etc., on to Seventhly]." Martin Luther, "Concerning the Jews and Their Lies" (1543), in *The Christian in Society* IV, ed. Franklin Sherman, Luther's Works 47, ed. Helmut T. Lehmann (Philadelphia: Fortress Press, 1971), p. 137. Those who have not had the "pleasure" should read this essay in its entirety.

Sherman's Introduction to the essay, p. 123, contains a brief account of the pervasive anti-Semitism of the late medieval period, which led him to assert that Luther's essay, despite "the crudity of its language at many points and the inhumanity of its proposals," was "largely repeating the anti-Semitic commonplaces of the time [and that] much of his theological argumentation is borrowed from earlier Christian polemics against Judaism. . . ."

239. Extensive citation is plainly superogatory, but see, e.g., George L. Mosse, *Toward the Final Solution: A History of European Racism* (New York: H. Fertig, 1978), especially pp. 171–214; Irving Greenberg, "Cloud of Smoke, Pillar of Fire: Judaism, Christianity, and Modernity after the Holocaust," in *Auschwitz: Beginning of a New Era? Reflections on the Holocaust*, ed. Eva Fleischner (New York: KTAV Publishing, 1977), pp. 7–20.

Joseph Cardinal Bernadin has given us an unflinching acknowledgment of the connection between historic Christian anti-Semitism and the rise of Hitler: "[T]here is little doubt that classical Christian anti-Semitism was a central factor in generating popular support for the Nazi undertaking, along with economic greed, religious and political nationalism, and ordinary human fear. For many baptized Christians, it constituted the primary reason for their personal collaboration with the Nazi movement. . . . In the Church today, we must not minimize the extent of Christian involvement with Hitler and his associates." "Anti-Semitism: A Catholic Critique," in *Toward Greater Understanding: Essays in Honor of John Cardinal O'Connor*, ed. Anthony J. Cernera (Bridgeport, Conn.: Sacred Heart University Press, 1995), p. 27.

For a challenging argument that, in a very complex way, implicates the entire theology of Christianity in a stance toward Jews that stands in the way of regarding them (us) as simply human beings, see Rubenstein, *After Auschwitz*, chap. 2.

240. "Remarks of President Reagan at Bitburg Air Force Base, May 5, 1968," in *Bitburg in Moral and Political Perspective*, ed. Geoffrey H. Hartman (Bloomington: Indiana University Press, 1986), p. 258. As part

of a fortieth anniversary "ceremony of reconciliation," Reagan announced plans to join West German Chancellor Kohl in laying a wreath at a German military cemetery. He initially rejected suggestions that he visit a concentration camp as part of his trip, on the ground that his intention was not to "reawaken the memories," but to observe the day that "peace began," adding that "none of [the German people] who were adults and participating in any way" in the War were still alive [!], and the "guilt feeling that's been imposed upon them" was "unnecessary" (p. 92). It was disclosed that the cemetery chosen contained the graves of several dozen members of SS units that had engaged in infamous massacres during the war. The President's response was to stand his ground regarding Bitburg (although agreeing to add Bergen-Belsen to his itinerary); he referred to the Bitburg soldiers as "young men [who] were victims of the Nazis also. . . . They were victims just as surely as the victims in the concentration camps" (p. 94). At Bergen-Belsen, as at Bitburg, he spoke of "the awful evil started by one man—an evil that victimized all the world with its destruction" (pp. 94–95).

241. Cooney, *American Pope*, pp. 132–133. A number of specific instances of such efforts by Archbishop Roncalli are recounted in Morley, *Vatican Diplomacy and the Jews During the Holocaust*; see pp. 43, 61, 91–92, 122, 161; See also Oesterreicher, *New Encounter Between Christians and Jews*, pp. 113–14. Roncalli shared, however, the prevalent Catholic hostility to any resettlement of Jews in the Holy Land, on account of his antipathy to the creation of a large Jewish presence or a Jewish State there. See Morley, *Vatican Diplomacy and the Jews During the Holocaust*, pp. 94, 206.

242. The central Conciliar document is the Declaration *Nostra Aetate* (On the Relationship of the Church to Non-Christian Religions), Section 4. Msgr. John M. Oesterreicher, Director of the Institute of Judaeo-Christian Studies, Seton Hall University, and the principal draftsperson on the project that led to the promulgation of *Nostra Aetate*, attributes "its existence to an express mandate of John XXIII." *New Encounter Between Christians and Jews*, p. 103. (The Declaration is published as the frontispiece of Oesterreicher's book.)

For earlier initiatives of Pope John, see ibid, pp. 108–13. For the tortuous gestation of the document, past some relatively modest theological resistance and much fierce political opposition from the Arab States and Catholic clergy resident in them, see ibid., pp. 103–277. In the hindsight of the past three decades, Section 4 reads like a very modest, even grudging statement, but it set in motion a process that has far outrun its tentative beginnings. See International Catholic-Jewish Liaison Committee, "The Evolution of a Tradition: From *Nostra Aetate* to the 'Notes,' " *Fifteen Years of Catholic-Jewish Dialogue, 1970–1985* (Vatican City: Libreria Editrice Vaticana, 1988), chap. 10.

243. See the documents of the Vatican and the National Conference of Catholic Bishops (U.S.) reprinted as Appendixes A though C in *Faith Without Prejudice*, ed. Fisher, pp. 123–94. These documents, and Dr. Fisher's book, call for and embody a thorough-going reexamination of the traditional understandings of Scripture and liturgy.

One individual example that I find especially stunning is an inquiry by a Roman Catholic theologian, Sister Mary Boys, regarding the Cross itself: "Should a Symbol Betrayed Be Reclaimed?" The "betrayal" is of Paul's "radical act of folly": In place of its proclamation of the extent to which "the Holy One had identified with human wretchedness," the Cross became a symbol of temporal dominance, and of anti-Semitism. Professor Boys seriously considers whether in light of that history the Cross should now be "laid aside." Ultimately, it was an experience more than reasoned argument that made her desist from proposing that response. In its place, she calls for a "reclaiming" of the Cross, through honestly repenting for its misuse and "reappropriating" it to "embody the power of reconciliation for which Jesus lived and died." Mary C. Boys, "The Cross: Should a Symbol Betrayed Be Reclaimed?" *Cross Currents*, Spring 1994, pp. 8, 18–23.

244. See Eugene J. Fisher and Leon Klenicki, *Pope John Paul II on Jews and Judaism, 1979–1986* (1987), a joint publication of the Committee for Ecumenical and Interreligious Dialogue, National Conference of Catholic Bishops, and the Anti-Defamation League, B'nai B'rith.

245. *"[H]odu la Adonai ki tob/ki le olam hasdo. . . .* O give thanks to the Lord for he is good / his steadfast love endures for ever!" Ibid. pp. 84–85. It is impossible for me, and I believe for any Jew for whom the liturgy rings in his or her ears, to read of these words on the Pope's lips, uttered in a synagogue, without understanding him to have been praying. I can only imagine their effect on those Jews who heard them.

Rabbi David Blumenthal has recounted his family's experience of an audience (along with seven thousand others) with Pope John Paul. Seated in the front row, they were among those whom the Pope greeted personally. At the conclusion of a remarkable exchange, the Pope invoked God's blessing on each of them, omitting to make the customary sign of the Cross. David R. Blumenthal, "Letter from Rome," *Cross Currents*, Fall 1996, pp. 388, 392.

246. See the documents reproduced in *Faith Without Prejudice*, ed. Fisher; also Philip A. Cunningham, *Education for Shalom: Religion Textbooks and the Enhancement of the Catholic and Jewish Relationship* (Philadelphia: American Interfaith Institute, 1995); *Removing Anti-Judaism from the Pulpit*, ed. Howard Clark Kee and Irvin J. Borosky (Philadelphia: American Interfaith Institute; New York: Continuum, 1996). For radical theological expressions of philo-Semitic thought, see Paul Van Buren,

Discerning the Way: A Theology of the Jewish Reality (New York: Seabury Press, 1980); Paul Van Buren, "Judaism in Christian Theology," *Journal of Ecumenical Studies*, 18 (1981), 114–127.

247. A document like the new Catechism is probably of far greater salience in affecting the outlook of lay Catholics than the official pronouncements of the Vatican or the writing of theologians. For a careful statement of a Catholic theologian's disappointment in the enduring supersessionism that animates the portrayal of Judaism and Jews in the revised Catechism, see Mary C. Boys, "How Shall We Christians Understand Jews and Judaism? Questions about the New Catechism," *Theology Today*, 53 (1996), 165–170.

On the related problem of the Catholic Lectionary, the use in the Good Friday liturgy of "The Reproaches" (against the Israelites for their response to Jesus), and the Gospels themselves, see Gerard S. Sloyan, "The Jews and the New Roman Lectionary," *Face to Face: An Interreligious Bulletin*, 2 (1976), 5–11.

248. Quoted in Heschel's, "No Religion Is an Island," p. 18.

249. See, e.g., E. P. Sanders, *Paul and Palestinian Judaism: A Comparison of Patterns of Religion* (Minneapolis: Fortress Press, 1977); Leonard Swidler, *Yeshua: A Model for Moderns* (Kansas City: Sheed & Ward, 1988), pp. 33–57; Clark M. Williamson, "The New Testament Reconsidered: Recent Post-Holocaust Scholarship," *Quarterly Review*, Winter 1984, p. 337. For a study by a Protestant theologian, rejecting supersessionism on theological grounds, see R. Kendall Soulen, *The God of Israel and Christian Theology* (Minneapolis: Fortress Press, 1996). A brief, telling personal account is by Catholic theologian John C. Merkle, "Heschel's Attitude Toward Religious Pluralism," in *No Religion Is an Island*, ed. Harold Kasimow and Byron L. Sherwin (Maryknoll, N.Y.: Orbis Books, 1991), pp. 107–108.

See also the thorough-going revision of the scriptural text, in *The Inclusive New Testament*, note 127, above. Interestingly enough—and I note this not intending to detract from the magnitude of their achievement—the authors evidently saw no difficulty in continuing to use the supersessionist term "New Testament." Kendall Soulen does not merely abjure the "Old" and "New" usage, but refers to the Hebrew Scriptures simply as the "Scriptures" ("because it follows the usage of Jesus and the first Christians") and uses the term "Apostolic Witness," identifying the "characteristic" that to the Church renders them authoritative, for the Christian Scriptures (pp. 179–80*n*32).

250. It is for this reason extremely offensive to Muslims for Westerners to refer to their religion, Islam, as "Mohammedanism." The confession of faith in Islam is, "There is no God but God, and Muhammed is the messenger of God." See Thomas W. Lippman, *Understanding Islam:*

An Introduction to the Muslim World (New York: New American Library, 1990), pp. 1, 6. There is an analogous misunderstanding regarding the word "Allah," which is Arabic for God, unambiguously understood in Islam as the God of Abraham. "It is therefore misleading to say that Muslims worship Allah as if Allah were some God other than the God of the Jews and Christians." Ibid., p. 7.

251. This is the stance of Marcus Borg; see *Meeting Jesus Again for the First Time*, pp. viii, 44n42, at 45.

252. On the Holiness Code, see pp. 28–37, above. The difference may be one of degree. See the discussion of my mindset that Judaism, like other religions, "belongs" to its orthodox variants, pp. 40–41, above.

Part of Borg's difficulty with the idea of Jesus's uniqueness is its link, as he sees it, with the claim that Christianity "is exclusively true and that Jesus is 'the only way' " (p. 37). I question the inexorability of the link. Jesus is unique from *within* the Christian religion; in Christianity, no other holy person, or great teacher, has the same status. But Christianity is *one way* to approach God, a language by which Christians seek to express what is beyond speech (see pp. 38, above). It is not the only language. What one must avow, credally, in order to be able legitimately to "speak the Christian language" is a question primarily for Christians to grapple with. I consider a comparable problem in Chapter 2, the section entitled "The Challenge of Warrant," pp. 39–43, above.

253. The first Shaffer quotation is from "Jurisprudence in the Light of the Hebraic Faith," *Notre Dame Journal of Law, Ethics, and Public Policy*, 1 (1984), 77; the second, from "On Thinking Theologically about Lawyers as Counselors," *Florida Law Review*, 42 (1990), 471.

Dean Gaffney made the statement quoted in the text at the annual dinner of the *Journal of Law and Religion*, Hamline University. See Edward McGlynn Gaffney, "In Praise of a Gentle Soul," *Journal of Law and Religion*, 10 (1994), 287–88. Compare Robert Bellah's assertion that, today as in Paul's time, one must be converted to Judaism before he or she can be converted to Christianity. "At Home and Not at Home," 423–24.

For an indication that this view has ancient credentials, see Snape, "Rabbinical and Early Christian Ethics," p. 627: "Christian theology, holding fast to the historical connection between Christianity and Judaism, held also that the God of Old Testament and New was one. . . ."

The Protestant theologian John B. Cobb, writing to espouse a "Christocentric catholic theology," says this: "When we seriously take Jesus as the center of our history, we cannot be satisfied with the partisan rejection of Jesus' people that has characterized our gentile Christianity through the centuries. We look forward with Paul to the time when our gentile misappropriation of Jesus will not compel Jews to disown him. We believe that our destiny as Christians is bound up with the destiny of the Jews in one destiny of Jews-and-Christians. Indeed we understand that we are all Jews whether we are the natural or the engrafted branches. "Toward a Christocentric Catholic Theology," p. 90.

Antony Fernando, a Sri Lankan Christian theologian, writes: "In my mind, a Christian can be truly a Christian only if he is truly a Jew in spirit. . . . The only novel outcome of [Christ's] teaching is that he made it possible for people who are not Jews in the flesh to still be believers in the God of the Jews." Antony Fernando, "An Asian Perspective," in *No Religion Is an Island*, ed. Harold Kasimow and Byron Sherwin (Maryknoll, N.Y.: Orbis Books, 1991), p. 176.

254. Thomas L. Shaffer, "The Tension Between Law in America and the Religious Tradition," in *Law and the Ordering of Our Life Together*, ed. Richard John Neuhaus (Grand Rapids, Mich.: W. B. Eerdmans, 1989), p. 32. (The Pastoral Letter is cited in note 95, above).

255. See Philip Hallie, *Lest Innocent Blood Be Shed: The Story of the Village of Le Chambon and How Goodness Happened There* (New York: Harper & Row, 1979).

256. Schulweis, *For Those Who Can't Believe*, p. 146. See Rabbi Schulweis's additional examples, and his discussion of their significance, pp. 145–158.

257. For fuller accounts, see Philip Friedman, *Their Brothers' Keepers* (New York: Crown Publishers, 1978); Carol Rittner and Sondra Myers, *The Courage to Care: Rescuers of Jews During the Holocaust* (New York: New York University Press, 1986) (containing accounts of some dozen individual "stories of rescue," along with reflective essays by several Jews and Christians); and Thomas Merton's account of "Danish Nonviolent Resistance to Hitler," in Thomas Merton, *The Nonviolent Alternative* (New York: Farrar, Straus & Giroux, 1980), pp. 166ff..

258. *Mishnayoth*, trans. Philip Blackman, 3rd ed. (New York: The Judaica Press, 1963), Order Nezikin, Tractate Sanhedrin 5, pp. 254–255.

259. It is part of the story of the Polish woman that, when the mother she had hidden returned after the war to thank her, the woman implored her not to return, saying, "It would not be safe for my neighbors to know that I had harbored a Jewish family."

260. The Vietnamese Buddhist monk, Thich Nhat Hanh, has recounted a startlingly similar odyssey in his "path to discovering Jesus as one of [his] spiritual ancestors." Initially, his realization of the pernicious role played by the Catholic clergy in the colonization of Viet Nam, and later in supporting "an atmosphere of discrimination and injustice against non-Christians," made "the beauty of Jesus' teachings" inaccessible to him. "It was only later," he continues, "through friendships with

Christian men and women who truly embody the spirit of understanding and compassion of Jesus, that I have been able to touch the depths
of Christianity." Thich Nhat Hanh, *Living Buddha, Living Christ* (New
York: Riverhead Books, 1995), pp. 4–5.

261. *The Journal of George Fox* I, ed. Norman Penney (Philadelphia:
John C. Winston Co., 1911), p. 113.

262. O'Meara, *Fundamentalism: A Catholic Perspective*, p. 89.

263. Borg, *Meeting Jesus Again for the First Time*, p. 137. For a candid,
reflective account by an English Quaker of her struggles with this question, see Joyce Neill, *Credo: A Quaker Booklet* (London: Quaker Home
Service, 1986). "I have," she reports, "come now to a position where I
can listen quite comfortably to language and imagery that previously
upset and distressed me, and I can, as it were, make my own 'simultaneous translation' and feel at one with the speaker" (p. 14). She recounts a
similar spirit in an Irish Quaker of her acquaintance, who responded to
a friendly question from a neighbor, "It has always seemed to me that
you are one who has given her heart to the Lord Jesus—Is this so?"
"Those are not the words I would use, but I know what you mean, and
yes, I have" (p. 15).

Contemporary Christian theologians struggle to harmonize their faith
with their skepticism about the propositional truth of Christian theology. One such attempt, focusing on the avowal that "Jesus is God,"
finds merit in the insight that I embraced, p. 36, above, that "God" is
not a noun. See Leonard Swidler, "Yeshua: Messiah? Christ? Human?
Divine?" in *Bursting the Bonds? A Jewish-Christian Dialogue on Jesus and
Paul* (Maryknoll, N.Y.: Orbis Books, 1990), pp. 85–89. Although I respect this struggle, and find disturbing the ready willingness of some
conservative Christians to scorn or caricature it, it is not for me to en-
dorse it.

264. Hershel Matt, "How Shall a Believing Jew View Christianity?"
Judaism, 1975, p. 403.

265. See p. 55, above.

266. Johnson, *Real Jesus*, pp. 135–36, 141, 143.

267. To the extent that the statement in the text carries an unspoken
judgment, I disavow it. After writing those words, I happened to attend
an Episcopal Mass, and found the following excerpt from the Catechism
in the Book of Common Prayer: "Q. What do we mean when we say
that Jesus is the only Son of God? A. We mean that Jesus is the only
perfect image of the Father, and shows us the nature of God." Episcopal
Church, *The (Proposed) Book of Common Prayer* (New York: Church
Hymnal Corporation and Seabury Press, 1977), p. 849. I find this response stunning. I should expect that the Book of Common Prayer is
no longer the repository of orthodoxy that it was in the days of Arch-

bishop Laud, but this language transforms the term "Son of God" for me. It moves "Son of" squarely into a metaphoric plane: The assertion that, as an image of God, Jesus was both perfect and unique, is recognizable to me as the basic Christian affirmation of the incarnation of divinity in Jesus (see, e.g., p. 27, above). The statement that he "shows us the nature of God" is resonant with the statements of many; see p. 108, above, about Jesus as teacher. In neither aspect does "Son of God" add a new and more challenging mystery to the profession of Christian belief.

Will I have a similar experience with respect to the idea of vicarious atonement? Christian scholar Marcus Borg asserts that, "taken metaphorically, this story can be very powerful." *Meeting Jesus Again for the First Time*, p. 131. All I can say is that I have not (yet?) had or read of such an experience. Borg goes on to say that, "taken literally, [the idea] is a profound obstacle to accepting the Christian message. To many people, it simply makes no sense, and I think we need to be straightforward about that" (p. 131).

268. Albert Nolan, *Jesus Before Christianity* (Maryknoll, N.Y.: Orbis Books, 1992), p. 167. This teaching reinforces the moral (rather than the metaphysical) dimension of the belief in Jesus as Son of God; see the preceding note.

269. National Conference of Catholic Bishops, *Economic Justice for All*, p. 15.

270. Kamenetz, *Jew in the Lotus*, p. 233. Rabbi Abraham Joshua Heschel has put the thought with characteristic eloquence: "To meet a human being is a major challenge to mind and heart. . . . To meet a human being is an opportunity to sense the image of God, *the presence* of God. According to a rabbinical interpretation, the Lord said to Moses: 'Wherever you see the trace of man there I stand before you. . . .'

"When engaged in a conversation with a person of differing religious commitment I discover that we disagree in matters sacred to us, does the image of God I face disappear? Does God cease to stand before me? . . . Does the fact that we differ in our conceptions of God cancel what we have in common: the image of God?" "No Religion Is an Island," pp. 7–8.

271. The quoted words are from a central moment in the liturgy, the prayer beginning (according to the traditional translation), "Lord, Lord, God full of compassion and mercy." Compare the closing passage of the *U'nsaneh Tokef*, p. 98, above: "Even until his dying day Thou waitest for him, perchance he will repent and Thou wilt straightway receive him."

272. Nancy Fuchs-Kreimer, Kavanah [meditation introducing a prayer] for Yom Kippur (unpublished, 1993). Compare, to similar import, Kaufman, "Reconstructing the Concept of God," p. 111.

273. Merton, *Nonviolent Alternative*, p. 112.

274. "All this is from God, who reconciled us to him through Christ, and has given us the ministry of reconciliation; that is, in Christ, God was reconciling the world to himself, not counting their trespasses against them, and entrusting the message of reconciliation to us." 2 Corinthians 5:18–19.

275. See note 36 above.

276. Albert Jonsen attributes to Dietrich Bonhoeffer, the German Lutheran anti-Nazi martyr, the view that reconciliation is "the central message" of the Christian Scriptures. "This reconciliation is accomplished because the beloved Son became flesh, took upon himself true and complete humanity, its suffering and its joy, even its sin. . . . In accepting [Jesus], who is our brother in the flesh, [God] accepts all men and all of human life." Albert R. Jonsen, *Responsibility in Modern Religious Ethics* (Washington, D.C.: Corpus Books, 1968), p. 115.

277. In the words that Rev. Matthew Fox attributes to the second-century bishop Irenaeus: "God became human so that humans might become God." *Original Blessing: A Primer in Creation Spirituality*, (Santa Fe, N.M.: Bear & Co., 1983), p. 48. A passage in the Catholic Sunday prayer service expresses the thought simply and directly: "You sent him as one like ourselves, though free from sin, that you might see and love in us what you see and love in him." Quoted in J. A. Di Noia, "Jesus and the World Religions," *First Things*, June–July 1995, p. 26.

278. Mesters, *God, Where Are You?* p. 235. "Emmaus never happened," concludes the Catholic biblical historian John Dominic Crossan—and goes on immediately to conclude as well: "Emmaus always happens." *Jesus: A Revolutionary Biography* (San Francisco: HarperSanFrancisco, 1989), p. 197.

For a staggeringly beautiful and powerful account of how "Emmaus happens" every day, in his life, and in that of any who open themselves to it, see Nouwen, *With Burning Hearts*, p. 66: "Every time we invite Jesus into our homes, that is to say, into our life with all its light and dark sides, and offer him the place of honor at our table, he takes the bread and the cup and hands them to us saying: 'Take and eat, this is my body. Take and drink, this is my blood. Do this to remember me.' "

279. There is contemporary relevance in an admonition that Thomas Merton attributes to an elder of the fourth-century Desert Fathers: "Do not judge a fornicator if you are chaste, for if you do, you too are violating the law as much as he is. For He who said thou shall not fornicate also said thou shall not judge." *Wisdom of the Desert*, p. 41.

Contrast Rev. Richard John Neuhaus's criticism of the Jesuits for "relativizing" and "muting" their condemnation of abortion by including with it other concerns—racism, women's rights, and drug addiction were among them—in their reaction to the contemporary scene. "A Jesuit Awakening," *First Things*, August–September 1994, pp. 73–74. The value of the continued existence of the Society should be judged, Neuhaus concludes (p. 74), by the "public urgency" of its concern for "the children killed and the women exploited by abortion."

Neuhaus has more recently asserted explicitly that "there is a strong connection between religious commitment and conservatism on a very broad range of questions." "Anti-Semitism and Our Common Future," p. 62. Yes, for many there is; but for many others, there is an equally strong connection between (their) religious commitment and much of the political liberalism, indeed, radicalism, that Neuhaus deplores. See, to choose only among Christian thinkers quoted in this book, the work of Marcus Borg, John Dominic Crossan, Daniel Maguire, and Merold Westphal. To Neuhaus, of course, these folks are to be derided as not true believers, but pending proof that *he* has been given the keys to the kingdom, we need not tarry over that response. The broader point is that, for them as for him (and for me), there certainly is a "connection" between the characteristics of our religious consciousness and our politics. Authoritarian religion fits well with conservative politics, and a religion not built on hierarchy fits well with egalitarian politics. (I am reminded of an advertisement [*The New York Times Book Review*, February 10, 1991, p. 16] for a pictorial history of the civil rights movement, Michael S. Durham's *Powerful Days: The Civil Rights Photography of Charles Moore*. It has two pictures—one of Rev. Martin Luther King, Jr., and the other of a leader of the Ku Klux Klan—flanking a picture of the book jacket. Each man stands before the same symbol, the Cross.)

The more elusive question is as to the direction of the causal connection. My own inclination is to believe that neither religion nor politics drives the other, but that the same aspects of our consciousness that make us responsive to one brand of religious faith account for our political orientation as well. For a brief analysis congruent with this thought, see George Lakoff, "Moral Politics: What Conservatives Know That Liberals Don't," in *Two Models of Christianity* (Chicago: The University of Chicago Press, 1996), chap. 14, esp. p. 262.

280. See pp. 9–10, above.

281. Max Savelle, *Seeds of Liberty: The Genesis of the American Mind* (New York: Alfred A. Knopf, 1948), p. ix.

282. The quoted phrase is from a letter by Judge Learned Hand, probably the most widely respected judge of his time. The letter was read at a Harvard Law School ceremony in 1960, and a portion of it is set forth in my article, "The Gravamen of the Secondary Boycott," *Columbia Law Review*, 62 (1962), 1393–1394n155.

283. Obviously, no short set of references could document or illus-

trate the assertions contained in the last several paragraphs. If one book exemplifies what I have described, it is Henry Hart and Albert Sacks's coursebook, "The Legal Process: Basic Problems in the Making and Application of Law" (tentative edition, 1958), "published" in mimeographed versions during my law school days and for a generation justly called the legal world's "most influential unpublished book." Ironically, now that the deep contestability of its premises has been made clear, it has for the first time been published in hard covers, under the original title, prepared for publication with an introductory historical and analytical essay by William N. Eskridge, Jr., and Philip P. Frickey (Westbury, N.Y.: Foundation Press, 1994).

284. 347 U.S. 483 (1954).

285. For examples, see Justice Harlan's opinions in *Greene v. McElroy*, 360 U.S. 474, 509 (1959); *Vitarelli v. Seaton*, 359 U.S. 535 (1959); and *Service v. Dulles*, 354 U.S. 363 (1957).

286. *U.S. ex rel. Goldsby v. Harpole*, 263 F.2d 71 (5th Cir. 1959).

287. On the constitutionality of capital punishment, see the Justice's opinion in *McGautha v. California*, 402 U.S. 183 (1990). His aversion to it is suggested, but only weakly, by his opinions in *Kinsella v. Singleton*, 361 U.S. 249, 255–256 (1960), and *Reid v. Covert*, 354 U.S. 1, 65 at 77–78 (1957).

288. See, e.g., *Local 1424, Int'l Ass'n of Machinists v. NLRB*, 362 U.S. 411 (1960); *NLRB v. Drivers Union*, 362 U.S. 274 (1960); *NLRB v. Insurance Agents' Union*, 361 U.S. 477 (1960), and, in adjacent Terms of Court, *Local 357, Int'l Bhd. of Teamsters v. NLRB*, 365 U.S. 667 (1961); *Local 1976, United Bhd. of Carpenters v. NLRB*, 357 U.S. 93 (1958).

289. For a painstakingly careful and detailed appraisal of the judicial work-product of Justice Harlan's successor, William Rehnquist, written relatively early in the latter's career, see David L. Shapiro, "Mr. Justice Rehnquist: A Preliminary View," *Harvard Law Review*, 90 (1976), 293–357. His conclusion, that, while Justice Rehnquist "is a man of considerable intellectual power and independence of mind, the unyielding character of his ideology has had a substantial adverse effect on his judicial product" has hardly been undermined in the two decades since.

290. See the brief report of the speech, Anthony Lewis, "Robert Kennedy Bids the Bar Join Fight Against Social Ills," *The New York Times*, May 2, 1964, p. 22.

291. *Shapiro v. Thompson*, 394 U.S. 618 (1968). Appropriately enough, the argument that I made in my draft was substantially more far-reaching than the approach taken by lead counsel Archibald Cox, then recently Solicitor General and soon to be Watergate Special Prosecutor. His argument won the case, but on a narrow ground, which permitted the welfare rights campaign soon thereafter to lose the war in

Dandridge v. Williams, 397 U.S. 271 (1970). Although my argument would have governed the far more important Dandridge litigation had it prevailed, it probably would have lost, sooner rather than later.

292. See Law School Task Force on Entitlement to Governmental Benefits, Report to the Biennial Conference of ACLU (unpublished, 1968).

293. Howard Lesnick, "What Does *Bakke* Require of Law Schools? The SALT Board of Governors Statement," *University of Pennsylvania Law Review*, 128 (1979), 141–158.

294. I have been unable to find any contemporaneous report of this statement. I remember it vividly, presumably from the television coverage of the ceremony, but have to acknowledge more than one occasion on which I have "remembered" something that did not in fact happen.

295. The story is—or at least was—well known. See, e.g., Fred Emery, *Watergate: The Corruption of American Politics and the Fall of Richard Nixon* (New York: Times Books, 1994); Stanley I. Kutler, *The Wars of Watergate: The Last Crisis of Richard Nixon* (New York: Alfred A. Knopf, 1990).

296. The myth propagated at the time of Nixon's death that Watergate was some sort of "tragic flaw" in the career of a great statesman was, to me, little more than a sick joke. For post-mortem confirmation of the depth of the man's venality, corruption, and limitless meanness of spirit, see Stanley Kutler, *Abuse of Power: The New Nixon Tapes* (New York: The Free Press, 1997).

297. For the account, see Plato, *Meno*, in *Collected Dialogues*, pp. 353, 365–370. To Socrates, the fact that the boy, ignorant of geometry, could be led to understand the relation between the length of one side of a square and its area proved that "learning" was the recalling to awareness of knowledge that the immortal soul had acquired in earlier lives.

298. I teach the course out of a book I prepared, *Being a Lawyer: Individual Choice and Responsibility in the Practice of Law* (St. Paul, Minn.: West Publishing Company, 1992), along with *Becoming a Lawyer*, cited in note 20, above, and Plato's *Gorgias*, which poses all the central questions about the moral justification of the traditional conception of a lawyer's role.

299. An essay that I developed in tandem with the course, and which examines many of its themes, is "The Wellsprings of Legal Responses to Inequality: A Perspective on Perspectives," *Duke Law Journal* (1991), 413–454. For some fragmentary beginnings toward an understanding of this goal of "subjectivizing" one's fundamental premises, see the final section of the essay, pp. 441–454.

300. It is difficult to "document" this evaluation without writing more than I want to about politics, and even if I wrote for pages I

would persuade only the persuaded. I am thinking, for example, of the insistence that we cannot afford to spend money on education, social services, and the reduction of unemployment, but must spend more and more on border guards and prisons (as long as the prison authorities do not spend money on recreation or other minimal amenities of confinement); the fantasy that we help poor people to "reduce dependency" by cutting them loose (even more than they are) into a world that we are simultaneously making harsher for the poorly educated, poorly housed, etc. For one demonstration, a generation old, of the shopworn and infirm quality of today's "reform" ideas, see "Comment, The Failure of the Work Incentive Program," *University of Pennsylvania Law Review*, 119 (1971), 485–501.

A brief, telling account, focusing on prisons, is James S. Kunen's "Teaching Prisoners a Lesson," *The New Yorker*, July 10, 1995, pp. 34–37.

301. David Remnick, "Lost in Space," ibid., December 5, 1994, p. 81.

302. For a sample of their recent published works, which of course reflects only a fraction of their influence in the world, see Karl E. Klare, "Workplace Democracy and Market Reconstruction: An Agenda for Legal Reform," *Catholic University Law Review*, 38 (1988), 1–68; Julius Getman, *In the Company of Scholars: The Struggle for the Soul of Higher Education* (Austin: University of Texas Press, 1992); Julius Getman, with F. Ray Marshall, "Industrial Relations in Transition: The Paper Industry Example," *Yale Law Journal*, 102 (1993), 1803–1896; Clyde W. Summers, "Employee Voice and Employment Rights: Preliminary Guidelines and Proposals," *University of Pennsylvania Law Review*, 141 (1992), 457–546.

303. For descriptions of the ways in which we reconceived the goals, methods, and content of legal education, see Charles R. Halpern, "A New Direction in Legal Education: The CUNY Law School at Queens College," *Nova Law Journal*, 10 (1986), 549–574, and two essays of mine, "Infinity in a Grain of Sand: The World of Law and Lawyering as Portrayed in the Clinical Teaching Implicit in the Law School Curriculum," *U.C.L.A. Law Review*, 37 (1990), 1182–1198; "The Integration of Responsibility and Values: Legal Education in an Alternative Consciousness of Law and Lawyering," *Nova Law Journal*, 10 (1986), 633–644.

304. Berthold Brecht, "To Posterity," in *Selected Poems* (New York: Reynal & Hitchcock, 1947), p. 177.

Eulogizing his Yale Law School colleague Robert Cover, Guido Calabresi described him in terms that set a high standard for all who struggle for justice, one that we seldom approached at CUNY: "He was a passionate activist. And yet he understood instinctively how destructive passion can be if it does not forgive and even love those individuals on whom it must, on whom it *must*, turn its fire. He was deeply devoted to his heritage. And yet he never let its great traditions exclude others, but made of them a light for all peoples, and a searing criticism of injustice everywhere, within as well as without." Guido Calabresi, "Dedication: Robert M. Cover," *Journal of Law and Religion*, 5 (1987), 1.

305. Since 1986, employers have been required by law to offer employment only to applicants able to prove the lawfulness of their presence here. 8 U.S.C. Section 1324a(a) (1). I worked on a brief in support of the American Friends Service Committee's unsuccessful attempt to challenge on religious grounds this conscription of its board and staff in enforcing governmental policy by withholding a means of livelihood to otherwise qualified people. *AFSC v. Thornburgh*, 961 F.2d 1405 (9th Cir. 1992). More recent policy debates seem to have considered only methods of extending and strengthening this law; of depriving aliens facing exclusion or deportation of fundamental procedural protections, while greatly extending the grounds of "removal" (as it is currently termed); and of denying even lawfully admitted immigrants an array of social services and payments to which they have historically been entitled equally with citizens. See the demagogically misnamed "Illegal Immigration Reform and Immigrant Responsibility Act of 1996," 110 Stat. 3009, and "Personal Responsibility and Work Opportunity Reconciliation Act of 1996," 110 Stat. 2105, Sections 401, 411. At the state level, the popularity of California's Proposition 187 bespeaks widespread popular support for excluding "illegal" aliens almost entirely from access to health and education.

306. See, e.g., the entries on "Immigration" and "Immigration Restriction" in the *Dictionary of American History*, ed. Louise Bilebof Katz and James Trustow Adams, rev. ed., 8 vols. (New York: Charles Scribner's Sons, 1976), 3:332–341, 3:341–343, respectively, referring to the "crowded and relatively backward" communities of eastern and southern Europe, and the "drive to limit 'new' immigrants, particularly the 'less American' Asians, Slavs, Italians, and Jews."

307. A former colleague from my earliest days as a law teacher, Louis Henkin, now a widely esteemed expert in many areas of law bearing on immigration policy, has written an eloquent essay, "An Immigration Policy for a Just Society?" *San Diego Law Review*, 31 (1994), 1017–1024, challenging us (United States citizens) not only to ask what justice demands with respect to immigration policy, but to consider that question recalling that (except for Native Americans and the descendants of those brought here as slaves) we are all immigrants. He recounts the story of President Franklin Roosevelt, invited after many years to address the

annual convention of the Daughters of the American Revolution, a fiercely nativist group in those days. Roosevelt, whose Dutch forebears had left him with impeccable family credentials, "came to the podium, and addressed the group: 'My fellow immigrants' " (p. 1020).

308. See Deuteronomy 26:1–11. The "first fruits" of the harvest are to be given to God, and in the celebration of "the bounty" of the harvest that is to follow, we are specifically enjoined to include "the aliens who reside among" us (26:11).

309. The rabbis have pondered the question how love can be commanded. See Wineberg, *Lessons in Tanya*, p. 818.

310. Handleman, "*Emunah*," pp. 302–303.

311. Handleman notes, ibid, that the rabbis read the opening line of Genesis ("In the beginning God created the heavens and the earth") as "referring to the Torah, as in the verse, 'The Lord made me as the beginning of His way' (Prov. VIII, 22)." In the passage from Proverbs, the speaker is Sophia (a transliteration of the Greek word translated as Wisdom). Hence, Handleman's conclusion quoted in the text.

312. Cobb, "Toward a Christocentric Catholic Theology," p. 88. In English, the text is, "In the beginning was the Word, and the Word was with God, and the Word was God" (John 1:1); Cobb expresses the wish that the Greek text had "spoken of *Sophia* instead of *Logos*." Ibid. See also Harold G. Wells, "Trinitarian Feminism: Elizabeth Johnson's Wisdom Christology," *Theology Today*, October 1995, p. 337.

313. Richard Stith, "Images, Spirituality, and Law," *Journal of Law and Religion*, 10 (1995), 43.

314. *Jeremiah*, trans. H. Freedman, ed. A. Cohen, The Soncino Books of the Bible 14 (London: Soncino, 1961), p. 211*n*32.

315. *Southern Pacific R.R. Co. v. Jensen*, 244 U.S. 205 (1917) (dissenting opinion).

316. The natural law tradition denies that law is no more than the command of one with recognized political power—simply posited by the sovereign, hence "positivism"—asserting that "human law is in some sense derived from moral norms that are universally valid and discoverable by reasoning about human nature and true human goods." Kent Greenawalt, "The Natural Duty to Obey the Law," *Michigan Law Review*, 84 (1985), 8. A classic statement of the positivist position is, again, by Justice Holmes: "[A] legal duty so called is nothing more than a prediction that if a man does or omits certain things he will be made to suffer in this way or that. . . ." Oliver Wendell Holmes, Jr., "The Path of the Law," *Harvard Law Review*, 10 (1897), 458. For a widely read interchange on the subject, see H. L. A. Hart, "Positivism and the Separation of Law and Morals," *Harvard Law Review*, 71 (1958), 593–629; Lon L. Fuller, "Positivism and Fidelity to Law—A Reply to Professor Hart," *Harvard Law Review*, 71 (1958), 630–672.

Within the natural law camp, there is a further debate over its relation to belief in God.

317. Fredelle Zaiman Spiegel, *Women's Wages, Women's Worth: Politics, Religion, and Equity* (New York: Continuum, 1994), p. 133.

318. Joseph Boyle, "Duties to Others in Roman Catholic Thought," in *Duties to Others*, ed. Courtney S. Campbell and B. Andrew Lustig (Dordrecht, The Netherlands: Kluwer Academic, 1994), p. 84. Compare Matthew Berke, "A Jewish Appreciation of Catholic Social Teaching," in *Catholicism, Liberalism, and Communitarianism: The Catholic Intellectual Tradition and the Moral Foundations of Democracy*, ed. Kenneth L. Grasso et al. (Lanham, Md.: Rowman & Littlefield, 1995), p. 239: "[T]he commandments are not regarded here as arbitrary, life-denying impositions that are alien to man's real impulses. . . . Ethical requirements bind the conscience because they are *true*. 'In fact [he is quoting Pope John Paul II's encyclical *Veritatis Splendor* (1993)], human freedom finds its authentic and complete fulfillment precisely in the acceptance of that law.' " To the extent that I understand it (see my account of the Sinaitic revelation, p. 27, above), the Jewish tradition is entirely in accord.

319. I recognize that I am egregiously transplanting a category here, by moving from the biblical Wisdom, the meaning of which is shrouded in variousness and uncertainty—see the entries on "Wisdom" and "Wisdom Literature" in *The Encyclopedia of Religion*, ed. Mircea Eliade, 15 vols. (New York: Macmillan, 1967), 15:392–395 and 15:401–409, respectively—to a contemporary conception of wisdom as a quality of mind and spirit, which may float seriously loose from its moorings. All I will say by way of justification is that I am using the concept heuristically, not historically or theologically.

320. For an introduction to the positions of two leading contemporary philosophers, see Leora Batnitzky, "A Seamless Web? John Finnis and Joseph Raz on the Obligation to Obey the Law," *Oxford Journal of Legal Studies*, 15 (1995), 153–176.

321. Lewis, *Surprised by Joy*, pp. 231–232. A similar understanding (but without Lewis's commitment of belief) may be that of the late law professor Arthur Leff: "[I]n a God-based system, we do not define God's utterances as unquestionable. *We* are not doing the defining. Our relation to God's moral order is the triangle's relationship to the order of Euclidean plane geometry, not the mathematician's. We are defined, constituted, as beings whose [acts inconsistent with God's will are] wrong, bad, unlawful." Arthur Leff, "Unspeakable Ethics, Unnatural Law," *Duke Law Journal*, 1979, 1231.

322. Niebuhr, *Responsible Self*, p. 67.

323. "Our action is responsible . . . when it is response to action

upon us in a continuing discourse or interaction among beings forming a continuing society." Ibid., p. 65.

324. Miriam Starhawk, "Ethics and Justice in Goddess Religion," in *The Politics of Women's Spirituality: Essays on the Rise of Spiritual Powers Within the Feminist Movement*, ed. Charlotte Spretnak (Garden City, N.Y.: Doubleday Anchor, 1982), p. 415. She adds: "'What you send, returns three times over' is the saying. . . . [A]ll things are interdependent and interrelated and, therefore, mutually responsible." Ibid.

325. Jonsen, *Responsibility in Modern Religious Ethics*, pp. 186–187, 191–197.

326. Borg, *Meeting Jesus Again for the First Time*, pp. 75–80. He understands Jesus as teaching the "subversion" of conventional wisdom; see pp. 80–88.

327. *Office of Disciplinary Counsel v. Michaels*, 38 Ohio St. 248, 527 N.E.2d 299 (1988).

328. The subject has produced a considerable body of law, responding to wide variations in the factual bases for belief in the possibility of rehabilitation, and also in the judges' willingness to use the sanction to facilitate it. For an extensive discussion, in an extreme case of a pattern of serious misconduct, see *Attorney Grievance Commission v. Kenney*, 664 A.2d 854 (Md. 1995).

329. Nel Noddings, "Moral Obligation or Moral Support for High-Tech Home Care," *Hastings Center Report*, 24 (September–October 1994), S6.

330. Perhaps the most chilling manifestation of this spirit in contemporary politics has to do with prisons. We are witnessing not merely a venomous dismissal of any talk of "rehabilitation" in setting the length and conditions of imprisonment, but also the combination of an insatiable willingness to spend scarce tax dollars to build and maintain prisons with a malevolent desire to save a few of those tax dollars by dismissing as "pork" any services that are designed to make life more tolerable to those in prison and calculated to reduce recidivism. The elimination of "Pell" grants for prisoners, which for a minuscule cost brought education and its resulting credentials to many prisoners, is the most serious example. The vicious furor in 1994 over "midnight basketball" illustrated how young, largely black men who have not committed any crime are nonetheless embraced within the spirit of this hate.

A recent RAND study suggests that an investment in crime-prevention programs, graduation incentives, and parent training in an amount less than an additional twenty per cent more than the cost of California's "three strikes" law alone could double the crime-reduction effect of that provision. Peter W. Greenwood et al., *Diverting Children from a Life of Crime: Measuring Costs and Benefits* (Santa Monica, Calif.: RAND 1996).

Only an overly committed rationalist would expect such findings to generate legislative attention to measures like those described.

More recently, we are seeing the growth of the imposition of charges for health services to prisoners. See Andrew Metz, "Fees Lowering Costs of Prison Infirmary," *The Philadelphia Inquirer*, September 3, 1995, p. A1. Assertedly prompted by "a public perception that inmates are coddled," the move to charge prisoners for visits to medical personnel and medication is said to reflect the fact that taxpayers are "fed up with paying for anything for prisoners."

331. Compare the readings of the Parable by theologian James B. Tubbs, Jr., and philosopher Joseph Boyle: "In the end, the parable's message does not deal with how one identifies those others who are 'neighbors,' anyway. Instead it exemplifies what it means to be a neighbor to others, regardless of their identity. The prescription Jesus offers is that one should meet the stranger as his/her neighbor or friend. Every encounter with a stranger, then, provides the context and the opportunity for 'loving the neighbor as oneself.'" James B. Tubbs, Jr., "Theology and the Invitation of the Stranger," in *Duties to Others*, ed. Courtney S. Campbell and B. Andrew Lustig (Dordrecht, The Netherlands: Kluwer Academic, 1994), p. 43.

"If 'neighbor' is defined broadly, as Jesus insisted . . . , those to whom people have responsibilities comprise an extensive group. For this parable plainly indicates that ethnic community is not necessary to make people neighbors, and strongly suggests that the capacity to help others is sufficient. If that capacity is a sufficient condition, then the circle of a person's neighbors cannot decisively exclude any human being whom one can help." Joseph Boyle, "Duties to Others in Roman Catholic Thought," ibid., p. 76.

332. See Ben Zion Eliash, "To Leave or Not to Leave: The Good Samaritan in Jewish Law," *St. Louis University Law Journal*, 38 (1994), 619–628. The author recounts Maimonides's rendition of the "undisputed Talmudic teaching about the bystander's duty of rescue": "If one person is able to save another and does not save him he transgresses the commandment 'neither shall thou stand idly by the blood of thy neighbor'" (p. 622). Because the breach of duty "involves no action" (which is the reason that there is no breach in American law), there is no sanction, but nonetheless "the offense is most serious" (p. 623 [again, quoting Maimonides]). Eliash concludes: "Those of us familiar with John Austin's theory that only what is sanctioned is law, will have doubts whether the Jewish duty of helping and saving is a legal one. But in Jewish law there was not and there is not such a doubt. Neither the Talmudic scholars nor later scholars have had even the slightest doubt that the duty is a legal one" (p. 623). The article examines several examples under contemporary Israeli law; see pp. 625 and 628.

For a discussion of "Duties to Others in Roman Catholic Thought," see philosopher Joseph Boyle's chapter by that name in *Duties to Others*, ed. Campbell and Lustig, p. 73.

333. Aharon Lichtenstein, "Does Jewish Tradition Recognize an Ethic Independent of Halakha?" in *Modern Jewish Ethics*, ed. Marvin Fox (Columbus: Ohio State University Press, 1975).

334. Ibid., p. 81. This single excerpt does not do justice to the subtlety of Rabbi Lichtenstein's analysis; see ibid., pp. 76–83.

335. Postema, "Moral Responsibility in Professional Ethics," 69–70. To Postema, "morality is not merely a matter of getting things right—as in solving a puzzle or learning to speak grammatically—but a matter of relating to people in a special and specifically human way." Ibid. See p. 90, above.

336. Thich Nhat Hanh, *Interbeing: Commentaries on the Tiep Hien Precepts* (Berkeley, Calif.: Parallax Press, 1987), p. 34.

337. Charles Fried, "The Lawyer as Friend: The Moral Foundations of the Lawyer-Client Relation," *Yale Law Journal*, 85 (1976), 1066.

338. Richard Wasserstrom, "Lawyers as Professionals: Some Moral Issues," *Human Rights*, 5 (1975), 1–24.

339. For a rich, textured and careful exposition of the "limits and ordering" of duties to others, see Boyle, "Duties to Others in Roman Catholic Thought," pp. 79–86. Especially valuable are his discussion of the Catholic idea of the "order of charity," neutralizing the polarizing tendency of thoughts like that of Fried; his response to the charge of "moral rigorism"; and his espousal of the obligation to develop a "personal vocation," by which, through "careful reflection and deliberation, one seeks to match one's talents and opportunities for service to the needs of the world in which one finds oneself."

A meditation that is no little bit more challenging introduces John Dominic Crossan's *Jesus: A Revolutionary Dialogue*. He presents (p. xiv) this "imaginary dialogue":

"I've read your book, Dominic, and it's quite good. So now you're ready to live by my vision and join me in my program?"

"I don't think I have the courage, Jesus, but I did describe it quite well, didn't I, and the method was especially good, wasn't it?"

"Thank you, Dominic, for not falsifying the message to suit your own incapacity. That at least is something."

"Is it enough, Jesus?"

"No, Dominic, it is not."

340. As translated and quoted by William Ewald; see note 159, above. I have deleted the word, "however," which follows the first word in the text.

341. *Antigone*, p. 115.

342. Hart, *Concept of Law*, pp. 82–85.

343. Even Hart's paradigm case is complicated for one who believes, with the rabbinic tradition, that the moral law forbids not only suicide but any act that puts our lives at risk except for the most compelling cause. See Basil F. Herring, *Jewish Ethics and Halakhah for Our Time: Sources and Commentary* (New York: KTAV Publishing House and Yeshiva University Press, 1984), p. 74, attributing to Maimonides the principle that "one's person belongs to no one but God himself."

344. I mean to sidestep the question of the validity of the claim, made by theologians from Thomas Aquinas to Martin Luther King, that an enactment is not "law" if it is contrary to the moral law. For a brief discussion (and rejection) of the thesis that "a bad law is not a law, or at any rate a law of a government without moral authority is not a law," see Joseph Raz, *Practical Reason and Norms* (Princeton, N.J.: Princeton University Press, 1990), pp. 164–165. I believe that the definitional claim is made in order to ground the claim of non-obligation. I have sought to focus directly on that latter claim, without taking on the question of the meaning of law.

345. If I may repeat here what is set forth in text in Chapter 2, pp. 30–31, above: "I do not find in the fact that the Torah *says*, 'The Lord said to Moses,' a sufficient reason for me to believe it (or a sufficient reason for me to act as if I did). I do not give the Scriptures, even the Pentateuch, that sort of authority. . . .

"The evident fact of the belief of Moses and the Israelite community through the centuries does play a substantial part in the process of my coming to my beliefs. The beliefs of a great teacher or of a community of faith are a powerful heuristic, and on this ground the fact of Moses's and traditional Judaism's belief leads me no little part of the way toward sharing it. Indeed, on this ground, through its authority as teacher, the entire Torah deserves the most respectful attention.

"But I do not find the fact of another's belief sufficient reason for my own, for my own efforts at discernment are (necessarily) involved, in interaction with those of my teachers. I therefore need to take into account the *content* of Moses's and the Israelites' belief. . . . [T]he mere fact that a belief has a given source—what philosophers call a 'content-independent' reason—does not end the inquiry."

See pp. 94–101, above, for a discussion of the value of Scripture, and of religious language, practices, and symbols generally, in serving to strengthen the ability to act on one's understanding of God's will.

346. Hurd, "Challenging Authority," 1676.

347. In my view, much of the emotional fervor behind the conservative rallying cry of "political correctness" is grounded in the implicit belief that all that has changed in recent years is the direction in which

social pressure has pushed the public expression of views, that there has not been a genuine change in moral awareness. I find a large ingredient of wish-fulfillment in that belief. Such a dismissive reaction is, however, facilitated by the reluctance of many liberals to ground their responses in moral judgments—for example, accusing those who express racist or sexist attitudes merely of "insensitivity," which allows one to believe that the offense is failing to take special account of the (exaggerated) sensibilities of the other ("We all know how touchy 'they' are").

348. Bolt, *Man for All Seasons*, p. 73.

349. Jonsen, *Responsibility in Modern Religious Ethics*, p. 192.

350. Michael S. Moore, "Torture and the Balance of Evils," *Israel Law Review*, 23 (1989), 315.

351. Boyle, "Duties to Others in Roman Catholic Thought," pp. 75–76.

352. See, e.g., the discussion in chapter 3 of Herring, *Jewish Ethics and Halakhah for Our Time*. The Supreme Court of Israel recently dismissed a petition by the mother of a three-year-old child suffering from Tay-Sachs disease to authorize her, on behalf of the child, to refuse to receive any medical treatment, other than that designed to relieve pain or suffering, or any assistance in breathing. See the account of *Shefer v. State of Israel* in *The Jerusalem Post*, December. 6, 1993, p. 7. (I have been unable to find an English-language version of the decision.) In the course of his opinion, Justice Menahem Elon, who is a renowned scholar of Jewish law, reportedly concluded that Jewish law, "clearly and beyond any doubt," prohibited active euthanasia, but that acts "interrupting the means" of prolonging life were permissible in some cases "to relieve suffering." The substantive ground for the adverse ruling was a narrow one, that the child in the case before the court did not experience pain or suffering, which suggests the real possibility of a contrary result as to passive euthanasia in many cases.

Apparently, the opinion did not discuss the basis for giving controlling ethical significance, where there is pain or suffering, to the distinction between an act (such as suffocation or administration of a toxic substance) that ends life and an act (such as removal of a feeding or breathing implement) that intentionally "interrupts" the means of sustaining it long enough for death to result.

353. For discussion of my ultimate responsibility for my own discernment, see pp. 87–88, above. For relevant analyses by others, see note 159, above.

354. Seth Kreimer, "Does Pro-Choice Mean Pro-Kevorkian? An Essay on *Roe, Casey*, and the Right to Die," *American University Law Review*, 44 (1995), 807.

355. Professor Fingarette's words are quoted in Thomas L. Shaffer,

American Legal Ethics: Text, Readings, and Discussion Topics (New York: Matthew Bender, 1985), p. 17.

I take substantial, although probably unintended, support for my view from the opening sentences of a review by University of Pennsylvania bioethicist Arthur Caplan of a book recounting the actual life experiences of five people caught in the vise of societal disapproval of assisted suicide: "By the time I finished reading Lonny Shavelson's book [*A Chosen Death: The Dying Confront Assisted Suicide*], I disliked it. I disliked it because I found the book so moving, so gripping that I could not get it out of my head. I disliked it because it whipsawed my convictions that ours is a society that should not legalize assisted suicide on demand [sic]. I disliked it because the five people whose lives and deaths are chronicled persuasively insist on every page that their case for physician-assisted suicide be heard." Art Caplan, "Using Real Stories to Argue the Case for Assisted Suicide," *The Philadelphia Inquirer,* July 9, 1995, p. L1.

Caplan disliked the book, I suggest, because it brought home to him, if only momentarily, the horrific pain that he would subject these five (and many more) innocent people to, in order to protect unnamed others from possible future harm. (I am here not so much doubting the justification for his policy initiatives as suggesting that perhaps he was. It may have been that dissonance that led him to reinvigorate his resolve by referring to suicide "on demand," a bit of demagoguery as shameless as it is unscholarly.)

356. This is not to adopt the more lurid versions of the notion of "original sin" that have afflicted religious people for centuries. To say that we are fallible in our discernments, and often weak in our moral resolve, is not to say that we are "depraved" or on the road to hell.

357. P. 143, above.

358. Section 701(b), 42 U.S.C. § 2000e(b).

359. Dwelling units with no more than four units, one of which is occupied by the owner, are exempted from the prohibition on certain forms of discrimination in housing. See 42 U.S.C. § 3603(b) (1994).

360. I refer in the text to the obligatory quality of "the core" of the statute because in some circumstances it prohibits conduct not motivated by racial or other relevant animus, but unjustifiably having the effect of hindering employment opportunities for racial minorities or women. (The is the "disparate impact" principle, grounded in the decision in *Griggs v. Duke Power Co.,* 401 U.S. 424 (1971).) The extent to which this norm binds an "exempt" employer is complex. For example, assume that the Griggs principle would interdict such practices as filling positions in a manner that is not likely to bring their existence to the attention of prospective minority applicants—for example, hiring only by word-of-mouth generated among (largely white) incumbent workers,

or preferring relatives of the (white) employer. An exempt employer who found more elaborate publication of vacancies genuinely burdensome would be justified, in my view, in taking advantage of the exemption to save itself from having to justify its claim of excessive burden (which, under the law, would be the recognized defense of "business necessity"); similarly, an employer with two or three employees would be justified in hiring only close relatives for the positions, on the ground that so striking a change in the workplace as would attend introduction of strangers (of whatever race or sex) would far outweigh the trivial "disparate impact" of the practice. In contrast, an employer with a dozen employees would, I believe, have a moral obligation (notwithstanding the exemption) to refrain from acting on its belief that to hire only members of a particular ethnic group would make for a more harmonious work force.

361. Law teacher Stephen Pepper has graphically described the ways in which "the law" has come to be viewed wholly instrumentally, and its normative content collapsed into the "potential cost" flowing from the sanctions likely to be imposed for non-compliance (discounted by the likelihood of non-enforcement). Stephen L. Pepper, "The Lawyer's Amoral Role: A Defense, a Problem, and Some Possibilities," *American Bar Foundation Research Journal*, 1986, pp. 624–28. In the area of tort liability, the "cost" is often taken to be simply the likely increase in insurance premiums.

362. The absence of police is the result of a complex set of public decisions regarding the level of desirable monitoring and enforcement expenditures, in light of competing priorities. I recently heard an indignant caller on a radio "talk show" complain of having been "entrapped" by a police officer who parked in plain view alongside a highway on which he was speeding, because the officer was sitting in a car that was older and more decrepit in appearance than he had reason to expect of unmarked police cars.

363. I will not further burden this chapter by examining the question of obligation vis-à-vis civil tort liability, which normatively is meant to prohibit negligent conduct, but which provides for monetary liability as the sole remedy. See note 361, above.

364. A widely known expression of this view is by former Governor Mario Cuomo. His opposition to laws punishing, or even strongly discouraging, abortions is based on three grounds: Those who disagree with his (and his Church's) moral stance on the matter "are not a ruthless, callous alliance of anti-Christians determined to overthrow our moral standards," but "in many cases . . . the very people who have worked with Catholics to realize the goals of social justice set out in papal encyclicals"; all Americans are protected by our traditions of lib-

erty of conscience; and "a constitutional amendment would allow people to ignore the causes of many abortions instead of addressing them." Mario M. Cuomo, "Religious Belief and Public Morality: A Catholic Governor's Perspective," *Notre Dame Journal of Law and Public Policy* 1 (1984), 13.

365. For an absorbing and illuminating exploration of this problem, via a hypothetical interaction between two lawyers over the propriety of engaging in "aggressive tax planning," see George Cooper, "The Avoidance Dynamic: A Tale of Tax Planning, Tax Ethics, and Tax Reform," *Columbia Law Review*, 80 (1980), 1553–1622.

366. Al Kamen, "Belize, the Billionaire, and Sarasota," *The Washington Post*, September 11, 1995, p. A21.

367. Se, e.g., Jennifer Lin, "How Campbell's Heir Cut His Taxes: He Left," *The Philadelphia Inquirer*, July 9, 1995, p. A1 (relinquishment of American citizenship by Dorrance heir reportedly worth, in Campbell Soup stock alone, over $1.3 billion).

368. Martha Vazquez, "Notre Dame Law School: Catholicism, Conscience and Commitment," *Notre Dame Law Review*, 69 (1994), 1005–1006.

369. Seth Kreimer, "The Responsibilities of the Jewish Lawyer" (unpublished, 1993), p. 3.

370. Beck, *Mature Christianity*, p. 33.

371. *One Hundred Poems of Kabir*, ed. Rabindranath Tagore (New York: Macmillan, 1961), p. 9.

372. Nolan, *Jesus Before Christianity*, p. 367.

BIBLIOGRAPHY

ARTICLES

Alexander, Frank S. "Speaking Theologically." *Emory Law Journal*, 42 (1993), 1081–1097.

Alston, William P. "Realism and the Christian Faith." *International Journal for the Philosophy of Religion*, 38 (1995), 37–60.

Batnitzky, Leora. "A Seamless Web? John Finnis and Joseph Raz on the Obligation to Obey the Law." *Oxford Journal of Legal Studies*, 15 (1995), 153–176.

Bellah, Robert N. "At Home and Not at Home: Religious Pluralism and Religious Truth." *Christian Century*, April 19, 1995, pp. 423–427.

Blumenthal, David R. "Letter from Rome." *Cross Currents*, Fall 1996, pp. 388–394.

Borg, Marcus J. "The Historian, the Christian, and Jesus." *Theology Today*, April 1995, pp. 6–16.

Boys, Mary. "The Cross: Should a Symbol Betrayed Be Reclaimed?" *Cross Currents*, Spring 1994, pp. 5–27.

———. "How Shall We Christians Understand Jews and Judaism? Questions About the New Catechism." *Theology Today*, 53 (1996), 165–170.

Calabresi, Guido. "Dedication: Robert M. Cover." *Journal of Law and Religion*, 5 (1987), 1–2.

Callahan, Sidney. "The Role of Emotion in Ethical Decision-making." *Hastings Center Report*, 18 (June–July 1988), 9–14.

Caplan, Art. "Using Real Stories to Argue the Case for Assisted Suicide." *The Philadelphia Inquirer*, July 9, 1995, p. L1.

Carson, Ronald A. "Sensibility and Rationality in Bioethics." *Hastings Center Report*, May–June 1994, pp. 23–24.

"Comment: The Failure of the Work Incentive Program." *University of Pennsylvania Law Review*, 119 (1971), 485–501.

Conscience: A Journal of Prochoice Catholic Opinion, 18, No. 2 (Summer 1997).

Cooper, George. "The Avoidance Dynamic: A Tale of Tax Planning, Tax Ethics, and Tax Reform." *Columbia Law Review*, 80 (1980), 1553–1622.

Cuomo, Mario M. "Religious Belief and Public Morality: A Catholic Governor's Perspective." *Notre Dame Journal of Legal Ethics and Public Policy*, 1 (1984), 13–32.

Di Noia, J. A. "Jesus and the World Religions." *First Things*, June–July 1995, pp. 24–28.

Dinter, Paul E. "Christ's Body as Male and Female," *Cross Currents*, Fall 1994, pp. 390–399.

Dulles, Avery, s.j. "The Challenge of the Catechism." *First Things*, January 1995, 46–53.

————. "*Sensus Fidelium*" [The Sense of the Faithful], *America*, November 1, 1986, 240–246.

Elbow, Peter. "The Uses of Binary Thinking." *Journal of Advanced Composition*, 13 (1993), 51–78.

Eliash, Ben Zion. "To Leave or Not to Leave: The Good Samaritan in Jewish Law." *St. Louis University Law Journal*, 38 (1994), 619–628.

Ewald, William. "Comparative Jurisprudence (1): What Was It Like to Try a Rat?" *University of Pennsylvania Law Review*, 143 (1995), 1889–2150.

Foot, Philippa. "Does Moral Subjectivism Rest on a Mistake?" *Oxford Journal of Legal Studies*, 15 (1995), 1–14.

Fried, Charles. "The Lawyer as Friend: The Moral Foundations of the Lawyer–Client Relation." *Yale Law Journal*, 85 (1976), 1060–1089.

Frymer-Kensky, Tikva. "Toward a Liberal Theory of Halakha." *Tikkun*, July–August 1995, pp. 42–43.

Fuchs-Kreimer, Nancy. "God as 'Fuehrer.'" *Reconstructionism Today*, Autumn 1993, p. 13.

Fuller, Lon L. "Positivism and Fidelity to law—A Reply to Professor Hart." *Harvard Law Review*, 71 (1958), 630–672.

Gaffney, Edward McGlynn. "In Praise of a Gentle Soul." *Journal of Law and Religion*, 10 (1994), 279–290.

Getman, Julius, with F. Ray Marshall. "Industrial Relations in Transition: The Paper Industry Example." *Yale Law Journal*, 102 (1993), 1803–1896.

Gillman, Neil. "Authority and Parameters in Jewish Decision-Making." *The Reconstructionist*, Fall 1994, pp. 73–79.

Goetz, Ronald. Review of *The Religious Critic in American Culture* by William Dean. *Theology Today*, 52 (1995), 414–418.

Greenawalt, Kent. "The Natural Duty to Obey the Law." *Michigan Law Review*, 84 (1985), 1–62.

Griffiths, Paul J. "Why We Need Interreligious Polemics." *First Things*, June–July 1994, pp. 31–37.

Gruchy, John W. de. "Waving the Flag." *Christian Century*, June 15–22, 1994, pp. 596–597.

Gustafson, James M. "Moral Discourse About Medicine: A Variety of Forms." *Journal of Medicine and Philosophy*, 15 (1990), 125–142.

Halpern, Charles R. "A New Direction in Legal Education: The CUNY Law School at Queens College." *Nova Law Journal*, 10 (1986), 549–574.

Halstead. James. "The Orthodox Unorthodoxy of John Dominic Crossan: An Interview." *Cross Currents*, 45 (1995–1996), 510–530.

Hamm, Dennis. "Burning Bush, Barren Fig Tree," *America*, March 7, 1998.

Handelman, Susan. "*Emunah*: The Craft of Faith." *Cross Currents*, Fall 1992, pp. 293–313.

Hart, H. L. A. "Positivism and the Separation of Law and Morals." *Harvard Law Review*, 71 (1958), 593–629.

Hartigan, Emily Fowler. "From Righteousness to Beauty: Reflections on *Poethics* and *Justice as Translation*." *Tulane Law Review*, 57 (1992), 455–484.

———. "The Power of Language Beyond Words: Law as Invitation." *Harvard Civil Rights–Civil Liberties Law Review*, 26 (1991), 67–112.

Henkin, Louis. "An Immigration Policy for a Just Society?" *San Diego Law Review*, 31 (1994), 1017–1024.

Hoffman, Lawrence A. "Jewish-Christian Services—Babel or Mixed Multitude?" *Cross Currents*, Spring 1990, pp. 5–17.

Holmes, Jesse. "To the Scientifically-Minded." *Friends Journal*, June 1992, pp. 22–23.

Holmes, Oliver Wendell, Jr. "The Path of the Law." *Harvard Law Review*, 10 (1897), 457–478.

Hurd, Heidi. "Challenging Authority." *Yale Law Journal*, 100 (1991), 1611–1678.

Johnson, Elizabeth A. "Trinity: To Let the Symbol Sing Again." *Theology Today*, 54 (1997), 299–311.

Kamen, Al. "Belize, the Billionaire, and Sarasota." *The Washington Post*, September 11, 1995, p. A21.

Klare, Karl E. "Workplace Democracy and Market Reconstruction: An Agenda for Legal Reform." *Catholic University Law Review*, 38 (1988), 1–68.

Korn, Eugene. "*Tselem Elokim* [Image of God] and the Dialectic of Jewish Morality." *Tradition*, 31 (1997), 5–30.

Kreimer, Seth. "Does Pro-Choice Mean Pro-Kevorkian? An Essay on *Roe, Casey*, and the Right to Die." *American University Law Review*, 44 (1995), 803–854.

Kunen, James S. "Teaching Prisoners a Lesson." *The New Yorker*, July 10, 1995, pp. 34–37.

Lamm, Norman. "The State of Jewish Belief." *Commentary*, August 1966, pp. 110–112.

Leff, Arthur. "Unspeakable Ethics, Unnatural Law." *Duke Law Journal*, 1979, pp. 1229–1250.

Lehman, Warren. "The Pursuit of a Client's Interest." *Michigan Law Review*, 77 (1979), 1078–1098.

Lesnick, Howard. "The Gravamen of the Secondary Boycott." *Columbia Law Review*, 62 (1962), 1363–1430.

———. "Infinity in a Grain of Sand: The World of Law and Lawyering as Portrayed in the Clinical Teaching Implicit in the Law School Curriculum." *U.C.L.A. Law Review*, 37 (1990), 1157–1198.

———. "The Integration of Responsibility and Values: Legal Education in an Alternative Consciousness of Law and Lawyering." *Nova Law Journal*, 10 (1986), 633–644.

———. "What Does *Bakke* Require of Law Schools? The SALT Board of Governors Statement." *University of Pennsylvania Law Review*, 128 (1979), 141–158.

———. "The Wellsprings of Legal Responses to Inequality: A Perspective on Perspectives." *Duke Law Journal*, 1991, pp. 413–454.

———. "Why Pro Bono in Law Schools." *Law and Inequality: A Journal of Theory and Practice*, 13 (1994), 25–38.

Levinson, Sanford. "Some Reflections on Multiculturalism, 'Equal Concern and Respect,' and the Establishment Clause of the First Amendment." *University of Richmond Law Review*, 27 (1993), 489–506.

Lewis, Anthony. "Robert Kennedy Bids the Bar Join Fight Against Social Ills." *The New York Times*, May 2, 1964, p. 22.

Lin, Jennifer. "How Campbell's Heir Cut His Taxes: He Left." *The Philadelphia Inquirer*, July 9, 1995, p. A1.

Luban, David. "A Theological Argument Against Theopolitics." *Report from the Institute for Philosophy and Public Policy*, 16 (1996), 12–18.

Matt, Daniel. "Beyond the Personal God." *The Reconstructionist*, Spring 1994, pp. 38–47.

Matt, Hershel. "How Shall a Believing Jew View Christianity?" *Judaism*, 1975, pp. 391–405.

Metz, Andrew. "Fees Lowering Costs of Prison Infirmary." *The Philadelphia Inquirer*, September 3, 1995, p. A1.

Moore, Michael. "Choice, Character, and Excuse." *Social Philosophy and Policy*, 7 (1990), 29–58.

———. "Moral Reality." *Wisconsin Law Review*, 1982, 1061–1166.

———. "Torture and the Balance of Evils." *Israel Law Review*, 23 (1989), 280–344.

National Conference of Catholic Bishops. "1992: A Time for Remembering, Reconciling, and Recommitting Ourselves as a People." Statement on Native Americans. *Origins: Catholic News Documentary Service*, January 9, 1992, pp. 493, 495–499.

———. "One in Christ Jesus: A Pastoral Response to the Concerns of Women for Church and Society." *Origins: Catholic News Documentary Service*, April 5, 1990, pp. 717, 719–740.

Neuchterlein, James. "Some of My Best Friends." *First Things*, December 1994, pp. 7–8.

Neuhaus, Richard John. "Anti-Semitism and Our Common Future." *First Things*. June–July 1995, pp. 58–63.

———. "A Jesuit Awakening." *First Things*. August–September 1994, pp. 73–74.

———. "The Public Square." *First Things*, February 1995, pp. 60–71.

Noddings, Nel. "Moral Obligation or Moral Support for High-Tech Home Care." *Hastings Center Report*, 24 (September–October 1994), S6–S10.

Nussbaum, Martha C. "Valuing Values: A Case for Reasoned

Commitment." *Yale Journal of Law and the Humanities*, 6 (1994), 197–218.

O'Sullivan, Owen. "The Silent Schism." *Cross Currents* (Winter 1994–95), 518–526.

Owen, Dennis E., and Barry Mesch. "Protestants, Jews and the Law." *Christian Century*, June 6–13, 1984, pp. 601–604.

Pannenberg, Wolfhart. "Christianity and the West: Ambiguous Past, Uncertain Future." *First Things*, December 1994, pp. 18–23.

Pepper, Stephen L. "The Lawyer's Amoral Role: a Defense, a Problem, and Some Possibilities." *American Bar Foundation Research Journal*, 1986, pp. 613–628.

Postema, Gerald. "Moral Responsibility in Professional Ethics." *New York University Law Review*, 55 (1980), 63–91.

"Reassessing Law Schooling: The Sterling Forest Group." *New York University Law Review*, 53 (1978), 561–591.

Remnick, David. "Lost in Space." *The New Yorker*. December 5, 1994, pp. 79–86.

Reuther, Rosemary Radford. "Watershed for Faithful Catholics." *Conscience: A Journal of Prochoice Catholic Opinion* (Winter 1993–94), 31–32.

Shaffer, Thomas L. "Judges as Prophets." *Texas Law Review*, 67 (1989), 1327–1342.

———. "Jurisprudence in the Light of the Hebraic Faith." *Notre Dame Journal of Law, Ethics, and Public Policy*, 1 (1984), 77–114.

———. "On Thinking Theologically About Lawyers as Counselors." *Florida Law Review*, 42 (1990), 467–478.

Shapiro, David L. "Mr. Justice Rehnquist: A Preliminary View." *Harvard Law Review*, 90 (1976), 293–357.

Sloyan, Gerard S. "The Jews and the New Roman Lectionary." *Face to Face: An Interreligious Bulletin*, 2 (1976), 5–11.

Smolin, David M. "Cracks in the Mirrored Prison: An Evangelical Critique of Secularist Academic and Judicial Myths Regarding the Relationship of Religion and American Politics." *Loyola of Los Angeles Law Review*, 29 (1996), 1487–1512.

Society of Jesus. 34th General Congregation. "Interim Documents of General Congregation." *National Jesuit News*, April 1995.

Soloveitchik, Joseph B. "Confrontation." *Tradition: A Journal of Orthodox Thought*, 5 (1964), 18–25.

Stith, Richard. "Images, Spirituality, and Law." *Journal of Law and Religion*, 10 (1993–1994), 33–48.

———. "Why the Taint to Religion: The Interplay of Chance and Reason." *Brigham Young University Law Review*, 1993, 467–474.

Summers, Clyde W. "Employee Voice and Employment Rights: Preliminary Guidelines and Proposals." *University of Pennsylvania Law Review*, 141 (1992), 457–546.

Taylor, Gabriele. "Justifying the Emotions." *Mind*, 84 (1975), 390–402.

Umansky, Ellan M. "Creative Adjustment and Other Kaplanian Principles of Change." *The Reconstructionist*, Fall 1995, pp. 31–40.

Van Buren, Paul. "Judaism in Christian Theology." *Journal of Ecumenical Studies*, 18 (1981), 114–127.

Vasquez, Martha. "Notre Dame Law School: Catholicism, Conscience and Commitment." *Notre Dame Law Review*, 69 (1994), 1005–1010.

Waskow, Arthur. "Out of the Tomb of Abraham." *Tikkun*, March–April 1995, pp. 37–40, 89–90.

Wasserstrom, Richard. "Lawyers as Professionals: Some Moral Issues." *Human Rights*, 5 (1975), 1–24.

Weintraub, Samuel H. "The Spiritual Ecology of Kashrut." *The Reconstructionist*, Winter 1991–1992, pp. 12–14.

Wells, Harold G. "Trinitarian Feminism: Elizabeth Johnson's Wisdom Christology." *Theology Today*, October 1995, 330–344.

White, James Boyd. "Response to Roger Cramton's Article." *Journal of Legal Education*, 37 (1987), 533–534.

———. "What Can a Lawyer Learn from Literature?" *Harvard Law Review*, 102 (1989), 2014–2047.

Williamson, Clark M. "The New Testament Reconsidered: Recent Post-Holocaust Scholarship." *Quarterly Review*, Winter 1984, pp. 316–350.

BOOKS

Adler, Mortimer. *Truth in Religion: The Plurality of Religions and the Unity of Truth.* New York: Macmillan, 1990.

Alpert, Rebecca, and Jacob Staub. *Exploring Judaism: A Reconstructionist Approach.* New York: Reconstructionist Press, 1985.

Angelou, Maya. *I Know Why the Caged Bird Sings.* New York: Bantam Books, 1971.

Armstrong, Karen. *A History of God: The 4000-Year Quest of Judaism, Christianity, and Islam.* New York: Alfred A. Knopf, 1993.

———. *Jerusalem: One City, Three Faiths.* New York: Ballantine Books, 1996.

The Babylonian Talmud. Ed. Isidore Epstein. London, The Soncino Press, 1935. Repr. 1961.

Baker, William J. *Jesse Owens: An American Life.* New York: The Free Press, 1986.

Beck, Norman. *Mature Christianity: The Recognition and Repudiation of the Anti-Jewish Polemic of the New Testament.* Selinsgrove, Penn.: Susquehnna University Press/Associated University Presses, 1985.

Bellah, Robert N. *The Broken Covenant: American Civil Religion in Time of Trial.* New York: Seabury Press, 1975.

Bendall, Kent, and Frederick Ferre. *Exploring the Logic of Faith: A Dialogue on the Relation of Modern Philosophy to Christian Faith.* New York: Association Press, 1962.

Berke, Matthew. "A Jewish Appreciation of Catholic Social Teaching." In *Catholicism, Liberalism, and Communitarianism: The Catholic Intellectual Tradition and the Moral Foundations of Democracy.* Ed. Kenneth L. Grasso et al. Lanham, Md.: Rowman & Littlefield, 1995. Pp. 235–271.

Bernardin, Joseph Cardinal. "Anti-Semitism: A Catholic Critique." In *Toward Greater Understanding: Essays in Honor of John Cardinal O'Connor.* Ed. Anthony J. Cernera. Bridgeport, Conn.: Sacred Heart University Press, 1995. Pp. 15–31.

Besdin, Abraham R. *Reflections of the Rav: Lessons in Jewish Thought Adapted from Lectures of Rabbi Joseph B. Soloveitchik.* Jerusalem: World Zionist Organization, Department for Torah Education and Culture in the Diaspora, 1979.

Bianco, Frank. *Voices of Silence: Lives of the Trappists Today.* Garden City, N.Y.: Doubleday Anchor, 1992.

Bieber, Nancy. *Communion for a Quaker.* Wallingford, Penn.: Pendle Hill Publications, 1997.

Bishops' Committee on the Liturgy. "God's Mercy Endures Forever: Guidelines on the Presentation of Jews and Judaism in

Catholic Preaching (1988)." In *Faith Without Prejudice: Rebuilding Christian Attitudes Toward Judaism.* Ed. Eugene J. Fisher. New York: Crossroad, 1993. Pp. 170–185.

Bitburg in Moral and Political Perspective. Ed. Geoffrey H. Hartman. Bloomington: Indiana University Press, 1986.

Bjarkman, Peter C. "Six-Pointed Diamonds and the Ultimate Shiksa: Baseball and the American-Jewish Immigrant Experience." In *Cooperstown Symposium on Baseball and the American Culture.* Ed. Alvin L. Hall. Westport, Conn.: Meckler, 1991. Pp. 306–347.

Blake, William. "Auguries of Innocence." In *Blake's Poetry and Designs.* Ed. Mary Lynn Johnson and John Ernest Grant. New York: W. W. Norton, 1979. P. 209.

Blanshard, Paul. *American Freedom and Catholic Power.* Boston: Beacon Press, 1949.

Bolt, Robert. *A Man for All Seasons.* New York: Random House, 1962.

Borg, Marcus J. *Meeting Jesus Again for the First Time: The Historical Jesus and the Heart of Contemporary Faith.* San Francisco: HarperSanFrancisco, 1994.

Boyle, Joseph. "Duties to Others in Roman Catholic Thought." In *Duties to Others.* Ed. Courtney S. Campbell and B. Andrew Lustig. Dordrecht, The Netherlands: Kluwer Academic, 1994. Pp. 73–90.

Brecht, Berthold. *Selected Poems.* New York: Reynal & Hitchcock, 1947.

Buber, Martin. *Eclipse of God: Studies in the Relation Between Religion and Philosophy.* New York: Harper, 1952.

———. *I and Thou.* Trans. Walter Kaufmann. New York: Charles Scribner's Sons, 1970.

———. *Two Types of Faith.* Trans. Norman P. Goldhawk. London: Routledge & Paul, 1951.

Carlson, John Roy. *Under Cover: My Four Years in the Nazi Underworld of America.* New York: E. P. Dutton, 1943.

Carter, Stephen L. *The Culture of Disbelief: How American Law and Politics Trivializes Religious Devotion.* New York: Basic Books, 1993.

Carter, Sydney. "George Fox." In *Rise Up Singing.* Ed. Peter Blood and Annie Patterson. Bethlehem, Penn.: Sing Out Corp., 1988. P. 42.

Cheri. *That Which You Are Seeking Is Causing You to Seek.* Mountain View, Calif. Center for the Practice of Zen Buddhist Meditation, 1990.

The Complete Parallel Bible. New York: Oxford University Press, 1993.

Cobb, John B., Jr. "Toward a Christocentric Catholic Theology." In *Toward a Universal Theology of Religion.* Ed. Leonard Swidler. Maryknoll, N.Y.: Orbis Books, 1987. Pp. 86–100.

Cohen, A. *Everyman's Talmud.* New York: E. P. Dutton, 1949.

Cooney, John. *The American Pope: The Life and Times of Francis Cardinal Spellman.* New York: Times Books, 1984.

Covington, Dennis. *Salvation on Sand Mountain: Snake Handling and Redemption in Southern Appalachia.* Reading, Mass.: Addison-Wesley, 1995.

Crossan, John Dominic. *Jesus: A Revolutionary Biography.* San Francisco: HarperSanFrancisco, 1989.

Cunningham, Philip A. *Education for Shalom: Religion Textbooks and the Enhancement of the Catholic and Jewish Relationship.* Philadelphia: American Interfaith Institute, 1995.

Cupitt, Don. *Taking Leave of God.* New York: Crossroad, 1981.

Dawidowicz, Lucy S. *The War Against the Jews, 1933–1945.* Toronto: Bantam Books, 1986.

Dinnerstein, Leonard. *Antisemitism in America.* New York: Oxford University Press, 1994.

Dorr, Donal. *Option for the Poor: A Hundred Years of Vatican Social Teaching.* Maryknoll, N.Y.: Orbis Books, 1983.

Dvorkin, Elizabeth, Jack Himmelstein, and Howard Lesnick. *Becoming a Lawyer: A Humanistic Perspective on Legal Education and Professionalism.* St. Paul, Minn.: West Publishing Company, 1981.

Eliade, Mircea. Preface. *The Encyclopedia of Religion.* Ed. Mircea Eliade. 15 vols. New York: Macmillan, 1987. 1:ix–xii.

———. *The Sacred and the Profane: The Nature of Religion.* Trans. Willard R. Trask. New York: Harcourt, Brace, 1959.

Eliot, George. *Adam Bede.* Everyman edition. New York: Charles E. Tuttle, 1994.

———. *Romola.* New York: E. P. Dutton, 1956.

Eliot, T. S. *Murder in the Cathedral.* New York: Harcourt, Brace, 1935.

Elon, Ari. *From Jerusalem to the Edge of Heaven*. Philadelphia: Jewish Publication Society, 1995.

Emery, Fred. *Watergate: The Corruption of American Politics and the Fall of Richard Nixon*. New York: Times Books, 1994.

The Empty Chair: Finding Hope and Joy—Timeless Wisdom from a Hasidic Master, Rebbe Nachman of Breslav. Ed. Moshe Mykoff. Woodstock, Vt.: Jewish Lights Publishing, 1994.

Episcopal Church. *The (Proposed) Book of Common Prayer*. New York: Church Hymnal Corp., 1977.

Faith Without Prejudice: Rebuilding Christian Attitudes Toward Judaism. Ed. Eugene J. Fisher. New York: Crossroad, 1993.

Fernando, Antony. "An Asian Perspective." In *No Religion Is an Island: Abraham Joshua Heschel and Interreligious Dialogue*. Ed. Harold Kasimow and Byron L. Sherwin. Maryknoll, N.Y.: Orbis Books, 1991. Pp. 175–184.

Final Harvest: Emily Dickinson's Poems. Ed. Thomas H. Johnson. Boston: Little, Brown, 1961.

Finkelstein, Louis. *Akiba: Scholar, Saint, and Martyr*. Cleveland: World; Philadelphia: Jewish Publication Society of America, 1962.

Fisher, Eugene J., and Leon Klenicki. *Pope John Paul II on Jews and Judaism, 1979–1986*. Washington, D.C.: Office of Publishing and Promotion Services of the United States Catholic Conference and the Anti-Defamation League of B'nai B'rith, 1987.

Flannery, Edward H. *The Anguish of the Jews: Twenty-Three Centuries of Anti-Semitism*. New York: Macmillan, 1965.

Flexner, Helen Thomas. "Had Jesus What Thee Calls Common Sense, James?" In *A Quaker Reader*. Ed. Jessamyn West. New York: The Viking Press, 1962. Pp. 129–144.

Fox, George. *The Journal of George Fox* I. Ed. Norman Penney. Philadelphia: John C. Winston Co., 1911. P. 50.

Fox, Margaret. "The Testimony of Margaret Fox." In *The Works of George Fox* I. Repr. ed. New York: AMS Press, 1975.

Fox, Matthew. *Original Blessing: A Primer in Creation Spirituality*. Santa Fe, N.M.: Bear & Co., 1983.

Franz Rosenzweig: His Life and Thought. Ed. Nahum N. Glatzer. New York: Schocken Books, 1953.

Fraser, Steve. *Labor Will Rule: Sidney Hillman and the Rise of American Labor*. New York: The Free Press, 1991.

Friedman, Philip. *Their Brothers' Keepers*. New York: Crown Publishers, 1978.

Fuchs, Emil. *Christ in Catastrophe*. Wallingford, Penn.: Pendle Hill Publications, 1996.

Geertz, Clifford. *Islam Observed: Religious Development in Morocco and Indonesia*. New Haven, Conn.: Yale University Press, 1968.

Genesis Rabbah I. Ed. H. Freedman and Maurice Simon. 3rd ed. London: The Soncino Press, 1983.

Getman, Julius. *In the Company of Scholars: The Struggle for the Soul of Higher Education*. Austin: University of Texas Press, 1992.

Gillman, Neil. *Sacred Fragments: Recovering Theology for the Modern Jew*. Philadelphia: Jewish Publication Society of America, 1990.

Green, Arthur, and Barry W. Holtz. *Your Word Is Fire: The Hasidic Masters and Contemplative Prayer*. Woodstock, Vt.: Jewish Lights Publications, 1993.

Green, Ronald M. *Religious Reason: The Rational and Moral Basis of Religious Belief*. New York: Oxford University Press, 1978.

Greenawalt, Kent. *Religious Convictions and Political Choice*. New York: Oxford University Press, 1988.

Greenberg, Irving. "Cloud of Smoke, Pillar of Fire: Judaism, Christianity, and Modernity after the Holocaust." In *Auschwitz: Beginning of a New Era? Reflections on the Holocaust*. Ed. Eva Flieschner. New York: KTAV Publishing House, 1977. Pp. 7–20.

Greenwood, Peter W., et al. *Diverting Children from a Life of Crime: Measuring Costs and Benefits*. Santa Monica, Calif.: RAND, 1996.

Gustafson, James A. *Theology and Christian Ethics*. Philadelphia: United Church Press, 1974.

Gwyn, Douglas. *Apocalypse of the Word: The Life and Message of George Fox*. Richmond, Ind.: Friends United Press, 1986.

Hallie, Philip. *Lest Innocent Blood Be Shed: The Story of the Village of Le Chambon and How Goodness Happened There*. New York: Harper & Row, 1979.

Hamilton, Alexander, James Madison, and John Jay. Madison, James. *The Federalist Papers*. Ed. Clinton Rossiter. New York: Penguin Books, 1961.

Hart, H. L. A. *The Concept of Law*. 2nd ed. Oxford: Clarendon, 1994.

Hart, Henry, and Albert Sacks. *The Legal Process: Basic Problems in the Making and Application of Law.* Westbury, NY: Foundation Press, 1994.

Harvey, Andrew. *The Essential Mystics: The Soul's Journey into Truth.* San Francisco: HarperSanFrancisco, 1996.

———. *A Journey in Ladakh.* Boston: Houghton Mifflin, 1983.

A Hebrew and English Lexicon of the Old Testament. Ed. Francis Brown et al. Chicago: Moody Press, 1973.

Herring, Basil F. *Jewish Ethics and Halakhah for Our Time: Sources and Commentary.* New York: KTAV Publishing House and Yeshiva University Press, 1984.

Hertz, Joseph H. *The Authorised Daily Prayer Book.* Rev. ed. New York: Bloch Publishing, 1961.

Heschel, Abraham Joshua. *God in Search of Man: A Philosophy of Judaism.* New York: Harper & Row, 1955.

———. *Man Is Not Alone.* New York: Farrar, Straus, & Giroux, 1951.

———. "On Prayer." In *Moral Grandeur and Spiritual Audacity.* Ed. H. Susannah Heschel. New York: Farrar, Straus & Giroux, 1996. Pp. 257–267.

———. "No Religion Is an Island." In *No Religion Is an Island: Abraham Joshua Heschel and Interreligious Dialogue.* Ed. Harold Kasimow and Byron L. Sherwin. Maryknoll, N.Y.: Orbis Books, 1991. Pp. 343–359.

———. *The Sabbath–The Earth Is the Lord's.* Cleveland: World Publishing Co., 1963.

Heschel, H. Susannah. "My Father." In *No Religion Is an Island.* Ed. Harold Kasimow and Byron L. Sherwin. Maryknoll, N.Y.: Orbis Books, 1991. Pp. 23–41.

Heyward, [Isabel] Carter. *The Redemption of God: A Theology of Mutual Relation.* Washington, D.C.: University Press of America, 1982.

High Holiday Prayer Book. Ed. Morris Silverman. Hartford, Conn.: Prayer Book Press, 1939.

Holmes, Oliver Wendell, Jr. *The Common Law.* Ed. Mark De-Wolfe Howe. Cambridge, Mass.: The Belknap Press of Harvard University Press, 1963.

Hurd, Heidi M. "Interpreting Authorities." In *Law and Interpretation: Essays in Legal Philosophy.* Ed. Andrei Marmor. New York: Oxford University Press, 1995. Pp. 405–432.

"Immigration." In *Dictionary of American History.* Ed. Louise Bilebof Katz and James Trustow Adams. Rev. ed. 8 vols. New York: Charles Scribner's Sons, 1976. 3:332–341.

"Immigration Restriction." In *Dictionary of American History*. Ed. Louise Bilebof Katz and James Trustow Adams. Rev. ed. 8 vols. New York: Charles Scribner's Sons, 1976. 3:341–343.

International Catholic–Jewish Liaison Committee. "The Evolution of a Tradition: From *Nostra Aetate* to the 'Notes.'" *Fifteen Years of Catholic–Jewish Dialogue, 1970–1985*. Vatican City: Libreria Editrice Vaticana, 1988. Pp. 239–254.

The Inclusive New Testament. Brentwood, Md.: Priests for Equality, 1994.

International Council on Biblical Inerrancy. *Hermeneutics, Inerrancy, and the Bible*. Ed. Earl D. Radmacher and Robert D. Preus. Grand Rapids, Mich.: Academic Books/Zondervan, 1984.

Jeansonne, Glen. *Gerald L. K. Smith: Minister of Hate*. New Haven, Conn.: Yale University Press, 1988.

Jeremiah. Trans. H. Freedman. Ed. A. Cohen. The Soncino Books of the Bible 14. London: The Soncino Press, 1961.

Johnson, Luke Timothy. *The Real Jesus: The Misguided Quest for the Historical Jesus and the Truth of the Traditional Gospels*. San Francisco: HarperSanFrancisco, 1996.

Jonsen, Albert. *Responsibility in Modern Religious Ethics*. Washington, D.C.: Corpus Books, 1968.

Jorstad, Erling. *The Politics of Moralism: The New Christian Right in American Life*. Minneapolis: Augsburg Publishing House, 1981.

Kabir. *One Hundred Poems of Kabir*. Ed. Rabindranath Tagore. New York: Macmillan, 1961.

Kamenetz, Rodger. *The Jew in the Lotus: A Poet's Rediscovery of Jewish Identity in Buddhist India*. San Francisco: HarperSanFrancisco, 1994.

Kaplan, Mordecai A. *The Future of the American Jew*. New York: Macmillan, 1948.

Kaufman, Gordon D. "Reconstructing the Concept of God: De-Reifying the Anthropomorphisms." In *The Making and Remaking of Christian Doctrine*. Ed. Sarah Coakley and David A. Pailin. Oxford: Clarendon Press, 1993. Pp. 95–166.

Kazantzakis, Nikos. *God's Pauper: St. Francis of Assisi*. Trans. Peter A. Bien. London and Boston: Faber, 1975.

King, Martin Luther, Jr. "I See the Promised Land." In *I Have a*

Dream: Writings and Speeches That Changed the World. Ed. James Melvin Washington. San Francisco: HarperSan Francisco, 1992. Pp. 194–210.

Kol HaNeshama. New York: The Reconstructionist Press, 1994.

Kushner, Harold S. *When Children Ask About God*. New York: Schocken Books, 1989.

Kushner, Lawrence. *Honey from the Rock: Ten Gates of Jewish Mysticism*. San Francisco: Harper & Row, 1983.

Kutler, Stanley I. *Abuse of Power: The New Nixon Tapes*. New York: The Free Press, 1997.

———. *The Wars of Watergate: The Last Crisis of Richard Nixon*. New York: Alfred A. Knopf, 1990.

Lakoff, George. "Two Models of Christianity," *Moral Politics: What Conservatives Know and Liberals Don't*. Chicago: The University of Chicago Press, 1996.

Lamm, Norman. *Torah Umadda: The Encounter of Religious Learning and Worldly Knowledge in the Jewish Tradition*. Northvale, N.J.: J. Aronson, 1990.

Lens, Sidney. *Radicalism in America*. New York: Thomas Y. Crowell, 1969.

Lerner, Michael. *Jewish Renewal: A Path to Healing and Transformation*. New York: G. P. Putnam's Sons, 1994.

Lesnick, Howard. *Being a Lawyer: Individual Choice and Responsibility in the Practice of Law*. St. Paul: West Publishing Co., 1992.

Lewis, C. S. *Surprised by Joy: The Shape of My Early Life*. New York: Harcourt, Brace, 1956.

Lichtenstein, Aharon. "Does Jewish Tradition Recognize an Ethic Independent of Halakha?" In *Modern Jewish Ethics*. Ed. Marvin Fox. Columbus: Ohio State University Press, 1975. Pp. 62–88.

Lippman, Thomas W. *Understanding Islam: An Introduction to the Muslim World*. New York: New American Library, 1990.

London Yearly Meeting. *Faith and Practice*. London: Headley Brothers, Ltd, 1960.

Longman, Tremper III. "The Literature of the Old Testament." In *A Complete Literary Guide to the Bible*. Ed. Leland Ryken and Tremper Longman III. Grand Rapids, Mich.: Zondervan, 1993. Pp. 95–111.

Louth, Andrew. *Discerning the Mystery: An Essay on the Nature of Theology*. Oxford: Clarendon, 1983.

Ludlow, Robert. "Revolution and Compassion." In *A Penny a Copy: Readings from* THE CATHOLIC WORKER. Ed. Thomas C. Cornell et al. Maryknoll, N.Y.: Orbis Books, 1995. Pp. 64–67.

Luther, Martin. "Concerning the Jews and Their Lies." In *The Christian in Society* IV. Ed. Franklin Sherman. Luther's Works 47. Ed. Helmut T. Lehmann. Philadelphia: Fortress Press, 1971.

Maguire, Daniel. *The Moral Core of Judaism and Christianity: Reclaiming the Revolution*. Minneapolis: Fortress Press, 1993.

Mahzor for Rosh Hashanah and Yom Kippur: A Prayer Book for the Days of Awe. Ed. Rabbi Jules Harlow. New York: Rabbinical Assembly, 1978.

Maslow, Abraham. *The Farther Reaches of Human Nature*. New York: The Viking Press, 1971.

McClory, Robert. *The Turning Point: The Inside Story of the Papal Birth Control Commission*. . . . New York; Crossroad, 1995.

McFague, Sallie. *Speaking in Parables: A Study in Metaphor and Theology*. Philadelphia: Fortress Press, 1975.

Melville, Herman. *Moby-Dick*. Ed. Howard Mumford Jones. New York: W. W. Norton, 1967.

Mendes-Flohr, Paul. *Divided Passions: Jewish Intellectuals and the Experience of Modernity*. Detroit: Wayne State University Press, 1991.

Merkle, John C. "Heschel's Attitude Toward Religious Pluralism." In. *No Religion Is an Island: Abraham Joshua Heschel and Interreligious Dialogue*. Ed. Harold Kasimow and Byron L. Sherwin. Maryknoll, N.Y.: Orbis Books, 1991. Pp. 97–109.

Merton, Thomas. *The Nonviolent Alternative*. New York: Farrar, Straus & Giroux, 1980.

———. *The Wisdom of the Desert*. New York: New Directions, 1960.

Mesters, Carlos. *God, Where Are You? Rediscovering the Bible*. Maryknoll, N.Y.: Orbis Books, 1995.

The Midrash on Psalms I. Trans. William G. Braude. New Haven, Conn.: Yale University Press, 1959.

The Midrash Rabbah. I. *Genesis*. Ed. H. Freedman. 3rd ed. London: The Soncino Press, 1983.

The Midrash Rabbah. III. *Exodus*. Trans. S. M. Lehrman. Ed. H. Freedman and Maurice Simon. London: The Soncino Press, 1983.

Mishnayoth. Trans. Philip Blackman. 3rd ed. New York: The Judaica Press, 1963.

Morley, John F. *Vatican Diplomacy and the Jews During the Holocaust, 1939–43.* New York: KTAV Publishing House, 1980.

Mosse, George L. *Toward the Final Solution: A History of European Racism.* New York: H. Fertig, 1978.

Nasr, Seyyed Hossein. *Ideals and Realities of Islam.* London: George Allen & Unwin, 1975.

National Conference of Catholic Bishops. *Economic Justice for All:. Pastoral Letter on Catholic Social Teaching and the U.S. Economy.* Washington, D.C.: U.S. Catholic Conference, 1986.

Neill, Joyce. *Credo: A Quaker Booklet.* London: Quaker Home Service, 1986.

Nhat Hanh, Thich. *Being Peace.* Berkeley, Calif.: Parallax Press, 1987.

———. *Interbeing: Commentaries on the Tiep Hien Precepts.* Berkeley, Calif.: Parallax Press, 1987.

———. *Living Buddha, Living Christ.* New York: Riverhead Books, 1995.

Niebanck, Richard J. *By What Authority? The Making and Use of Social Statements.* New York: Lutheran Church in America, Division for Mission in North America, 1977.

Niebuhr, H. Richard. *The Responsible Self: An Essay in Christian Moral Philosophy.* New York: Harper & Row, 1963.

Niebuhr, Reinhold. *Man's Nature and His Communities.* New York: Charles Scribner's Sons, 1965.

Nolan, Albert. *Jesus Before Christianity.* Maryknoll, N.Y.: Orbis Books, 1992.

No Religion Is an Island: Abraham Joshua Heschel and Interreligious Dialogue. Ed. Harold Kasimow and Byron L. Sherwin. Maryknoll, N.Y.: Orbis Books, 1991.

Norris, Kathleen. *The Cloister Walk.* New York: Riverhead Books, 1997.

Nouwen, Henri J. M. *With Burning Hearts: A Meditation on the Eucharistic Life.* Maryknoll, N.Y.: Orbis Books, 1994.

Novak, Michael. *Freedom with Justice: Catholic Social Thought and Liberal Institutions.* San Francisco: Harper & Row, 1984.

Nussbaum, Martha. *Love's Knowledge: Essays on Philosophy and Literature.* New York: Oxford University Press, 1990.

O'Brien, David J., and Thomas A. Shannon. *Catholic Social*

Thought: The Documentary Heritage. Maryknoll, N.Y.: Orbis Books, 1992.

Ochs, Vanessa. *Words on Fire: One Woman's Journey into the Sacred.* San Diego: Harcourt Brace Jovanovich, 1990.

Oesterreicher, John M. *The New Encounter Between Christians and Jews.* New York: Philosophical Library, 1986.

O'Meara, Thomas J. *Fundamentalism: A Catholic Perspective.* New York: Paulist Press, 1990.

On Wings of Awe. Ed. Richard Levy. Washington, D.C.: B'nai B'rith Hillel Foundations, 1985.

O'Reilley, Mary Rose. *The Peaceable Classroom.* Portsmouth, N.H.: Boynton, 1993.

Otto, Rudolf. *The Idea of the Holy.* Trans. John W. Harvey. London: Oxford University Press, 1972.

Perry, Michael J. *Love and Power: The Role of Religion and Morality in American Politics.* New York: Oxford University Press, 1991.

———. *Morality, Politics, and Law.* New York: Oxford Univeristy Press, 1988.

Pieper, Josef. "The Philosophical Act." *Leisure: The Basis of Culture.* Trans. Alexander Dru. New York: Pantheon Books, 1952. Pp. 127–46.

Plaskow, Judith. *Standing Again at Sinai: Judaism from a Feminist Perspective.* New York: Harper & Row, 1990.

Plato. *The Collected Dialogues of Plato.* Ed. Edith Hamilton and Huntington Cairns. Princeton, N.J.: Princeton University Press, 1961.

Polanyi, Michael. *Personal Knowledge: Toward a Post-Critical Philosophy.* Chicago: The University of Chicago Press, 1958.

The Portable Walt Whitman. Ed. Malcolm Crowley. New York: The Viking Press, 1974.

Prager, Marcia. *The Path of Blessing.* New York: Bell Tower, 1998.

The (Proposed) Book of Common Prayer. Place: Church Hymnal Corp., 1977.

A Rabbinic Anthology. Ed. C. G. Montefiore and H. M. Loewe. Cleveland: World Publishing Co., 1963.

Rawls, John. *A Theory of Justice.* Cambridge, Mass.: The Belknap Press of Harvard University Press, 1971.

Raz, Joseph. *Practical Reason and Norms.* Princeton, N.J.: Princeton University Press, 1990.

Reagan, Ronald. "Remarks at Bitburg Air Force Base, May 5,

1968." In *Bitburg in Moral and Political Perspective*. Ed. Geoffrey H. Hartman. Bloomington: Indiana University Press, 1986.

Removing Anti-Judaism from the Pulpit. Ed. Howard Clark Kee and Irvin J. Borosky. Philadelphia: American Interfaith Institute; New York: Continuum, 1996.

Ribuffo, Leo P. *The Old Christian Right: The Protestant Far Right from the Great Depression to the Cold War*. Philadelphia: Temple University Press, 1983.

Rittner, Carol, and Sondra Myers. *The Courage to Care: Rescuers of Jews During the Holocaust*. New York: New York University Press, 1986.

Robinson, Jo Ann. *A. J. Muste, Pacifist and Prophet: His Relation to the Society of Friends*. Wallingford, Penn.: Pendle Hill Publications, 1981.

Rubenstein, Richard L. *After Auschwitz: History, Theology, and Contemporary Judaism*. Baltimore: The Johns Hopkins University Press, 1992.

Ruether, Rosemary Radford. "Anti-Semitism and Christian Theology." In *Auschwitz: Beginning of a New Era? Reflections on the Holocaust*. Ed. Eva Fleischner. New York: KTAV Publishing House, 1977. Pp. 79–92.

———. *Faith and Fratricide: The Theological Roots of Anti-Semitism*. New York, Seabury Press, 1974.

Russell, Bertrand. *Selected Papers of Bertrand Russell*. 2nd ed. New York: The Modern Library, 1955.

Salkin, Jeffry K. *Being God's Partner*. Woodstock, Vt.: Jewish Lights Publishing, 1994.

Sanders, E. P. *Paul and Palestinian Judaism: A Comparison of Patterns of Religion*. Minneapolis: Fortress Press, 1977.

Saperstein, Marc. *Moments of Crisis in Jewish-Christian Relations*. London: SCM Press, 1989.

Savelle, Max. *Seeds of Liberty: The Genesis of the American Mind*. New York: Alfred A. Knopf, 1948.

Scherman, Nosson. *The Complete ArtScroll Machzor: Rosh Hashanah*. Brooklyn, N.Y.: Nesorah Publications, 1985.

Schlesinger, Arthur M., Jr. *The Politics of Upheaval*. Boston: Houghton Mifflin, 1960.

Schulweis, Harold M. *For Those Who Can't Believe: Overcoming the Obstacles to Faith*. New York: HarperCollins, 1994.

Shaffer, Thomas L. *American Legal Ethics: Texts, Readings, and Discussion Topics.* New York: Matthew Bender, 1985.

——— "The Tension Between Law in America and the Religious Tradition." In *Law and the Ordering of Our Life Together.* Ed. Richard John Neuhaus. Grand Rapids, Mich.: W. B. Eerdmans, 1989. Pp. 28–53.

Shapiro, Rami M. *Wisdom of the Jewish Sages: A Modern Reading of* Pirke Avot. New York: Bell Tower, 1993.

Sievers, Joseph. "Where Two or Three . . . : The Rabbinic Concept of *Shekhinah* and Matthew 18:20." In *The Jewish Roots of Christian Liturgy.* Ed. Eugene J. Fisher. New York: Paulist Press, 1990. Pp. 47–64.

Sivarska, Sulak. *Seeds of Peace: A Buddhist Vision for Renewing Society.* Berkeley, Calif.: Parallax Press, 1992.

Smith, Mark A. "Jews and Judaism in the Catholic Lectionary." In *Fireball and the Lotus: Emerging Spirituality from Ancient Roots.* Ed. Ron Miller and Jim Kenney. Santa Fe, N.M.: Bear & Co., 1987. Pp. 56–64.

Snape, R. H. "Rabbinical and Early Christian Ethics." *A Rabbinic Anthology.* Ed. C. G. Montefiore and H. M. Loewe. Cleveland: World Publishing Co., 1963. Pp. 616–640.

Soelle, Dorothy, with Shirley A. Cloyes. *To Work and to Love: A Theology of Creation.* Philadelphia: Fortress Press, 1984.

Soloveitchik, Joseph B. *Halakhic Man.* Philadelphia: Jewish Publication Society of America, 1983.

Songs of the Spirit. Philadelphia: Friends General Conference Religious Education Committee, 1978.

Sophocles. *Antigone.* In *Anthology of Greek Drama.* Ed. Charles A. Robinson, Jr. New York: Holt, Rinehart and Winston, 1968.

Soulen, R. Kendall. *The God of Israel and Christian Theology.* Minneapolis: Fortress Press, 1996.

Spiegel, Fredelle Zaiman. *Women's Wages, Women's Worth: Politics, Religion, and Equity.* New York: Continuum, 1994.

Spiegel, Shalom. *The Last Trial: On the Legends and Lore of the Command to Abraham to Offer Isaac as a Sacrifice—The Akedah.* Trans. Judah Goldin. New York: Behrman House, 1979.

Spong, John Shelby. *Liberating the Gospels: Reading the Bible with Jewish Eyes.* San Francisco: HarperSan Francisco, 1996.

Spretnak, Charlotte. *The Spiritual Dimension of Green Politics.* Santa Fe, N.M.: Bear & Co., 1986.

Starhawk, Miriam. "Ethics and Justice in Goddess Religion." In *The Politics of Women's Spirituality: Essays on the Rise of Spiritual Power Within the Feminist Movement.* Garden City, N.Y.: Doubleday Anchor, 1982. Pp. 415–422.

The State of the Union Messages of the Presidents, 1790–1966. 3 vols. New York: Chelsea House, 1966.

Steere, Douglas V. *Traveling In.* Ed. E. Glenn Hinson. Wallingford, Penn.: Pendle Hill Publications, 1995.

————. *Where Words Come From: An Interpretation of the Ground and Practice of Quaker Worship and Ministry.* London: Friends Home Service Committee, 1968.

Stout, Jeffrey. *Ethic After Babel: The Languages of Morals and Their Discontents.* Boston: Beacon Press, 1988.

Streng, Frederick J. "Truth." In *The Encyclopedia of Religion.* Ed. Mircea Eliade. 15 vols. New York: Macmillan, 1987. 15:77–79.

Swidler, Leonard. *Bursting the Bonds? A Jewish-Christian Dialogue on Jesus and Paul.* Maryknoll, N.Y.: Orbis Books, 1990. Pp. 5–50.

————. "Interreligious and Interideological Dialogue: The Matrix for All Systematic Reflection Today." In *Toward a Universal Theology of Religion.* Ed. Leonard W. Swidler. Maryknoll, N.Y.: Orbis Books, 1987.

————. *Yeshua: A Model for Moderns.* Kansas City: Sheed & Ward, 1988.

Tamara, Teruyasu. *A Zen Buddhist Encounters Quakerism.* Wallingford, Penn.: Pendle Hill Publications, 1992.

Thompson, Barbara Balzac. *Passover Seder: Ritual and Menu for an Observance by Christians.* Minneapolis: Augsburg Publishing House, 1984.

Tubbs, James B., Jr. "Theology and the Invitation of the Stranger." In *Duties to Others.* Ed. Courtney S. Campbell and B. Andrew Lustig. Dordrecht, The Netherlands: Kluwer Academic, 1994. Pp. 39–54.

Tucker, Robert C. *Philosophy and Myth in Karl Marx.* 2nd ed. Cambridge: Cambridge University Press, 1972.

Turner, James. *Without God, Without Creed: The Origins of Unbelief in America.* Baltimore: The John Hopkins University Press, 1985.

Unger, Roberto. *Knowledge and Politics.* New York, The Free Press, 1975.

Van Buren, Paul. *Discerning the Way: A Theology of the Jewish Reality.* New York: Seabury Press, 1980.

Waida, Manabu. "Elephants." In *The Encyclopedia of Religion.* Ed. Mircea Eliade. 15 vols. New York: Macmillan, 1987. 5:81–86.

The Way of Response: Martin Buber—Selections from His Writings. Ed. Nahum N. Glatzer. New York: Schocken Books, 1966.

West, Cornel. *The Ethical Dimensions of Marxist Thought.* New York: Monthly Review Press, 1991.

Westphal, Merold. *Suspicion and Faith: The Religious Uses of Modern Atheism.* Grand Rapids, Mich.: W. B. Eerdmans, 1993. Repr. New York: Fordham University Press, 1998.

Williams, Patricia J. *The Alchemy of Race and Rights: Diary of a Law Professor.* Cambridge, Mass.: Harvard University Press, 1991.

Willkie, Wendell L. *One World.* New York: Simon & Schuster, 1943.

Wills, Garry. *Under God: Religion and American Politics.* New York: Simon & Schuster, 1990.

Wineberg, Yosef. *Lessons in Tanya: The Tanya of R. Shneur Zalman of Liadi.* Brooklyn, N.Y.: Kehot, 1987.

"Wisdom." *The Encyclopedia of Religion.* Ed. Mircea Eliade. 15 vols. New York: Macmillan, 1987. 15:392–395.

"Wisdom Literature." *The Encyclopedia of Religion.* Ed. Mircea Eliade. 15 vols. New York: Macmillan, 1987. 15:401–409.

Yamauchi, Edwin M. *Persia and the Bible.* Grand Rapids, Mich.: Baker Book House, 1990.

JUDICIAL DECISIONS

AFSC v. Thornburgh, 961 F.2d 1405 (9th Cir. 1992).

Attorney Grievance Commission v. Kenney, 664 A.2d 854 (Md. 1995).

Brown v. Board of Education, 347 U.S. 483 (1954).

Dandridge v. Williams, 397 U.S. 271 (1970).

Greene v. McElroy, 360 U.S. 474, 509(1959).

Griggs v. Duke Power Co., 401 U.S. 424 (1971).

Kinsella v. Singleton, 361 U.S. 249, 255–256 (1960).

Local 357, Int'l Bhd. of Teamsters v. NLRB, 365 U.S. 667 (1961).

Local 1424, Int'l Association of Machinists v. NLRB, 362 U.S. 411 (1960).

Local 1976, United Bhd. of Carpenters v. NLRB, 357 U.S. 93 (1958).

McGautha v. California, 402 U.S. 183 (1990).

NLRB v. Drivers Union, 362 U.S. 274 (1960).

NLRB v. Insurance Agents' Union, 361 U.S. 477 (1960).

North Carolina Civil Liberties Union Legal Foundation v. Constangy, 947 F.2d 1145 (4th Cir. 1991)

Office of Disciplinary Counsel v. Michaels. 38 Ohio St. 248 N.E.2d 299 (1988).

Reid v. Covert, 354 U.S. 1 (1957).

Roberts v. Madigan, 921 F.2d 1047 (10th Cir. 199)

Service v. Dulles, 354 U.S. 363 (1957).

Shapiro v. Thompson, 294 U.S. 618 (1968)

Southern Pacific. R.R. Co. v. Jensen, 244 U.S. 205 (1917).

U.S. ex rel. Goldsby v. Harpole, 263 F.2d 71 (5th Cir. 1959).

United States v. Seeger, 326 F.2d (2d Cir. 1964) and 163 U.S. 65 (1965).

Vitarelli v. Seaton, 359 U.S. 535 (1959).

Statutes

Civil Rights Act of 1964, Section 701 (b), 42 U.S.C. Section 2000e(b).

Fair Housing Act of 1968 42 U.S.C. Section 3603(b).

Illegal Immigration Reform and Immigrant Responsibility Act of 1996, 110 Stat. 3009.

Immigration Reform and Control Act of 1986, 8 U.S.C. Section 1324a(a) (1).

Personal Responsibility and Work Opportunity Reconciliation Act of 1996, 110 Stat. 2105.

INDEX

SCRIPTURAL PASSAGES

NAMES

Subjects